MILITARY EQUIPMENT OF THE CONFEDERATE STATES

Books LLC®, Reference Series, Memphis, USA, 2011. ISBN: 9781155964911. www.booksllc.net. Copyright: http://creativecommons.org/licenses/by-sa/3.0/ceed.en

Table of Contents

Military equipment of the Confederate States
List of railroads of the Confederate States of America 2
Richmond Depot 3
Slouch hat 4
Uniforms of the Confederate States military forces 6

Naval ships of the Confederate States of America
CSS Alabama 11
CSS Albemarle 18
CSS Appomattox 21
CSS Archer 22
CSS Arkansas 22
CSS Baltic 24
CSS Beaufort 24
CSS Black Warrior 25
CSS Bombshell 25
CSS Charleston 25
CSS Chattahoochee 26
CSS Chickamauga 26
CSS Chicora 27
CSS Clarence 27
CSS Colonel Lovell 28
CSS Columbia 28
CSS Cotton Plant 28
CSS Curlew 0
CSS David 29
CSS Drewry 29
CSS Ellis 30
CSS Fanny 30
CSS Florida 31
CSS Florida (blockade runner) 31
CSS Florida (cruiser) 32
CSS Forrest 33
CSS Fredericksburg 33
CSS Gaines 33
CSS General Beauregard 34
CSS General Earl Van Dorn 34
CSS General M. Jeff Thompson 34
CSS George Page 35
CSS Georgia (battery) 35
CSS Georgia (cruiser) 35
CSS Governor Moore 36

CSS Grampus 37
CSS Grand Duke 37
CSS Hampton 37
CSS Isondiga 37
CSS Ivy 38
CSS Jackson 39
CSS Jamestown 39
CSS Lady Davis 40
CSS Lark 40
CSS Louisiana 41
CSS Manassas 42
CSS McRae 43
CSS Mississippi 43
CSS Morgan 45
CSS Muscogee 46
CSS Nashville (1861) 46
CSS Nashville (1864) 46
CSS Neuse 46
CSS New Orleans 47
CSS North Carolina 47
CSS Oregon 47
CSS Owl 48
CSS Palmetto State 48
CSS Patrick Henry 49
CSS Pedee 49
CSS Raleigh (1861) 50
CSS Raleigh (1864) 50
CSS Rappahannock 50
CSS Resolute 51
CSS Richmond 51
CSS Robert E. Lee 52
CSS Savannah (gunboat) 53
CSS Savannah (ironclad) 53
CSS Scorpion 53
CSS Sea Bird 54
CSS Selma (1856) 54
CSS Shenandoah 55
CSS Spray 57
CSS Stonewall Jackson 58
CSS Sumter 58
CSS Tacony 59
CSS Tallahassee 59
CSS Teaser 61
CSS Tennessee (1862) 62
CSS Tennessee (1863) 63
CSS Texas 64

CSS Tuscaloosa 0
CSS Virginia 64
CSS Virginia II 67
CSS Webb 69
CS Bayou City 69
CS Neptune 70
Danish ironclad Danmark 70
Era No. 5 70
Japanese ironclad Kōtetsu 71
Laurent Millaudon (1856) 72
List of ships of the Confederate States Navy 74
Monticello (privateer) 78
PS Alfred (1863) 78
SS Rob Roy 78
SS Scotia (1847) 79
Spanish cruiser Tornado 79
Star of the West 82
USS Atlanta (1861) 83
USS Cornubia (1858) 85
USS Planter (1862) 86
USS Red Rover (1859) 87
USS United States (1797) 88

Weapons of the Confederate States
Arkansas toothpick 92
Beaumont-Adams Revolver 93
Blakely rifle 93
Bowie knife 94
Brooke rifle 96
Burnside carbine 98
Colt 1851 Navy Revolver 98
Colt M1861 Navy 100
E. C. Singer 100
Fayetteville rifle 101
Gorgas machine gun 101
Hawken rifle 101
Hughes Breech-loading cannon 102
Kerr's Patent Revolver 102
LeMat Revolver 103
List of Confederate arms manufacturers 0
London Armoury Company 105
Long rifle 106
M1841 Mississippi Rifle 108
Maynard Carbine 109

2 - Introduction

Merrill Carbine 109
Pattern 1853 Enfield 109
Pattern 1861 Enfield Musketoon 111
Richmond Rifle 111
Rising Breech Carbine 111
Singer: Confederate Naval Mine 0
Tarpley carbine 112
Tranter (revolver) 112
Webley & Scott 113
Whitworth rifle 116
Williams Gun 117
Winans Steam Gun 117

Introduction

Purchase of this book entitles you to a free trial membership in the publisher's book club at www.booksllc.net. (Time limited offer.) Simply enter the barcode number from the back cover onto the membership form. The book club entitles you to select from hundreds of thousands of books at no additional charge. You can also download a digital copy of this and related books to read on the go. Simply enter the title or subject onto the search form to find them.

Each chapter in this book ends with a URL to a hyperlinked online version. Type the URL exactly as it appears. If you change the URL's capitalization it won't work. Use the online version to access related pages, websites, footnotes, tables, color photos, updates. Click the version history tab to see the chapter's contributors. Click the edit link to suggest changes.

A large and diverse editor base collaboratively wrote the book, not a single author. After a long process of discussion and debate, the chapters gradually took on a neutral point of view reached through consensus. Additional editors expanded and contributed to chapters striving to achieve balance and comprehensive coverage. This reduced the regional or cultural bias found in many other books and provided access and breadth on subject matter otherwise little documented.

List of railroads of the Confederate States of America

This is a list of Confederate Railroads in operation or used by the Confederate States of America during the American Civil War. See also Confederate railroads in the American Civil War. At the outset of the war, the Confederacy possessed the third largest set of railroads of any nation in the world, with about 9,000 miles of railroad track. Southern companies, towns, cities as well as state governments were heavy investors in railroad companies, which were typically designed as feeder lines linking farming centers to port cities.

Railroads and Railroad Companies

- Alabama and Florida Railroad of Alabama
- Alabama and Mississippi Rivers Railroad
- Alabama and Tennessee River Railroad
- Alabama and Florida Railroad of Florida
- Alabama Coal Company Railroad
- Alexandria, Loudoun and Hampshire Railroad
- Allen's Plantation Railroad
- Atlanta and West Point Railroad
- Atlantic and Gulf Railroad
- Atlantic and North Carolina Railroad
- Atlantic, Tennessee and Ohio Railroad
- Augusta and Milledgeville Railroad
- Augusta and Savannah Railroad
- Baton Rouge, Grosse Tete and Opelousa Railroad
- Baltimore and Ohio Railroad
- Blue Ridge Railroad
- Blue Ridge Railroad of South Carolina
- Brunswick and Albany Railroad
- Brunswick and Florida Railroad
- Buffalo Bayou, Brazos and Colorado Railroad
- Cahaba, Marion and Greensboro Railroad
- Central Railroad of Georgia
- Central Southern Railroad
- Centreville Military Railroad
- Charlotte and South Carolina Railroad
- Charleston and Savannah Railroad
- Cheraw and Darlington Railroad
- Clinton and Port Hudson Railroad
- Clover Hill Railroad
- East Tennessee and Virginia Railroad
- Eastern Texas Railroad
- Edgefield and Kentucky Railroad
- Etowah Railroad
- Florida Railroad
- Florida, Atlantic and Gulf Central Railroad
- Galveston, Houston and Henderson Railroad
- Galveston and Houston Junction Railroad
- Georgia Railroad
- Gordon's Mine Railroad
- Grand Gulf and Port Gibson Railroad
- Greenville and Columbia Railroad
- Houston & Texas Central Railroad
- Houston Tap and Brazoria Railroad
- Jefferson and Lake Pontchartrain Railroad
- King's Mountain Railroad
- Knoxville and Kentucky Railroad
- Laurens Railroad
- Louisville and Nashville Railroad
- Macon and Brunswick Railroad
- Macon and Western Railroad
- Manassas Gap Railroad
- McMinnville and Manchester Railroad
- Memphis and Charleston Railroad
- Memphis and Little Rock Railroad
- Memphis and Ohio Railroad
- Memphis, Clarksville and Louisville Railroad
- Memphis, El Paso and Pacific Railroad
- Mexican Gulf Railroad

- Milledgeville Railroad
- Mississippi Central Railroad
- Mississippi, Gainesville and Tuscaloosa Railroad
- Mississippi and Tennessee Railroad
- Mobile and Girard Railroad
- Mobile and Great Northern Railroad
- Mobile and Ohio Railroad
- Montevallo Coal Railroad
- Montgomery and Eufaula Railroad
- Montgomery and West Point Railroad
- Muscogee Railroad
- Nashville and Chattanooga Railroad
- Nashville and Decatur Railroad
- Nashville and Northwestern Railroad
- New Orleans and Carrollton Railroad
- New Orleans and Ohio Railroad
- New Orleans, Jackson and Great Northern Railroad
- New Orleans, Opelousas and Great Western Railroad
- Nashville and Decatur Railroad
- Norfolk and Petersburg Railroad
- North Carolina Railroad
- Northeast and Southwest Alabama Railroad
- Northeastern Railroad
- Northwestern Virginia Railroad
- Orange and Alexandria Railroad
- Pensacola and Georgia Railroad
- Pensacola and Mobile Railroad
- Petersburg Railroad
- Piedmont Railroad
- Pontchartrain Railroad
- Raleigh and Gaston Railroad
- Raymond Railroad
- Red River Railroad
- Richmond and York River Railroad
- Richmond, Fredericksburg and Potomac Railroad
- Roanoke Valley Railroad
- Rogersville and Jefferson Railroad
- Rome Railroad
- San Antonio and Mexican Gulf Railroad
- Savannah, Albany and Gulf Railroad
- Seaboard and Roanoke Railroad
- Selma and Meridian Railroad
- Shelby Iron Company Railroad
- South and North Alabama Railroad
- South Carolina Railroad
- Southside Railroad
- South Western Railroad
- Southern Railroad of Mississippi
- Southern Pacific Railroad
- Spartanburg and Union Railroad
- Spring Hill Railroad
- Tallahassee Railroad
- Tennessee and Alabama Railroad
- Tennessee and Alabama Central Railroad
- Tennessee Coal and Railroad
- Texas and New Orleans Railroad
- Tuckahoe and James River Railroad
- Tuskegee Railroad
- Upson County Railroad
- Vicksburg, Shreveport and Texas Railroad
- Virginia and Tennessee Railroad
- Virginia Central Railroad
- Washington County Railroad
- West Feliciana Railroad
- Western Railroad
- Western North Carolina Railroad
- Wills Valley Railroad
- Wilmington, Charlotte and Rutherford Railroad
- Wilmington and Manchester Railroad
- Wilmington and Weldon Railroad
- Winchester and Alabama Railroad
- Winchester and Potomac Railroad

Railroad Tunnels
- Blue Ridge Tunnel

Source (edited): "http://en.wikipedia.org/wiki/List_of_railroads_of_the_Confederate_States_of_America"

Richmond Depot

The Richmond Depot is a Confederate-issued shell jacket to troops in the Army of Northern Virginia during the American Civil War.

History

Richmond Depot jackets were not issued to western Confederates or the Army of Tennessee.

Design

Three types of Richmond Depot jackets were produced:
- The Richmond Depot Type I was issued late in 1861 or the beginning of 1862. The Richmond Depot Type I, was a jacket with a six piece body and two piece sleeves, with an eight or nine button front, shoulder straps and probably belt loops. There were generally two buttons on the cuffs. The lining was probably a cotton osnaburg. The distinctive point about the first pattern jacket and the feature that distinguished it from the Type II, was that it was trimmed on the collar, shoulder straps and cuffs with either tape or piping-which appears to be usually 1/4" inch dark colored. Today, there are no surviving Type I jackets, but based on photographs, these details can be deduced.
- In mid-1862, the Type I was phased out for the Type II. Due to scarce supplies, they were made of jeans (a mixture of wool and cotton) or satinette and cashmere. There are several extant examples of Type IIs throughout out the US, including in the Museum of the Confederacy. The Richmond Depot Type II jacket is characterized by a nine-button front, no buttons on the cuffs, top-stitched edges, shoulder straps, belt loops on each hip, an unbleached cotton osnaburg lining and interior pockets. It has a six piece body and two piece sleeves. Generally, it has no trim, although examples with partial trim do exist.
- The Type II was phased out in mid-1864 for the Richmond Depot Type III. This was the last Richmond Depot jacket issued to the Army of Northern Virginia. Seven of these jackets have survived, and there are a number of identifiable photographs that show them in use. Since these jackets were produced over a considerable period of time, and because they were made from materials available at different

times, variations in the coat material and the number of buttons have been noted.

Source (edited): "http://en.wikipedia.org/wiki/Richmond_Depot"

Slouch hat

Slouch hat during the American Civil War

A **slouch hat** is a wide-brimmed felt hat with a chinstrap most commonly worn as part of a military uniform. It is a survivor of the felt hats worn by 18th century armies. At varying periods since then the slouch hat has been worn by military personnel from many nations including Australia, Britain, India, New Zealand, Southern Rhodesia, France, the United States, Germany and many others, but Australia had a slouch as the standard issue headwear from around 1885, and still does to this day. Today, it continues to be worn by military personnel from a number of countries, although it is primarily associated with Australia, where it is considered to be a national symbol. The distinctive Australian slouch hat, sometimes called an **Australian bush hat**, (however in the Australian Army the term "bush hat" refers to a soft, short-brimmed hat similar to the US "Boonie hat") has one side of the brim turned up or pinned to the side of the hat with a special badge (the bayonet collection badge, or the rising sun badge) in order to allow a rifle to be slung over the shoulder. In the United States it was also called the Kossuth hat, after Lajos Kossuth.

History

Naik Agansing Rai VC, 5th Royal Gurkha Rifles (Frontier Force)

The name "Slouch Hat" refers to the fact that one side droops down as opposed to the other which is pinned against the side of the crown. This style of hat has been worn for many hundreds of years, especially during the English Civil War during the 17th century when it became associated with the forces of King Charles I, the Cavaliers, but it was also fashionable for the aristocracy throughout Europe during that time until it was superseded by the tricorn.

Despite being primarily associated with Australia, the slouch hat style did not originate in Australia, being introduced there around 1885 and was sometimes described as a 'Tyrolean' import, derived from the black 'Corsican hat' (Korsehut) with a feather and a leather chinstrap; this hat with an upturned brim was worn by the fifteen battalions of Austrian light troops formed in 1801 after the French Revolutionary Wars. A contemporary painting dated 1884 (in the regimental museum) of the pipe band of 1st Battalion Argyll & Sutherland Highlanders in service dress, crossing the veldt in Zululand, shows them wearing khaki slouch hats.

A shortage of cork helmets led to the widespread use of the slouch hat amongst British Empire forces during the Second Boer War, where it was used by units such as the City Imperial Volunteers (CIV), Imperial Yeomanry, and King Edward's Horse. After the war, however, many armies rejected the once-popular headwear (as the British Army did in 1905), although it came back into fashion briefly during World War II during the Burma campaign and amongst troops serving in India and Southeast Asia at this time.

The slouch hat in gray felt was worn by the Schutztruppe (protection force), the colonial armed force of Imperial Germany, as an alternative to the pith helmet, especially in South West Africa. Different coloured puggarees were worn by the Germans in South West Africa, German East Africa, German West Africa (Togo and Cameroon) and China. The hat had its brim pinned up on the right side with a cockade in the national colors and was worn with the home uniform as well. German colonial police units in South West Africa wore a khaki slouch hat with a small national cockade on the front and the right side pinned up by a metal Imperial crown device.

The slouch hat was frequently worn throughout Africa and in motion pictures about Africa such as Jungle Jim and safari films.

It became associated with the Australian military around the end of the 19th Century and since World War I it has been manufactured in Australia by the Akubra company for the Australian Army. This slouch hat is still worn by the Australian military today and it has become a national symbol in Australia. A Unit Colour Patch is also worn by members of the Australian Army on their Slouch Hat to indicate which unit they are from.

The slouch hat or Terai hat is also associated with the Gurkha regiments of the British Army and Indian Army (formerly the British Indian Army) and is still worn by the Gurkhas; the hat is no longer worn on active service. The 2nd Gurkha Rifles became the first Gurkha regiment to adopt the slouch hat when they were issued with the Australian variant in 1901. The Gurkha terai hat is created by fusing two hats into one to make the hat more rigid and is worn at an angle, tilted to the right.

The Chindits and other units of Field Marshal William Slim's British Fourteenth Army, who fought against the Japanese in the Far East during World War II, also became associated with the slouch hat (also known as the bush hat in the British Army). The slouch hat was also used by colonial units of the British Empire, including the Royal West African Frontier Force, the Canadian Yukon Field Force, Canadian Pacific Railway Militia, the Kenya Regiment and troops from Rhodesia.

Slouch hat in Australia

A Company of the Victorian Mounted Rifles on manoeuvres in Victoria in 1889.

The slouch hat was first worn by military forces in Australia in 1885 when the newly created Victorian Mounted Rifles wore the hat as part of their khaki uniform. On 22 December 1890, the military commanders of the then separate Australian Colonies prior to the Federation of Australia met to discuss the introduction of the khaki uniform throughout Australia. They agreed that all Australian Forces with the exception of the Artillery would wear the slouch hat. It was to be looped up on one side — Victoria and Tasmania on the right and the other colonies (later states) on the left. This was done so that rifles could be held at the slope without damaging the brim.

After Federation, the slouch hat became standard Australian Army headgear in 1903 and since then it has developed into an important national symbol.

Australian Light Horse troops wearing slouch hats, November 1914.

The Slouch hat (also known as a Hat KFF or Hat Khaki Fur Felt) is worn as the standard ceremonial headdress for all members of the army except those belonging to units or corps that have an official headdress, e.g. some units wear a beret. As such it is treated with the utmost care and respect. The Grade 1 Slouch hat is worn with a seven band puggaree, said to represent the six states and the territories of Australia, the soldiers' Unit Colour Patch (right of puggaree), Corps or Regiment Hat badge (front of puggaree) and the General Service Badge (The Rising Sun, on the left brim); and the left brim is folded up and clipped into place. The Grade 2 Slouch hat is the same but with the left brim down and is worn in some units as general duty dress - the wide brim giving excellent sun protection. Most soldiers will have a second hat to wear as their Grade 2 Slouch hat.

Australian Army Grade 1 Slouch Hat with Royal Australian Engineers corps badge

The Slouch Hat worn by the Army is one of the ADF's trademarks, but it is not theirs alone: the Royal Australian Air Force wears the HKFF with a dark blue or "Air Force Blue" Puggaree, as a Non Ceremonial head dress for the RAAF; the Royal Australian Navy is also known to wear the hat when wearing camouflage and other uniforms, and has the same features as the RAAF's HKFF. The RAAF and RAN Slouch Hats do not have unit colour patches, nor do they wear it brim up; instead the only badge worn is the RAAF or RAN cap badge, of a design appropriate to the wearer's rank, at the front of puggaree

The 1st Battalion, Royal Australian Regiment (1RAR) for their slouch hats wear a jungle green coloured puggaree with no colour patch, this dates back to traditions when serving in Malaya. Prior to the RAAF varying some of its Service Dress Uniform the RAAF also used to wear a Blue Slouch hat, with a black or blue puggaree and the Khaki for the HKFF puggaree had a blue band. Staff Cadets at the Royal Military College, Duntroon also wear a darker pugaree, although the origins of this are uncertain, while they also wear the chin strap of the hat the opposite way around from that of the rest of the Army.

Some units of the Royal Australian Armoured Corps such as cavalry and light horse regiments wear emu plumes behind the Rising Sun badge.

Within the Australian Army, mixing articles of uniform and civilian attire is known as mixed dress and prohibited. Removing all badges as well as the puggaree removes the hat's status as uniform and it may be worn with civilian

Slouch hat in New Zealand

The NZ version of the slouch hat, known in the New Zealand Army as the 'Mounted Rifles Hat', is currently worn by the various corps and regiments of the New Zealand Army. In all cases the puggaree is khaki-green-khaki, the original Mounted Rifles puggaree, with only the badge denoting the wearer's Regimental affiliation. It was originally reintroduced for wear by Queen Alexandra's Mounted Rifles in the mid-1990s, but in 2000 its issue was broadened to all Corps for wear with working dress (influenced by such use by QAMR) as well as with service dress. As an alternative to the typical NZ army lemon squeezer the NZ Mounted Rifles Hat is worn on all but the most important occasions, where the lemon squeezer takes precedence. The slouch hat predates the introduction of the lemon squeezer hat (which did not appear until after the Boer War) and is worn brim down. Historic photographs indicate the brim to have been worn up in the Australian style on occasion.

Slouch hat in the U.S. Military

Some American soldiers assigned to units in the China Burma India Theatre of World War II (CBI) such as the OSS Detachment 101 and the 1st Air Commando Group wore British Army issue bush hats with their uniforms without official authorisation.

In the early 1960s when American soldiers went to the Vietnam War, the standard headgear was a fatigue baseball or field cap that offered limited protection from the sun. Local tailors made a slouch hat in a style between a French type bush hat of the First Indochina War and an Australian type bush hat with a snap on the brim to pin one side up that was widely bought and unofficially worn by American troops in Vietnam. The local tailors usually used green fatigue cloth or leopard skin pattern military camouflage from old parachutes. The hat often had a cloth arc emblazoned with the word VIET-NAM on the brim. The U.S. 1st Air Commando Group members adopted the green slouch hat as their distinctive and practical headgear with an AIR COMMANDO arc.

In 1972 the U.S. Army authorized female Drill Sergeants to wear a similar type cloth bush hat with the brim pinned up on the side as their distinctive headgear. The U.S. Air Force female Military Training Instructors were given an Air Force blue slouch hat.

Slouch hat in the Indian Police

A few state police forces in India do use the Slouch Hats. The Armed Reserve wing of the Kerala Police used to wear slouch hats right up to the 1980s. Today the slouch hat is only worn by the Recruit Trainee Police Constables (RTPC) of Kerala Police during their training. The Armed Reserve policemen of Kerala Police now wear a blue peak cap. Karnataka Police continues to use slouch hats for its members in the lower rungs of the police force (Constables and Head Constables). The slouch hat will have the colours of the police unit embroidered on the brim which is put up. The police number of the officer is also fixed onto this side of the brim.

Slouch hat in Ireland

The uniform of the Irish Volunteers included a slouch hat and it was worn by many of the rebels during the 1916 Easter Rising (though it was not part of the uniform of the Irish Citizens Army). The hat is the subject of the Irish republican song "The Broad Black Brimmer". Source (edited): "http://en.wikipedia.org/wiki/Slouch_hat"

Uniforms of the Confederate States military forces

Seal of the Confederate States of America

The **Uniforms of the Confederate States military forces** were the uniforms used by the Confederate Army and Navy during the American Civil War, from 1861 to 1865. The uniform varied greatly due to a variety of reasons, such as location, limitations on the supply of cloth and other materials, and the cost of materials during the war.

Confederate forces were often poorly supplied with uniforms, especially late in the conflict. Servicemen sometimes wore combinations of uniform pieces, also wearing captured Union uniforms, and items of personal clothing. They sometimes went without shoes altogether, and broad felt or straw hats were worn as often as kepis or naval caps. There are some controversies about some of the exact details of a few of the uniforms, since some of the records were lost or destroyed after the Civil War ended.

Overview

The original Confederate uniforms from all branches of the military closely followed the lines of the Union's uniforms. This was until 6 June, 1861 when the Confederate Council issued General Order 9 which was the new regulations for the Confederate Infantry, Cavalry and Artillery.

The new uniforms were designed by Nicola Marshall, a Prussian who was heavily influenced by the mid-1800's uniforms of the Austrian and French armies.

Although the regular Confederate military had a paper strength of 6,000 personnel, the first 100,000 volunteers from all over the South participated in a variety of dress. Many were from State Militia outfits which had their own State issued uniforms and in the early battles some Confederate units who wore dark blue outfits were often mistaken at the field of battle for the enemy, conversely, many Union units too which were originally militia units went to war wearing grey.

It was not until the Depot system was established in 1862 by the Confederate Quartermaster in Richmond Virginia that uniforms would be mass produced and supplied to troops. Until that time the "commutation system" was in place which allowed soldiers to have their own uniforms made to the new CSA regulations to be reimbursed by the CS government. Allowance was $21 per 6 months for uniforms.

Officers always had to buy their own until March 6, 1864 when General Order 28 was released which allowed Confederate officers to purchase uniforms from the same sources as the troops, and at cost price.

Following the Richmond Depot, other depots started up throughout the South to supply to their respective regional forces. Major depots were Columbus, Athens and Atlanta, Georgia for the Army of Tennessee and Houston, Texas and Shreveport, Louisiana for the Trans-Mississippi forces.

As the war progressed the image began to shift from the "ragged rebel" look to a well-uniformed Army in the Eastern and Western theaters. In the last 12 months of fighting these Confederate forces were well uniformed, the best they had ever appeared in terms of consistency, wearing clothing made of imported blue-grey cloth, used by the British Army and manufactured in Limerick Ireland, by Peter Tait specifically for the Confederacy.

Unfortunately in the Trans-Mississippi, problems of distribution of the plentiful uniforms made in Houston and Shreveport, meant that the South Western forces missed out. Many Trans-Mississippi troops were still wearing Federal uniforms until 1864, which were obtained from stock issued from a Federal depot in San Antonio that had been captured in 1861.

Confederate headgear was to be the chasseur cap or "kepi", a French military cap. These were not popular due to their inability to protect the wearer from the sun, and regular civilian hats, slouch hats, or other hats were often worn in the field instead. Confederate Cavalry troops often wore Hardee hats, much like the Union Cavalry which was a representative of the additional "flair" associated with the Cavalry troops. Two examples of CSA Cavalry officer's famous for wearing these hats are Colonel John S. Mosby and General J.E.B. Stuart.

Design

Confederate Battle Flag

The use of wool in the uniform meant that the uniforms were not suited to the warm climates that were common in the South. This helped contribute to the fact that many Confederate soldiers suffered from heatstroke on long marches.

Grey was not the best choice for camouflage, although at the time the usefulness of camouflage was not generally recognized. It was not until after the Spanish-American War that the United States Army instituted a khaki uniform. Grey was chosen for Confederate uniforms because grey dye could be made relatively cheaply.

Confederate States Army uniforms

Army officers

Generals

William Mahone wearing one version of Three Gold Stars and Wreath on a General's Collar

George Pickett wearing one version of Three Gold Stars and Wreath on a General's Collar

William "Extra Billy" Smith wearing one version of Three Gold Stars and Wreath on a General's Collar

John Wharton wearing one version of Three Gold Stars and Wreath on a General's Collar

Daniel Harvey Hill wearing one version of Three Gold Stars and Wreath on a General's Collar

"Stonewall Jackson" Example of the Three Gold Stars and Wreath on a General's Collar

On the upright collar of full generals, lieutenant generals, major generals, and brigadier generals three stars were stitched within a wreath, all embroidered in gold coloring. The center star was slightly larger than the other stars. It was not possible to know which grade of general an officer was by their collar insignia. However, major generals and lieutenant generals wore three groups of buttons down the front of the overcoat, and brigadiers wore groups of two. At least 3 Generals officers did not wear the prescribed uniform: Robert E. Lee who wore the uniform of a Colonel, refusing to wear a generals insignia until the Confederate victory; Joseph Hogg- died of a fever; and Benjamin McCulloch.

Other officers

CS General A. P. Hill wearing the 3 stars of a Colonel

CS General Joseph E. Johnston wearing the 3 stars of a Colonel

CS General Winfield Scott Featherston wearing the 3{?} stars of a Colonel

CS General Thomas R. R. Cobb wearing the 3 stars of a Colonel

Colonels wore three gold stars of the same size on their collar; the same as generals, but without the wreath. While lieutenant colonels wore two stars on their collars, majors wore one star, which was placed in the middle of the collar. Captains had three gold horizontal bars, first lieutenants wore two bars, and second lieutenants wore one bar. However, the Confederate Congress often created new commissions, and did not always standardize rank insignia immediately.

Army enlisted men

Chevrons

Chevrons in the Confederate Army were only worn by sergeants and corporals. Sergeants wore three chevrons on their sleeves, and corporals wore two chevrons.

Buttons

A brigadier general's coat had two rows of eight buttons, grouped in pairs. The other junior officers wore two rows of seven equally spaced buttons each.

Jackets

Confederate Army officers indicated their military affiliation with different colored facing on their coats or jackets.

Edmund Kirby Smith wearing one version of Three Gold Stars and Wreath on a General's Collar

PGT Beauregard wearing one version of Three Gold Stars and Wreath on a General's Collar

Albert Sidney Johnston wearing one version of Three Gold Stars and Wreath on a General's Collar

The colors were red for artillery, yellow for cavalry, light blue for infantry, and black for medical. Regimental officers wore the colors on the outer seam of their pants on one and one-quarter inch stripes. Generals wore two and five-eighths inch stripes on each pant leg. While the quartermasters, commissary, and engineer officers wore a single gold, one and one-quarter inch outer-seam stripe. Noncommissioned officers were to wear on their outer seams a one and one-quarter inch cotton stripe or braid of colors appropriate to their army branch. A very distinctive feature of the Condederate officers uniforms was the gold braid Austrian knots on their sleeves. More elaborate braiding indicated higher rank and some knots almost reached the shoulder.

Kepis

The "French" pattern kepi, was the standard issue headgear to all army personnel, with dark blue band, sides & crown for generals, staff officers, and engineers. For commissioned officers and enlisted personal they had bands of dark blue with different colors denoting the branch of service on the sides and crown. Theses were as follows, Red for artillery, yellow for cavalry, and light or sky blue for infantry. Cap visors were made from leather or "oilcloth" over paste board. Chin straps were also installed.

Trousers

The Confederate trousers were very similar to those of the Union forces. Early on the trousers were sky blue in color. They were most often made of wool, and were easily worn during long marches. If trousers did not arrive for the troops the soldiers would have to use their own pants to wear.

Example of a CS Belt Buckle

Example of a CSA Belt Buckle

Belt

There were numerous types of belts produced for the Confederate Military during the Civil War. There were two types of belts which were standard to all army personal. The CS, standing for Confederate States, and CSA belt, standing for Confederate States of America. The buckle themselves were made of brass and were produced in multiple plants in the South and throughout the World.. Whether the belt was one with a CS or CSA on the buckle depended on the location at which it was made and on the maker. Some Confederate soldiers were issued with, or otherwise obtained, belt buckles with insignias unique to the state they came from or served under the command of. At the beginning of the war, soldiers with experience in the U.S. Army could often be seen still wearing "US" belt buckles, as this would have been all that they had available. As supplies became more difficult to obtain near the end of the war, buckles captured from Union forces were also worn.

Cavalry Uniforms

1st Virginia Cavalry-Example of a Confederate cavalryman wearing the stag hat

Design

The first of the Cavalry uniforms were made by the cavalrymen themselves. By 1862, the Confederate regulations ordered the uniform to become organized, being cadet grey and lined with a thin layer around the sleeve. The pant legs were light blue with a yellow strip rising from the bottom of the leg to the top. Non-commissioned officers of the cavalry wore either regular clothes from home or a variety of different types of uniforms.

Buttons

A normal junior officer had two rows of evenly spaced seven buttons, grouped into pairs.

Hats

The kepi was also standard issue to all army personnel. In the cavalry the color of the kepi was to be yellow. More common than the kepi was the Confederate stag hat, which was worn by most of the Confederate Cavalry.

Artillery Uniforms

Design

The first of the Artillery uniforms were a variety of handmade and personally customized uniforms. By 1862, the Confederate uniforms became organized. They became cadet grey and were to be lined with a layer of red around the sleeve. The pant legs were light blue. Even after the uniforms were organized many of the artillerymen wore regular clothes due to the heat and discomfort caused by the regular uniforms.

Buttons

In the Confederate Artillery a normal junior officer had two rows of seven evenly spaced buttons, grouped into pairs, while a senior officer could have as many as eight buttons in two rows.

Hats

The kepi was also standard issue to the artillerymen, they were made red to match that of the rest of their uniforms. During the summer months they were also allowed to wear straw hats because of the heat.

Confederate States Navy uniforms

Design

Confederate States Navy Department

The first of the Navy uniforms were made in dark blue, but with the Southern style of rank insignia for the officers. The 1862 Confederate regulations ordered the uniform to be steel grey and lined with a dark black silk serge. They were also made in medium grey and cadet grey. They were made of wool, and these uniforms were not fit for the heat of the lower decks of a ship. Non-commissioned officers wore a variety of uniforms, or even regular clothing.

Shoulder Straps

Example of a Confederate Naval Officer's Uniform (Statue of Captain Raphael Semmes, Mobile, Alabama).

According to the dress code of the Confederate Navy, shoulder straps were to be worn differently by each rank.

- Admirals wore a shoulder strap of sky-blue cloth, edged with black, that was four inches long and one inch and three-eighths wide embroidered with gold one-quarter of an inch in width. They had five stars spaced equally, the two on the ends six-tenths of an inch in diameter, and the three intermediate stars six-eighths of an inch in diameter.
- Flag officers wore a shoulder strap of sky-blue cloth, edged with black, that was four inches long and one inch and three-eighths wide embroidered with gold one-quarter of an inch in width. They had four stars spaced equally, the two on the ends six-tenths of an inch in diameter, and the two intermediate stars six-eighths of an inch in diameter.
- captains wore the same shoulder straps as the flag officers, but with three equally spaced stars, each six-tenths of an inch in diameter.
- Commanders also had the same shoulder straps, but with only two stars.
- Lieutenants had the same shoulder straps, with a single, central, star.
- The shoulder straps worn by masters had the same design, but without any stars.
- Passed midshipmen wore a strip of gold lace four inches in length and a half an inch wide.
- For a midshipman, no shoulder straps were to be worn.

Caps

Confederate Naval Caps were made of steel grey cloth. They were not to be less than three inches and a half, nor more than four inches in height. They were also not to be more than ten, or less than nine inches and a half, at the top, and had a patent leather visor, to be worn by all officers in their service dress.

- For a flag officer, the cap had an anchor in an open wreath of oak leaves, with four stars above the anchor. They were to be embroidered in gold as per pattern.
- For a captain, the same as a flag officer's, except that there were only three stars above the anchor, and the gold band was one and one-half inches wide.
- For a commander it was to be the same as for a captain, except that there were only but two stars.
- For a lieutenant, the same as that of a captain, except there was only one star.
- For a master, the same as for a captain, except that there was no star.
- For a passed midshipman, an anchor without a wreath.
- For a midshipman, no caps were to be worn.

Confederate States Marine Corps uniforms

The uniform used by the Confederate States Marine Corps resembled that prescribed for the Confederate Army. However, there is controversy about some of the exact details of the uniform, since the CSMC was not as large, and many of its records were destroyed. In 1865, right after the war's end, Lloyd J. Beal, commander of the CSMC, had a fire at his home which destroyed most of the CSMC's records. It is clear, however, that the Marines were often equipped out of the stores of whichever garrison was nearest their location. One description has the Marines dressed in, frock coats of a particular (and undetermined) shade of gray, and dark blue or black trousers. It appears that Confederate Marines wore forage caps although it is unclear if there was any ornamentation on the cover. Much of the gear worn by the CSMC was imported from Russia, and from Great Britain and its empire, mainly Canada. This created a fairly unique look.

Source (edited): "http://en.wikipedia.org/wiki/Uniforms_of_the_Confederate_States_military_forces"

CSS Alabama

CSS *Alabama* was a screw sloop-of-war built for the Confederate States Navy at Birkenhead, United Kingdom, in 1862 by John Laird Sons and Company. *Alabama* served as a commerce raider, attacking Union merchant and naval ships over the course of her two-year career, during which she never laid anchor in a Southern port. She was sunk by the USS *Kearsarge* in 1864.

History

Construction

Deck scene Cruiser Alabama in August, 1863 - Lts Armstrong and Sinclair at Sinclair's 32 pounder station

Alabama was built in secrecy in 1862 by British shipbuilders John Laird Sons and Company in North West England at their shipyards at Birkenhead, Cheshire. This was arranged by the Confederate agent James Dunwoody Bulloch, who was leading the procurement of sorely needed ships for the fledgling Confederate States Navy. He arranged the contract through Fraser, Trenholm Company, a cotton broker in Liverpool with ties to the Confederacy.

Initially known as hull number 290, the ship was launched without fanfare on 29 July 1862 as *Enrica*. Agent Bulloch arranged for a civilian crew and captain to sail *Enrica* to Terceira Island in the Azores. With Bulloch staying aboard to witness her recommissioning, the new ship's captain, Raphael Semmes, left Liverpool on 5 August 1862 aboard the steamer *Bahama* to take command of the new cruiser. Semmes arrived at Terceira Island on 20 August 1862 and began overseeing the refitting of the new vessel with various provisions, including armaments, and 350 tons of coal, brought there by *Agrippina*, his new ship's supply vessel. After three days of back-breaking work by the three ship's crews, the new ship was transformed into a naval cruiser, designated a commerce raider, for the Confederate States of America.

Alabama's British-made ordnance was composed of six broadside, 32-pounder, naval smoothbores and two larger and more powerful pivot cannons. Both pivot cannons were positioned roughly amidships along the deck's centerline, fore and aft of the main mast. The fore pivot was a heavy, long-range 100-pounder 7-inch (178 mm) Blakely rifle, the aft pivot a heavy, 8-inch (203 mm) smoothbore.

The new Confederate cruiser was powered by both sail and by two John Laird Sons and Company 300 horsepower (220 kW) horizontal steam engines, driving a single, Griffiths-type, twin-bladed brass screw. With the screw retracted using the stern's brass lifting gear mechanism, *Alabama* could make up to ten knots under sail alone and 13.25 knots (24.54 km/h) when her sail and steam power were used together.

Commissioning and voyage

The ship was purposely commissioned about a mile off Terceira Island in international waters on 24 August 1862: All the men from *Agripinna* and *Bahama* had been transferred to the quarter deck of *Enrica*, where her 24 officers, some of them Southerners, stood in full dress uniform. Captain Raphael Semmes mounted a gun-carriage and read his commission from President Jefferson Davis, authorizing him to take command of the new cruiser. Upon completion of the reading, musicians that assembled from among the three ships' crews began to play the tune "Dixie" just as the quartermaster finished hauling down *Enrica*'s British colors. A signal cannon boomed and the stops to the halliards at the peaks of the mizzen gaff and mainmast were broken and the ship's new battle ensign and commissioning pennant floated free on the breeze. With that the cruiser became Confederate States Steamer *Alabama*.

Captain Semmes then made a speech about the Southern cause to the assembled seamen, asking them to sign on for a voyage of unknown length and destiny. Semmes had only his 24 officers and no crew to man his new command. When this did not succeed, Semmes changed his tack. It should be noted here that engraved in the bronze of the great double ship's wheel was *Alabama's* motto: *"Aide-toi et Dieu t'aidera" (God helps those who help themselves)*. Semmes then offered signing money and double wages, paid in gold, and additional prize money to be paid by the Confederate congress for all destroyed Union ships. When the men began to shout "Hear! Hear!" Semmes knew he had closed the deal: 83 seamen, many of them British, signed on for service in the Confederate Navy. Confederate agent Bulloch and the remaining seamen then returned to their respective ships for their return voyage to England. Semmes still needed another 20 or so men for a full crew complement, but enough had signed on to at least handle the new commerce raider. The rest would be recruited from among captured crews of raided ships or from friendly ports-of-call. Of the original 83 crewmen that signed on that day, many completed the full voyage.

Captain Raphael Semmes, Alabama's commanding officer, standing by his ship's 110-pounder rifled gun during her visit to Capetown in August 1863. His executive officer, First Lieutenant John M. Kell, is in the background, standing by the ship's wheel.

Under Captain Semmes, *Alabama* spent her first two months in the Eastern Atlantic, ranging southwest of the Azores and then redoubling east, capturing and burning northern merchant ships. After a difficult crossing, she then continued her path of destruction and devastation in the greater New England region. She then sailed south, arriving in the West Indies where she raised more havoc before finally cruising west into the Gulf of Mexico. There, in January 1863, *Alabama* had her first military engagement. She came upon and quickly sank the Union side-wheeler USS *Hatteras* just off the Texas coast, near Galveston, capturing that warship's crew. She then continued further south, eventually crossing the equator, where she took the most prizes of her raiding career while cruising off the coast of Brazil. After a second Atlantic crossing, *Alabama* sailed down the southwestern African coast where she continued her war against northern commerce. After stopping in Saldanha Bay on 29 July 1863 in order to verify that no enemy ships were in Table Bay, she finally made a much-needed refitting and reprovisioning visit to Cape Town, South Africa. She then sailed for the East Indies, where she spent six months destroying seven more ships before finally redoubling the Cape of Good Hope en route to France. Union warships hunted frequently for the elusive and by now famous Confederate raider, but the few times *Alabama* was spotted, she quickly outwitted her pursuers and vanished beyond the horizon.

All together, she burned 65 Union vessels of various types, most of them merchant ships. During all of *Alabama's* raiding ventures, captured ships' crews and passengers were never harmed, only detained until they could be placed aboard a neutral ship or placed ashore in a friendly or neutral port.

Expeditionary raids of the CSS *Alabama*

All together, *Alabama* conducted a total of seven expeditionary raids, spanning the globe, before heading back to France for refit and repairs and a date with destiny:

- The CSS Alabama's Eastern Atlantic Expeditionary Raid (August–September, 1862) commenced immediately after she was commissioned. She immediately set sail for the shipping lanes southwest and then east of the Azores, where she captured and burned ten prizes, mostly whalers.
- The CSS Alabama's New England Expeditionary Raid (October–November, 1862) began after Captain Semmes and his crew departed for the northeastern seaboard of North America, along Newfoundland and New England, where she ranged as far south as Bermuda and the coast of Virginia, burning ten prizes while capturing and releasing three others.
- The CSS Alabama's Gulf of Mexico Expeditionary Raid (December, 1862 – January, 1863) was centered around a needed rendezvous with her supply vessel, CSS *Agrippina*. After that, she rendered aid to Texas during Major General Banks invasion near Galveston, Texas. There, she quickly sank the Union side-wheeler USS *Hatteras*.
- The CSS Alabama's South Atlantic Expeditionary Raid (February–July, 1863) was her most successful raiding venture, taking 29 prizes while raiding off the coast of Brazil. Here, she recommissioned the bark *Conrad* as the CSS *Tuscaloosa*.
- The CSS Alabama's South African Expeditionary Raid (August–September, 1863) occurred primarily while ranging off the coast of South Africa, as she worked together the CSS *Tuscaloosa*.
- The CSS Alabama's Indian Ocean Expeditionary Raid (September–November, 1863) was composed of a long trek across the Indian Ocean. The few prizes she gathered were in the East Indies.
- The CSS Alabama's South Pacific Expeditionary Raid (December, 1863) was her final raiding venture. She took a few prizes in the Strait of Malacca before finally turning back toward France for a much needed refit and long overdue repairs.

Upon the completion of her seven expeditionary raids, *Alabama* had been at sea for 534 days out of 657, never visiting a single Confederate port. She boarded nearly 450 vessels, captured or burned 65 Union merchant ships, and took more than 2,000 prisoners without a single loss of life from either prisoners or her own crew.

Final Cruise

"*Kearsarge* and the *Alabama*" by Édouard Manet

Sternpost of USS *Kearsarge* containing unexploded 100-pound shell fired by CSS *Alabama*

On 11 June 1864, *Alabama* arrived in port at Cherbourg, France. Captain Semmes soon requested permission to dry dock and overhaul his ship, much needed after so long a time at sea and so many naval actions. Pursuing the raider, the American sloop-of-war, USS *Kearsarge*, under the command of Captain John Ancrum Winslow, arrived three days later and took up station just outside the harbor. While at his previous port-of-call, Winslow had telegraphed Gibraltar to send the old man-o-war USS *St. Louis* with provisions and to provide blockading assistance. *Kearsarge* now had *Alabama* boxed-in with no place left to run.

Having no desire to see his worn-out ship rot away at a French dock while quarantined by Union warships, and given his instinctive aggressiveness and a long-held desire once again to engage his enemy, Captain Semmes chose to fight. After preparing his ship and drilling the crew for the coming battle during the next several days, Semmes issued, through diplomatic channels, a bold challenge to the Kearsarge's commander, "my intention is to fight the Kearsarge as soon as I can make the necessary arrangements. I hope these will not detain me more than until tomorrow or the morrow morning at farthest. I beg she will not depart until I am ready to go out. I have the honor to be Your obedient servant, R. Semmes, Captain."

On 19 June, *Alabama* sailed out to meet the Union cruiser. As *Kearsarge* turned to meet her opponent, *Alabama* opened fire. *Kearsarge* waited patiently until the range had closed to less than 1,000 yards (900 m). According to survivors, the two ships steamed on opposite courses in seven spiraling circles, moving southwesterly with the 3-knot current, each commander trying to cross the bow of his opponent to deliver a heavy raking fire. The battle quickly turned against *Alabama* due to the superior gunnery displayed by *Kearsarge* and the deteriorated state of *Alabama*'s contaminated powder and fuses. Her most important shot, fired from the forward 7-inch (178 mm) Blakely pivot rifle, hit very near *Kearsarge*'s vulnerable stern post, the impact binding the ship's rudder badly. That rifled shell, however, failed to explode. If it had done so, it would have seriously disabled *Kearsarge*'s steering, possibly sinking the warship, and ending the contest. In addition, *Alabama*'s too rapid rate-of-fire resulted in frequent poor gunnery, with many of her shots going too high, thus sealing the fate of the Confederate raider. As a result, *Kearsarge* benefited little that day from the protection of her outboard chain armor, whose presence Semmes later said was unknown to him at the time of his decision to issue the challenge to fight. In fact, in the years that followed, Semmes steadfastly claimed he would have never fought *Kearsarge* if he had known she was armor-clad.

The ironclad frigate French battleship *La Gloire* was in the English Channel, near Cherbourg, during the battle between *Alabama* and *Kearsarge*

This hull armor had been installed in just three days, more than a year before, while *Kearsarge* was in port at the Azores. It was made using 120 fathoms (720 feet) of 1.7-inch (43 mm) single link iron chain and covered hull spaces 49 feet (15 m), six-inches (152 mm) long by 6-feet, 2-inches deep. It was stopped up and down to eye-bolts with marlines and secured by iron dogs. It was concealed behind 1-inch deal-boards painted black to match the upper hull's color. This chaincladding was placed along *Kearsarge*'s port and starboard midsection down to the waterline, for additional protection of her engines and boilers when the upper portion of her coal bunkers were empty. This armor belt was hit twice during the fight: First in the starboard gangway by one of *Alabama*'s 32-pounder shells that cut the chain armor, denting the hull planking underneath, then again by a second 32-pounder shell that exploded and broke a link of the chain armor, tearing away a portion of the deal-board covering. If those rounds had come from *Alabama*'s more powerful 100-pounder Blakely pivot rifle, the likely result would not have been too serious, as both struck the chain armor a little more than five feet above the waterline. Even if both shots had penetrated *Kearsarge*'s side, they would have completely missed her vital machinery.

A little more than an hour after the first shot was fired, *Alabama* was reduced to a sinking wreck by *Kearsarge*'s powerful 11-inch (280 mm) Dahlgrens, forcing Captain Semmes to strike his colors and to send one of his two surviving boats to *Kearsarge* to ask for assistance.

According to witnesses, *Alabama* fired 370 rounds at her adversary, averaging one round per minute per gun, while *Kearsarge*'s gun crews fired less than half that many, taking more careful aim. During the confusion of battle, five more rounds were fired at *Alabama* after her colors were struck. (Her gun ports had been left open and the broadside cannon were still run out, appearing to come to bear on *Kearsarge*.) Then a hand-held white flag came fluttering from *Alabama*'s stern spanker boom, finally halting the engagement. Prior to this, she had her steering gear compromised by shell hits, but the fatal shot came later when one of *Kearsarge*'s 11-inch (280 mm) shells tore open a mid-section of *Alabama*'s starboard waterline. Water quickly rushed through the defeated cruiser, eventually drowning her boilers and forcing her down by the stern to the bottom. *Kearsarge* rescued the majority of the survivors, but 41 of *Alabama*'s officers and crew, including Semmes, were rescued by the *Deerhound*, a private yacht, while the *Kearsarge* stood off to recover her rescue boats while waiting for *Alabama* to sink. Captain Winslow was forced to stand by helplessly and watch *Deerhound* spirit away to England his much sought after adversary, Captain Semmes and his surviving shipmates.

The battle between the *Alabama* and *Kearsarge* is honored by the United States Navy with a battle star on the Civil War campaign streamer.
Died in Saldanha Bay from accidental gun shot on 3 August 1863.

Medal and honor awarded for valor

Perhaps the most courageous and selfless act during the *Alabama's* last moments involved the ship's assistant surgeon, Dr. David Herbert Llewellyn. Dr. Llewellyn, a Briton, was much loved and respected by the entire crew. During the battle, he steadfastly remained at his post in the wardroom tending the wounded until the order to abandon ship was finally given. As he helped wounded men into the *Alabama's* only two functional lifeboats, an able bodied sailor attempted to enter one, which was already full. Llewellyn, understanding that the man risked capsizing the craft, grabbed and pulled him back, saying "See, I want to save my life as much as you do; but let the wounded men be saved first." An officer in the boat, seeing that Llewellyn was about to be left aboard the stricken *Alabama*, shouted "Doctor, we can make room for you." Llewellyn shook his head and replied, "I will not peril the wounded." Unknown to the crew, Llewellyn had never learned to swim, and he drowned when the ship went down.

His sacrifice did not go unrecognized. The Confederacy awarded him posthumously the Southern Cross of Honor . In his native Wiltshire, a memorial window and tablet were placed at Easton Royal Church. Another tablet was placed in Charing Cross Hospital, where he attended medical school.

Repercussions

During her two-year career as a commerce raider, *Alabama* caused disorder and devastation across the globe for Union merchant shipping. The Confederate cruiser claimed 65 prizes valued at nearly $6,000,000 (approximately $123,000,000 in today's dollars). In an important development in international law, the U. S. Government pursued the "Alabama Claims" against the British Government for the devastation caused, and following a court of arbitration, won heavy damages.

Ironically, a decade before the beginning of the Civil War, Captain Semmes had observed:

"(Commerce raiders) are little better than licensed pirates; and it behooves all civilized nations [...] to suppress the practice altogether." --Raphael Semmes, 1851

The wreck

In November 1984, the French Navy mine hunter *Circé* discovered a wreck under nearly 60 m (200 ft) of water off Cherbourg at 49°45′9″N 1°41′42″W. Captain Max Guerout later confirmed the wreck to be the *Alabama's* remains.

In 1988, a non-profit organization the Association CSS *Alabama* was founded to conduct scientific exploration of the shipwreck. Although the wreck resides within French territorial waters, the U. S. government, as the successor to the former Confederate States of America, is the owner. On October 3, 1989, the United States and France signed an agreement recognizing this wreck as an important heritage resource of both nations and establishing a Joint French-American Scientific Committee for archaeological exploration. This agreement established a precedent for international cooperation in archaeological research and in the protection of a unique historic shipwreck. This agreement will be in effect for five years and is renewable by mutual consent.

The Association CSS *Alabama* and the U.S. Navy/Naval Historical Center signed on March 23, 1995 an official agreement accrediting Association CSS *Alabama* as operator of the archaeological investigation of the remains of the ship. Association CSS *Alabama*, which is funded solely from private donations, is continuing to make this an international project through its fund raising in France and in the United States, thanks to its sister organization, the CSS *Alabama* Association, incorporated in the State of Delaware.

In 2002, a diving expedition raised the ship's bell along with more than 300 other artifacts, including cannons, structural samples, tableware, ornate commodes, and numerous other items that reveal much about life aboard the Confederate warship. Many of the artifacts are now housed in the Underwater Archaeology Branch, Naval History & Heritage Command conservation lab.

CSS *Alabama* folklore

"Roll Alabama, roll!"

The *Alabama* is the subject of a sea shanty, "'Roll Alabama, roll'":
When the Alabama's Keel was Laid, (Roll Alabama, roll!), 'Twas laid in the yard of Jonathan Laird (Roll, roll Alabama, roll!)
'Twas Laid in the yard of Jonathan Laird, 'twas laid in the town of Birkenhead.
Down the Mersey way she rolled then, and Liverpool fitted her with guns and

men.
From the western isle she sailed forth,
to destroy the commerce of the north.
To Cherbourg port she sailed one day,
for to take her count of prize money.
Many a sailor laddie saw his doom,
when the Kearsarge it hove in view.
When a ball from the forward pivot that
day, shot the Alabama's stern away.
Off the three-mile limit in '64, the
Alabama was seen no more.

"Daar kom die Alibama"

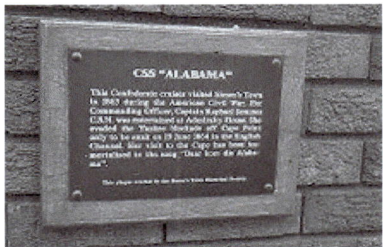

CSS *Alabama* plaque in Simonstown.

The *Alabama's* visit to Cape Town in 1863 has passed (with a slight spelling change) into South African folklore in the Afrikaans song, "'Daar Kom die Alibama'":
Daar kom die Alibama,
Die Alibama, die kom oor die see,
Daar kom die Alibama,
Die Alibama, die kom oor die see...
Nooi, nooi die rietkooi nooi,
Die rietkooi is gemaak,
Die rietkooi is vir my gemaak,
Om daarop te slaap...
O Alibama, die Alibama,
O Alibama, die kom oor die see,
O Alibama, die Alibama,
O Alibama, die kom oor die see...
There comes the Alabama,
The Alabama, it comes o'er the sea,
There comes the Alabama,
The Alabama, it comes o'er the sea...
Lass, lass, the reed bed calls,
The reed bed it is made,
The reed bed it is made for me,
To sleep upon...
Oh Alabama, the Alabama,
Oh Alabama, it comes o'er the sea,
Oh Alabama, the Alabama,
Oh Alabama, it comes o'er the sea...

CSS *Alabama*'s battle ensigns &

other naval flags
The practice of using primary and secondary naval flags after the British tradition was common practice for the Confederacy, linked as she was by both heritage and economy to the British Isles. The fledgling Confederate Navy therefore adopted and used jacks, commissioning pennants, battle ensigns, small boat ensigns, designating flags, and signal flags aboard its warships during the Civil War.

Jacks and commissioning pennants

The First Confederate Navy Jack, 1861–1863

The Second Confederate Navy Jack, 1863–1865

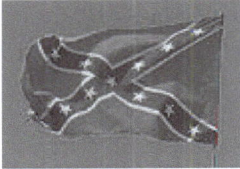

Navy Jack of the CSA

Alabama's original 7-star naval jack (first illustration, above) would have flown atop her foremast while she was in port, well forward of her battle ensign. At some point, it would have displayed the same asymmetrical, 8-star configuration as seen on one of her three still surviving battle ensigns (see "Surviving stars and bars" section below). A medium-blue color, early Confederate jacks duplicated the star arrangements seen on their ensigns' cantons. They were rectangular in shape, rather than square, because the Confederate Navy emulated the overall designs being used by their U. S. Navy counterparts. There is surviving evidence, the captured 7-star jack of the ironclad CSS *Atlanta*, which strongly suggests all early Confederate naval jacks were actually a dark blue, *matching* the color of their battle ensigns' cantons. Whatever its blue color, later versions of *Alabama*'s pre-1863 jack could have contained, like her ensign, 9, 11, 13, and up to 15 white, 5-pointed stars.

Alabama's naval jack design changed (second and third illustrations, above) when the Confederacy adopted the *Stainless Banner* Second National Flag (see that section, below). While her specific jack's dimensions are unknown, the Confederate naval regulations adopted on 26/28 May 1863 required that all new jacks be a larger version of the battle ensign's new 13-star canton, the red, blue, and white *Southern Cross*. Instead of being square, all jacks were required to be rectangular in shape, their width being one-and-a-half times their height, a ratio of 2:3. Their white-bordered diagonal saltires were a medium blue color rather than the dark blue seen on the *Stainless Banner*. However, virtually all surviving Confederate jacks show their proportions and specific details varied, despite the Confederate Navy regulation's precise requirements. Differences among both state and regional contractors' manufacturing methods and frequent materials shortages as the war progressed, likely account for the variations seen. Following the Civil War and up through today, the rectangular *Southern Cross* naval jack became the Confederate flag design most commonly associated with the post-war South, and racial controversy.

Both of *Alabama*'s pre-1863 commissioning pennants would have closely followed the pennant designs used by the U. S. Navy. They would have been long and narrow and one of five approved sizes, being anywhere from 25 feet (7.6 m) to 70 feet (21 m) in their overall lengths, and would have flown atop her main mast. Their medium or possibly dark blue cantons (hoists) would have been one-quarter of their overall flys (widths). Each could have carried from 7 to 15 white, 5-pointed stars, as the number of states in the Confederacy grew: 7 to 15 on *Alabama*'s daylight pennant but only 7 on her much smaller after-sunset pennant. Their star patterns could have been staggered either up and down or laid out in a single, horizonital row across their blue cantons (accounts vary). The remaining three-quarters of these very long, narrow streamers would have been divided equally with two stripes, red-over-white (some accounts say white-over-red), with both stripes termanating in twin-forked points. A slightly modified third pennant variant with *three* long, horizontal red-over-white-over-red stripes, also terminating in twin-forked points, was in use before 1863 by the Confederate Navy.

The stars and bars

On 4 March 1861, the committee of the first Provisional Congress of the Confederate States of America established the general requirements for the First National Flag of the Confederacy. Many designs were submitted by the public, but the new flag's approved design came from Marion, Alabama, Prussian artist Nicola Marschall, who had married into a Montgomery, Alabama family. The new Confederate flag and naval ensign was loosely adapted from his homeland's Austrian flag (with a dark blue canton added), quickly becoming known in the South as the *Stars and Bars*. Its hoist-to-fly (width-to-height) was later established by the committee with a ratio of 2:3. The flag's dark blue canton was to be in a 1:1 (square) ratio and contain seven white, 5-pointed stars arranged in a circular layout. The flag's three horizontal stripes were to be red over white over red and be of equal height. The newly adopted *Star and Bars* made its first public appearance outside the Ben Johnson House in Bardstown, Kentucky. It was then raised over the dome of the first Confederate capitol in Montgomery, Alabama and aboard all Condederate Navy ships, where it flew until 26 May 1863, when it was replaced with a new Second National Flag design.

Typical First National Flag (*Stars and Bars*) 13-star battle ensign design, possibly flown aboard CSS *Alabama*. (28 November 1861 – May 1863)

During *Alabama* 's long commerce raiding cruises, several revised versions of her *Stars and Bars* could have flown aboard when the news of additional stars being added eventually reached the ship. Their dark blue cantons could have contained at various times 9, 11, 13 (as pictured, right) and up to 15 white stars.

In addition to her own, *Alabama* is known to have carried both British Union Jack and U. S. Stars and Stripes ensigns in her flags locker. Both were flown at various times, along with the ensigns of other nations, to conceal *Alabama*'s true nationality as she overtook ships, looking for the North's commercial shipping.

Alabama's surviving stars and bars

At the beginning of *Alabama*'s raiding ventures, the newly commissioned cruiser may have been forced, out of necessity, to fly the only battle ensign available to Captain Semmes: an early 1861, 7-star First National Flag. Between 21 May and 28 November 1861, six more Southern states seceded and joined the Confederacy. Well before *Alabama* was launched as *Enrica* at Birkenhead, Merseyside in North West England, six more white, 5-pointed stars had been added to the *Stars and Bars* far away across the Atlantic on the Confederate mainland.

Typical First National Flag (*Stars and Bars*) 7-star battle ensign design. (4 May 1861 – 21 May 1861)

One such early *Stars and Bars* battle ensign was salvaged from *Alabama*'s floating debris, following her sinking by the *Kearsarge*. It still survives and is held by the Alabama Department of Archives and History. It is listed there as "Auxiliary Flag of the C.S.S. Alabama, Catalogue No. 86.3766.1." According to their provenence reconstruction, DeCost Smith, an American from New England, discovered this *Stars and Bars* ensign in a Paris upholstery shop in 1884, where he purchased it for 15 francs. Smith's nephew, Clement Sawtell of Lincoln Square, Massachusetts, later inherited the ensign from his uncle. At the suggestion of retired Rear Admiral Beverly M. Coleman, Sawtell donated it to the State of Alabama on 3 June 1975.

This battle ensign's overall dimensions are different from the Confederate regulations' required 2:3 ratio. It is 64-inches high (hoist) by 112-inches long (fly), a proportion of 5:9, and its dark blue canton contains *eight* white stars, 8-inches (203 mm) high, in an unusual arrangement: The stars are not organized in a circle but configured in three, centered, horizontal rows of two, then three, and finally two. The additional 8th star is tucked into the lower left corner (and in the lower right corner on the opposite side), giving the canton's layout a unique, asymmetrical appearance. It seems plausible this was *Alabama*'s original 7-star battle ensign, later altered at some point when the long-delayed news of an 8th state joining the Confederacy finally reached the far distant cruiser.

Two *Star and Bars* battle ensigns, labeled as having belonged to *Alabama*, also still exist. The first is a framed, *14-star* ensign located at the museum of Fort Monroe in Virginia. (A small number of these unusual 14-star national flags have survived to today and are held in several Civil War archives.) From the single, side-angled color photo available on the Internet, it appears to have an approximate hoist-to-fly aspect ratio of 1:2. A second *Stars and Bars* battle ensign is on display at the Pensacola Historical Museum. It's canton contains a circle of 12 stars surrounding a 13th at its center. While the provenance and specific details of these two *Alabama* ensigns are currently unavailable, such information will be added to this section when available.

The stainless banner

Typical 1:2 ratio Second National Flag (*Stainless Banner*) battle ensign design (adopted 1 May 1863).

By late 1863, a new battle ensign, the Second National Flag of the Confederacy, also known as the *Stainless Banner*, was flying aboard *Alabama*. The specifications for this new ensign, established on 1 May 1863 by the Confederate Congress, gave it a hoist-to-fly proportion of 1:2, the white area being twice as wide as the height. A short time later, however, the Confederate Navy Department revised these regulations, changing the Navy's battle ensign proportions to a 2:3 ratio. Its square canton was the established thirteen-star red, blue, and white *Southern Cross*, already in-use by the Southern army as the *Confederate Battle Flag*. This design was originally proposed in 1861 by South Carolina Congressman William Porcher Miles to be used as the original First National Flag, but it was supposedly rejected as appearing too much like a pair of crossed pants' suspenders.

Whatever its proportion, the white expanse of the *Stainless Banner* proved to have poor visibility at a distance, especially when viewed through the haze sometimes seen over water and or in contrast against soft gray skies. Both types of *Stainless Banner* ensigns ultimately wound of being used aboard Confederate ships, their proportions and specific details varying a bit from both ship-to-ship and state-to-state.

Typical 2:3 ratio revised Second National Flag (*Stainless Banner*) battle ensign (likely flying aboard CSS *Alabama* just before her surrender).

Accounts state that the *Stainless Banner* Second National Flag was flying high on a line attached to *Alabama*'s mizzen gaff until just before her sinking off Cherbourg, France, in 1864. At the close of her losing fight with the *Kearsarge*, *Alabama*'s battle ensign was ordered struck for the last time. What happened to it following the battle is unknown. All other colors in her flags locker, both old and new, except the one noted above, were lost with her destruction by the *Kearsarge*.

It is unknown which versions of all the above flags were flown at specific intervals during *Alabama*'s seven raiding campaigns. Captain Semmes, while visiting friendly or neutral foreign ports-of-call, may have simply commissioned multiple new battle ensigns, naval jacks, and pennants, as needed, while refitting and reprovisioning his ship. Or he may have ordered them altered or new ones made aboard when captured newspaper articles or official dispatches containing the changes finally caught up to *Alabama*.

Alabama's surviving stainless banners

Four of *Alabama*'s later-style ensigns have survived to the modern era. The first is a large, 67-inch x 114-inch (170-cm x 290-cm) battle ensign that is located in South Africa at the Cape Town Museum of History. Its *Southern Cross* canton is oversize and rectangular, instead of square, in roughly a 1:2 aspect ratio. It is also made without the usual white stripe outlines found around the diagonal saltires' blue bars. The central white star, located where the two blue saltires' cross, is also larger than the other twelve. This ensign is believed to have been made aboard by her British crew between *Alabama*'s two visits to Cape Town. For reasons unknown, this *Stainless Banner* was left ashore with a ship's chandler just before *Alabama* made her fateful return voyage to Cherbourg, France.

A second *Stainless Banner* ensign of South African origin was made in and then presented to *Alabama* on one of her two port visits to Cape Town. It resides in the Tennessee State Museum according to their website. No further information on this ensign or how it survived is available at this time. Those details will be added here as they become available.

The third surviving *Stainless Banner* is one of *Alabama*'s original small boat ensigns. This official-looking 25.5-inch x 41-inch ensign is marked in brown pigment on its hoist: "Alabama. 290. C.S.N. 1st Cutter." In 2007, it was offered for auction through Philip Weiss Auctions. This ensign was being sold by the grandson of its second owner, who had originally purchased it from the granddaughter of a USS *Kearsarge* sailor. Multiple photos of both sides of this ensign are still available at Weiss' liveauctioneers.com website.

A fourth surviving ensign appears, from various clues seen in photos, to be approximately 36-inches x 54-inches. Because *Alabama* was forced to replace several of her original small boats lost at different times during her lengthy cruise, this is likely a somewhat larger replacement boat ensign. While it could have been made aboard, its somewhat more accurate details suggest it might have been commissioned ashore during a port-of-call visit. This ensign was rescued from the sinking *Alabama* by W. P. Brooks, the cruiser's assistant-engineer. It was last flown, along with other historic flags, during a ceremony held on the parade ground at Fort Pulaski, GA, sometime during 1937. This ensign has since been mounted and framed and today continues to reside with the

Brooks family. Four photos of it can be found at the website for the "Alabama Crew," a British-based naval reinactor group. More detailed information on this Stainless Banner will be added here when it becomes available.

The Alabama Department of Archives and History also has in its collection one more important *Stainless Banner* ensign listed as "Admiral Semmes' Flag, Catalogue No. 86.1893.1 (PN10149-10150)." Their provenance reconstruction shows that it was presented to Semmes after the sinking of the *Alabama* by "Lady Dehogton and other English ladies." Such presentations of ceremonial colors were uncommon to ship's captains of the Confederate Navy, but a few are known to have received such honors. This Second National Flag is huge and made of pure silk, giving it an elegant appearance. Although this ensign is in a remarkable state of preservation, its very large size and delicate condition has precluded any up-close measurements, so its various details and dimensions are unavailable. When Semmes returned to the Confederacy from England, he brought this ceremonial *Stainless Banner* with him. It was inherited by his grandchildren, Raphael Semmes III and Mrs. Eunice Semmes Thorington. After his sister's death, Raphael Semmes III donated the ensign to the state of Alabama on 19 September 1929.

Source (edited): "http://en.wikipedia.org/wiki/CSS_Alabama"

CSS Albemarle

CSS *Albemarle* was an ironclad ram of the Confederate Navy (and later the second *Albemarle* of the United States Navy), named for a town and a sound in North Carolina and a county in Virginia. All three locations were named for General George Monck, the first Duke of Albemarle and one of the original Carolina Lords Proprietors.

Construction

On 16 April 1862, the Confederate Navy Department, enthusiastic about the offensive potential of armored rams following the victory of their first ironclad CSS *Virginia* (the rebuilt USS *Merrimack*) over the wooden-hulled Union blockaders in Hampton Roads, Virginia, signed a contract with nineteen year old detached Confederate Lieutenant Gilbert Elliott of Elizabeth City, North Carolina; he was to oversee the construction of a smaller but still powerful gunboat to destroy the Union warships in the North Carolina sounds. These men-of-war had enabled Union troops to hold strategic positions that controlled eastern North Carolina.

Since the terms of the agreement gave Elliott freedom to select an appropriate place to build the ram, he established a primitive shipyard, with the assistance of plantation owner Peter Smith, in a cornfield up the Roanoke River at a place called Edward's Ferry, near modern Scotland Neck, North Carolina; Smith was appointed the superintendent of construction. There, the water was too shallow to permit the approach of Union gunboats that otherwise would have destroyed the ironclad while still on its ways. Using detailed sketches provided by Elliott, the Confederate Navy's Chief Constructor John L. Porter finalized the gunboat's design, giving the ram an armored casemate with eight sloping sides. Within this thick-walled bunker were two 6.4-inch (160 mm) Brooke pivot rifles, one forward, the other aft, each capable of firing from three fixed gun ports. Both cannons were protected on all sides behind six exterior-mounted, heavy iron shutters. The ram was propelled by two 3-bladed screw propellers powered by two steam engines, each of 200 hp (150 kW), and built by Elliott.

Construction of the ironclad began in January 1863 and continued on during the next year. Word of the gunboat reached the Union naval officers stationed in the region, raising an alarm. They appealed to the War Department for an overland expedition to destroy the ship, to be christened *Albemarle* after the body of water into which the Roanoke emptied, but the Union Army never felt it could spare the troops needed to carry out such a mission; it was a decision that would prove to be very short-sighted.

Service on the Roanoke

CSS Albemarle

In April 1864 the newly commissioned Confederate States Steamer *Albemarle*, under the command of Captain James W. Cooke, got underway down-river toward Plymouth, North Carolina; its mission was to clear the river of all Union vessels so that General Robert F. Hoke's troops could storm the forts located there. She anchored about three miles (5 km) above the town, and the pilot, John Lock, set off with two seamen in a small boat to take soundings. The river was high and they discovered ten feet of water over the obstructions that the Union forces had placed in the Thoroughfare Gap. Captain Cooke immediately ordered steam and, by keeping to the middle of the channel, they passed safely over the obstructions. The ironclad's armor protected them from the Union guns of the forts at Warren's Neck and Boyle's Mill.

However, two paddle steamers, USS *Miami* and USS *Southfield*, lashed together with spars and chains, approached from up-river, attempting to pass on either side of *Albemarle* in order to trap her between them. Captain Cooke turned heavily to starboard, running dangerously close to the southern shore, and got outboard of *Southfield*. Turning back sharply into the river, he rammed the Union sidewheeler, driving her under; *Albemarle*'s ram became trapped in *Southfield*'s hull from the force of the blow, and her bow was pulled under as well. As *Southfield* sank she rolled over before settling on the riverbed; this action released the death grip that held the new Confederate ram.

Miami fired a shell into *Albemarle* at point-blank range while she was trapped by the wreck of *Southfield*, but the shell rebounded off *Albemarle*'s sloping iron armor and exploded on *Miami*, killing her commanding officer, Captain Charles W. Flusser. *Miami*'s crew attempted to board *Albemarle* to capture her but were soon driven back by heavy musket fire; *Miami* then steered clear of the ironclad and escaped into Albemarle Sound.

With the river now clear of Union ships, and with the assistance of *Albemarle*'s rifled cannon, General Hoke attacked and took Plymouth and the nearby forts.

The encounter at Albemarle Sound, May 5, 1864. From left to right are USS *Commodore Hull*, USS *Wyalusing*, USS *Sassacus*, CSS *Albemarle*, USS *Mattabesett* and the CSS *Bombshell*

On 5 May *Albemarle* and CSS *Bombshell*, a captured steamer, were escorting the troop-laden CSS *Cotton Plant* down the Roanoke River; they encountered four Union warships: USS *Miami*, now supported by USS *Mattabesett*, USS *Sassacus*, and USS *Wyalusing*. All four ships combined mounted more than sixty cannons. *Albemarle* opened fired first, wounding six men working one of *Mattabesett*'s two 100-pounder Parrott rifles, and then attempted to ram her, but the sidewheeler managed to round the ironclad's armored bow. She was closely followed by *Sassacus*, which then fired a broadside of solid 9-inch (229 mm) and 100-pound shot, all of which bounced off *Albemarle*'s casemate armor. However, *Bombshell*, being a softer target, was hulled by each heavy shot from *Sassucus*'s broadside and was quickly captured by Union forces, following her surrender.

Lieutenant Commander Francis Asbury Roe of *Sassacus*, seeing *Albemarle* at a range of about 400 yards (370 m), decided to ram. The Union ship struck the Confederate ironclad full and square, broadside-on, shattering the timbers of her own bow, twisting off her own bronze ram in the process, and jamming both ships together. With *Sassucus*'s hull almost touching the end of the ram's Brooke rifle, *Albemarle*' gun crew quickly fired two point-blank rifled shells, one of them puncturing *Sassucus*'s boilers; though live steam was roaring through the ship, she was able to break away and drift out of range. *Miami* first tried to use her spar torpedo and then to tangle the Confederate ram's screw propellers and rudder with a seine net, but neither ploy succeeded. More than 500 shells were fired at *Albemarle* during the battle; with visible battle damage to her smokestack and other areas on the ironclad, she easily steamed back up the Roanoke the victor, soon mooring at Plymouth.

Sinking

Albemarle successfully dominated the Roanoke and the approaches to Plymouth through the summer of 1864. By autumn the U. S. government decided that the situation should be studied to determine if something could be done: The U. S. Navy considered various ways to destroy *Albemarle*, including two plans submitted by Lieutenant William B. Cushing; they finally approved one of his plans, authorizing him to locate two small steam launches that might be fitted with spar torpedoes. Cushing discovered two 30-foot (9.1 m) picket boats under construction in New York and acquired them for his mission (some accounts have them as 45 feet (14 m) to 47-feet). On each he mounted a Dahlgren 12 pounder howitzer and a 14-foot (4.3 m) spar projecting into the water from its bow. One of the boats was lost at sea during the voyage from New York to Norfolk, Virginia, but the other arrived safely with its crew of seven officers and men at the mouth of the Roanoke. There, the steam launch's spar was fitted with a lanyard-detonated torpedo.

On the night of October 27 and 28, 1864, Cushing and his team began working their way upriver. A small cutter accompanied them, its crew having the task of preventing interference by the Confederate sentries stationed on a schooner anchored to the wreck of *Southfield*; both boats, under the cover of darkness, slipped past the schooner undetected. So Cushing decided to use all twenty-two of his men and the element of surprise to capture *Albemarle*.

Battle between the Sassacus and the Albemarle, May 1864

As they approached the Confederate docks their luck turned, and they were spotted in the dark. They came under heavy rifle and pistol fire from both the shore and aboard *Albemarle*. As they closed with the ironclad, they quickly discovered she was defended against approach by floating log booms. The logs, however, had been in the water for many months and were covered with heavy slime. The steam launch rode up and then over them without difficulty; with her spar fully against the ironclad's hull, Cushing stood up in the bow, pulled the lanyard, detonating the torpedo's explosive charge.

The explosion threw Cushing and his men overboard into the water; Cushing then stripped off most of his uniform and swam to shore, where he hid undercover until daylight, avoiding the hastily organized Confederate search parties. The next afternoon, he was finally able to steal a small skiff and began slowly paddling, using his hands and arms as oars, down-river to rejoin Union forces at the river's mouth. Cushing's long journey was quite perilous and he was nearly captured and almost drowned before finally reaching safety, totally exhausted by his ordeal; he was hailed a national hero of the Union cause for his daring exploits. Of the other men in Cushing's launch, one also escaped, two were drowned following to the explosion, and the rest were captured.

Cushing's daring commando raid blew a hole in *Albemarle*'s hull at the waterline "big enough to drive a wagon in." She sank immediately in the six feet of water below her keel, settling into the heavy river bottom mud, leaving the upper casemate mostly dry and the ship's large *Stainless Banner* ensign flying from the flagstaff at the rear of the casemate's upper deck. Confederate commander Alexander F. Warley, who had been appointed as her captain about a month earlier, later salvaged both of *Albemarle*'s rifled cannon and shells and used them to defend Plymouth against subsequent Union attack—futilely, as it turned out.

Lieutenant Cushing's successful effort to neutralize CSS *Albemarle* is honored by the U. S. Navy with a battle star on the Civil War campaign streamer.

Raising and later service

The United States Navy then raised and temporarily hull-patched the Confederate ram after the fall of Plymouth. After the end of the war, the Union gunboat USS *Ceres* towed *Albemarle* to the Norfolk Navy Yard where she arrived on 27 April, 1865. On 7 June orders were issued to repair her damaged hull, and she entered dry dock for that purpose soon thereafter. The work was completed on 14 August, 1865; two weeks later the ironclad was judged condemned by a Washington, D.C prize court. She saw no active naval service after being placed in ordinary at Norfolk, where she remained until finally being sold at public auction on 15 October, 1867 to J. N. Leonard and Company. No record of any subsequent career has been found; she was likely scrapped for salvage following purchase. One of her 6.4-inch (160 mm) double-banded Brooke rifled cannon was on display at the Headquarters of the Commander-in-Chief U. S. Atlantic Command at the Norfolk, Virginia Naval base. Her smokestack is on display at the Museum of the Albemarle in Elizabeth City, North Carolina.

Naval jack and battle ensign

The practice of using primary and secondary naval flags after the British tradition was common practice for the Confederacy, linked as she was by both heritage and economy to the British Isles. The fledgling Confederate Navy therefore adopted and used battle ensigns, naval jacks, small boat ensigns, commissioning pennants, designating flags, and signal flags aboard its warships during of the Civil War.

By both tradition and established regulations, both waring navies' jacks were flown forward of their ship's ensigns while in port. *Albemarle*'s likely flew atop a removable jack staff positioned either on her bow or in front of her pilot house on the upper casemate deck; historic and contemporary drawings and paintings show her jack being flown at either station.

Albemarle's naval jack was discovered below decks and preserved when her wreck was raised and refloated following the war. It's designated as "flag number 42" in the special collections catalog of the United States Naval Academy Museum at Annapolis and has been in the museum's collection for many years.

The jack's dimensions are 6 feet (1.8 m) x 8 feet, 2 inches (72 inches x 98 inches).

Albemarle's naval jack was a much larger version of her battle ensign's square, 13-star canton, known as the *Southern Cross*. There were, however, two noticeable differences from the ensign: As with all Confederate jacks, their diagonal saltires were a lighter, medium-blue color instead of the dark blue seen on the battle ensign. Instead of the canton's square proportion, all naval jacks were rectangular in shape, in a proportion of 2:3, required under the regulations issued on 26–28 May, 1863 by the Confederate Navy Department. But *Albemarle*'s naval jack is actually much closer to a proportion of 3:4, an example of just how loosely the official naval flag regulations were being followed by the time her jack was manufactured in 1864; this variation was likely due to regional differences in the flag making techniques employed by both the south's Carolinas at this time and to various material shortages common throughout the South during the later years of the war. Following the end of the Civil War and up through today, the rectangular *Southern Cross* naval jack became the single Confederate flag design most commonly associated with the post-war South, and controversy.

Albemarle's battle ensign was recovered from atop her casemate's flag staff by Sailing Master George F. Ford of the U. S. Navy, at some point after she was sunk at her moorings. This ensign was eventually donated by H. C. Havens of Hartford, CT, to the flag collection of the Museum of the Confederacy, where it resides today; Havens received it from William Faxon, the Assistant Secretary of the Navy.

The ensign's overall dimensions are 8.45 feet (2.58 m) x 16 feet about 101 inches x 192 inches (4,900 mm) and entirely hand-sewn and made of a very loose weave wool bunting.

Second National Flag *Stainless Banner* battle ensign (adopted 1 May 1863)

Albemarle's battle ensign was the Second National Flag of the Confederacy, also known as the Stainless Banner. Specifications for this new flag were established by the Confederate Congress on May 1, 1863, replacing the First National Flag, more commonly known as the Stars and Bars. This new flag's hoist-to-fly proportion (height-to-width) was in a 1:2 ratio, its white expanse being twice as wide as its height. A short time later, however, the Confederate Navy Department revised these regulations, changing the Navy's battle ensign proportions to a 2:3 ratio. Its square canton was the established thirteen-star red, blue, and white *Southern Cross*, already in-use by the Southern army as the Confederate Battle Flag. This design was originally proposed in 1861 by South Carolina Congressman William Porcher Miles to be used as the original First National Flag, but it was supposedly rejected at first as appearing too much like a pair of crossed pants' suspenders.

Revised 2:3 ratio *Stainless Banner* battle ensign (never flown aboard CSS *Albemarle*)

For reasons unknown, *Albemarle* retained her original 1:2 ratio ensign (see illustration above right) until its capture sometime after Lieutenant Cushing's daring raid. Whatever proportion used, the white expanse of the *Stainless Banner* proved to have poor visibility at a distance, especially when viewed through the haze sometimes seen around water and in contrast against soft gray southern skies.

Replica

Replica of CSS Albemarle taken in 2003

A 63 foot (19.2m) replica of the *Albemarle* has been at anchor near the Port O' Plymouth Museum in Plymouth since April, 2002; the ironclad replica is self-powered and capable of sailing on the river.

Source (edited): "http://en.wikipedia.org/wiki/CSS_Albemarle"

CSS Appomattox

CSS *Appomattox* was a small propellor-driven steamer used early in the war by the Confederate Navy to defend the sounds of northeastern North Carolina. After participating in the battle for Roanoke Island it was burned to prevent capture on February 10, 1862, near Elizabeth City, North Carolina.

Early history

The *Appomattox* was originally named the *Empire* when launched in Philadelphia in 1850. In May of 1861 she was chartered by the Virginia State Navy under Captain Milligan, towing blockships into position to obstruct the channels of the Elizabeth River around Norfolk. In that same month she twice sailed as a flag-of-truce boat under Captain Thomas T. Hunter of the Virginia Navy to arrange exchanges of wounded Union prisoners and passage north from Norfolk of certain families wishing to return to their Northern friends. In the latter part of June 1861 she again served as the bearer of a flag-of-truce off Fortress Monroe, this time for Brigadier General Huger, CSA.(ORN 5: 799ff)

Confederate Service in North Carolina

Renamed *Appomattox*, she was armed with two guns during early September and assigned to the waters along the North Carolina coast under the command of Lt. C. C. Simms, CSN. *Appomattox* was used to patrol Pamlico Sound in late January 1862. She was also used to obstruct channels in the Croatan Sound area by towing blockships to strategic points for sinking. On February 6, the eve of Burnside's attack, the *Appomattox* was sent down Croatan Sound to reconnoiter the invasion force. Burnside allowed her to do this unhindered, because he wished for the Confederates to know what they were up against. (ORN 6: 522, 789ff)

The *Appomattox* was one of 8 gunboats used to resist the Burnside Expedition's invasion of Roanoke Island on 7-8 February 1862. However, she missed the actual battle, having been sent to Edenton on an unspecified mission. She retreated with the surviving gunboats to Elizabeth City, N.C. On February 9, the *Appomattox* and the *Sea Bird* steamed back to Roanoke Island to see if any further assistance could be given to the defenders, and to evacuate the garrison at Fort Forrest on Redstone Point. They encountered the Union gunboats advancing up the sound, and immediately fled back to Elizabeth City to organize a defense there. (ORN 6:594ff)

The Confederate gunboats were attacked by the Federal gunboat fleet on February 10. The *Appomattox* kept up a brisk fire from her bow gun until it was accidentally spiked. She then retreated to the entrance of the Dismal Swamp Canal, using the stern howitzer to fire at pursuers. Upon reaching the first lock it was discovered that her beam was 2 inches too great to let her into the canal. As a result Lieutenant Simms had to destroy the *Appomattox* by setting her on fire.(Parker 1985: 254-259)

Rediscovery
On November 10, 2009 it was announced by the state Underwater Archaeology Branch that the wreck of the *Appomattox* had been found. The four-member diving team, comprising Philip Madre, Eddie Congleton, Jason Forbes, and Jason Madre, discovered the shipwreck in August 2007 in the Pasquotank River. They had been searching for the *Appomattox* for more than 10 years. The divers found a silver-plated spoon inscribed with the name of a crew member from *Appomattox*, thus confirming the ship's identity. (NC Dept Cultural Resources website, 2009)
Source (edited): "http://en.wikipedia.org/wiki/CSS_Appomattox"

CSS Archer

CSS *Archer* was originally a fishing schooner captured by the Confederate cruiser CSS *Tacony* during the American Civil War and converted into a Confederate cruiser for commerce raiding.

The CSS *Tacony*, commanded by Lt. Charles W. Read, captured the *Archer* on June 25, 1863 off the coast of Portland, Maine. Knowing that the Union was on a hunt for his ship, he transferred the crew and armaments to it and destroyed the *Tacony*.

Read decided to try and capture the revenue cutter *Caleb Cushing* on his way down the coast of New England. On June 27, 1863, the *Archer* sailed into Portland, Maine harbor in Maine and docked, disguising itself as schooner. At night, the *Cushing* was boarded and the crew placed below decks. The *Archer* and the *Caleb Cushing* then sailed out of the harbor in the dawn. When the disappearance of the *Cushing* was noticed, ships were sent in pursuit, and due to the failing wind, were able to catch up and capture the *Archer*, but not before Read had set the magazine onboard the *Cushing* on fire.

Officers and crew
- Lt. Charles W. Read, commander
- Billups, Matthewson, and Pride, master's mates
- Brown, engineer
- 16 men

Source (edited): "http://en.wikipedia.org/wiki/CSS_Archer"

CSS Arkansas

The **CSS *Arkansas*** was a Confederate Ironclad warship during the American Civil War. Serving in the Western Theater, the vessel ran through a U.S. Navy fleet at Vicksburg, Mississippi, on 15 July 1862, in a celebrated action in which she inflicted more damage than she received. She was later destroyed by her crew to prevent capture by Union forces.

History

Construction
Her keel was laid down at Memphis, Tennessee, by J.T. Shirley in October 1861. In April 1862, *Arkansas* was removed to Greenwood, Mississippi on the Yazoo River to prevent her capture when Memphis fell to the Union Navy. Her sister ship, CSS *Tennessee*, was burned on the stocks because she was not near enough to completion to be launched.

In May 1862 Capt. Isaac N. Brown of the Confederate States Navy received orders at Vicksburg from the Navy Department in Richmond, Virginia, to proceed to Greenwood, and there assume command of the *Arkansas*. His orders were to finish and equip the vessel. When Captain Brown arrived, he found a mere hull, without armor, engines in pieces, and guns without carriages. Supplies of railroad iron, intended as armor for the ship, were lying at the bottom of the river. A recovery mission was ordered, and the armor was pulled up out of the mud. Captain Brown then had the *Arkansas* towed to Yazoo City, where he pressed into service local craftsmen, and also got the assistance of 200 soldiers from the Confederate Army as construction crews. After five strenuous weeks of labor under the hot summer sun, the ship had to leave due to falling river levels. She had been fully outfitted, except for the curved armor intended to surround her stern and pilot house. Boiler plate was stuck on these areas "for appearances' sake".

Breaking through to Vicksburg
During this time, the Federal Navy had attacked Vicksburg with a large force made up of a squadron of ships, under Flag Officer David G. Farragut, that had come up from the Gulf of Mexico and a flotilla of United States Army gunboats and rams, under Flag Officer Charles H. Davis, from upriver.

Soon thereafter, General Earl Van Dorn, commanding the Confederate Army forces at Vicksburg, and as such in control of *Arkansas*, ordered Captain Brown to bring his ship down to the city. Brown filled out the crew of *Arkansas* with more than 100 sailors from vessels on the Mississippi, plus about 60 Missouri soldiers. These soldiers had never served big guns, and most of them had probably never even served aboard a ship before. Brown stated, "The only trouble they ever gave me was to keep them from running the *Arkansas* into the Union fleet before we were ready for battle." He then set sail for Vicksburg and the Union fleet.

After approximately 15 miles (24 km), it was discovered that steam from the boilers had leaked into the forward magazine and rendered the gunpowder wet and useless. Captain Brown and his men found a clearing along the bank of the Yazoo River, landed the wet powder and spread it out on tarpaulins in the sun to dry. With constant stirring and shaking the powder was dry enough to ignite by sundown. *Arkansas* proceeded on her way.

CSS *Arkansas* running through the Union fleet above Vicksburg, Mississippi, 15 July 1862

Shortly after sunrise on 15 July 1862, three Federal vessels were sighted steaming towards *Arkansas*—the ironclad *Carondelet*, the wooden gunboat *Tyler*, and the ram *Queen of the West*. The Federal vessels turned downriver, and a running battle ensued. *Carondelet* was quickly disabled with a shot through her steering mechanism, causing her to run aground. Attention was turned to *Tyler* and the ram, which ran for their fleet with the *Arkansas* pursuing. Soon the Federal fleet came into view around the river bend above Vicksburg, "a forest of masts and smokestacks." Captain Brown determined to steam as close to the enemy vessels as possible in order to prevent his vessel being rammed and to sow confusion. The Federal ships were largely immobile, as they did not have their steam up. They and *Arkansas* exchanged shots at close range, but she soon passed to safety beyond them. *Arkansas* arrived at Vicksburg to the sound of enthusiastic cheering from the citizens and within sight of the lower Federal fleet.

That night, Farragut's fleet ran past the batteries at Vicksburg and attempted to destroy *Arkansas* while doing so. They did not move until so late in the day, however, that they could not see their target. Only one shell hit home, killing two men and wounding three.

Although *Arkansas* did not destroy any enemy vessels, she inflicted severe losses among the personnel of the Federal fleets. In the engagement on the Yazoo and her passage of the fleet at Vicksburg, their total loss was 18 killed, 50 wounded, and an additional 10 missing (probably drowned). Farragut's fleet lost another 5 killed and 9 wounded when they ran past the Vicksburg batteries. The cost to *Arkansas* for the entire day's action was 12 killed and 18 wounded.

Under the Vicksburg bluffs

After repairs, the *Arkansas* again appeared to threaten her enemies, forcing them to keep up steam 24 hours a day in the hottest part of the summer. To remove the problem, the Union fleet tried once again to destroy the ironclad at her mooring. At this time, the severely reduced crew of *Arkansas* could man only three guns, so she depended for protection on the shore batteries. On the morning of 22 July, USS *Essex*, *Queen of the West*, and *Sumter* mounted an ill-coordinated attack. First *Essex* attempted to ram, but as she approached, the *Arkansas* crew were able to spring her. As a result, *Essex* missed her target and ran aground instead, where for ten minutes she remained under fire from both *Arkansas* and the shore batteries. The armor on *Essex* protected her crew, however, so she lost only one man killed and three wounded. On the other hand, one of her shots penetrated the iron plating on *Arkansas*, killing six and wounding six. When *Essex* worked off the bank, she continued downstream, where she joined Farragut's squadron.

Meanwhile, *Queen of the West* was making her run. Her captain misjudged her speed, so she ran past *Arkansas* and had to come back and ram upstream. Although she struck fairly, her reduced momentum meant that the collision did little damage. She then returned to the flotilla above the city. She had been riddled by shot from the batteries, but surprisingly suffered no serious casualties.

Farragut had already been pressing the Navy Department for permission to leave Vicksburg. It was clear that he would need assistance from the Army to capture the city, assistance that was not forthcoming. Sickness among his sailors, unacclimatised to the heat of summer in Mississippi, reduced their fighting strength by as much as a third. Furthermore, the annual drop in the level of the river threatened to strand his deep-draft ships. The constant vigilance now necessitated by the presence of *Arkansas* finally tipped the balance. He got permission to return to the vicinity of New Orleans, and on 24 June his fleet left.

With nothing his flotilla could do, Davis also withdrew. He took his vessels back to Helena, Arkansas, where he could still watch the river north of Vicksburg.

Final fight at Baton Rouge

With the Federal fleet gone, Captain Brown requested and was granted four days of leave, which he took in Grenada, Mississippi. Before leaving, he pointed out to General Van Dorn that the engines of his ship needed repairs before she could be used. He also gave positive orders to his executive officer, Lt. Henry K. Stevens, not to move her until he returned.

The *USS Essex* fires on the burning *Arkansas*

Unfortunately for the ship, Van Dorn disregarded his subordinate. He ordered Lt. Stevens to take *Arkansas* down to Baton Rouge, where she would support an attack on the Union position there by a Confederate Army force led by General John C. Breckinridge. Stevens demurred, citing his orders from Brown, and referred the question to "a senior officer of the Confederate navy." The "senior officer" chose not to intervene. Stevens, now under the orders of two superior officers, had to rush the ship down the river.

Confirming Brown's fears, the engines broke down several times between Vicksburg and Baton Rouge. Each time, the engineer was able to get them running again, but it was clear that they were unreliable. Nevertheless, the ship was able to get all the way to Baton Rouge, where she prepared for battle with a small Federal flotilla that included her old opponent USS *Essex*. On the morning of 6 August, *Essex* came in sight, and *Arkansas* moved into the stream to meet her. Just at this time, crank pins on both engines failed almost simultaneously, and *Arkansas* drifted helplessly to the shore.

Stevens prepared to abandon ship. He ordered the engines to be broken up, the guns to be loaded and excess shells spread around, and then the ship set afire. The crew then left. About this time, the ship broke free and began to drift down the river, and Stevens, the last man to leave, had to swim ashore. The burning vessel drifted down among the attacking Federal fleet, which watched from a respectful distance. At about noon, *Arkansas* blew up.

Current Disposition

The Arkansas currently rests, aligned north/south, deep under a levee roughly 1.4 miles south of the auto/rail bridge just below Free Negro Point. The wreck is 690 feet past river mile 233.
Source (edited): "http://en.wikipedia.org/wiki/CSS_Arkansas"

CSS Baltic

The **CSS *Baltic*** was an iron and cotton-clad sidewheeler ship built in 1860 in Philadelphia as a river tow boat belonging to the Southern Steamship Co. She was purchased by the State of Alabama, converted to an armored ram, and turned over to the Confederate States Navy in the middle of 1862. Her first commanding officer was Lieutenant James D. Johnston, CSN.

Throughout the American Civil War the *Baltic* operated in the Mobile Bay, Mobile, Alabama and Tombigbee Rivers. The *Baltic* was reported unfit for service in February 1863, with her deteriorating condition preventing her from joining the defense of Mobile Bay in June 1864. She was dismantled in July of 1864 and her armor transferred to CSS *Nashville*.

The *Baltic* was captured at Nanna Hubba Bluff, Tombigbee River, Alabama, on May 10, 1865, and sold to the U. S. Government on December 31, 1865.

This article includes text from the public domain Dictionary of American Naval Fighting Ships.
Source (edited): "http://en.wikipedia.org/wiki/CSS_Baltic"

CSS Beaufort

The **CSS *Beaufort*** was an iron hull gunboat that served in North Carolina and Virginia during the Civil War.

The *Beaufort* was originally called the *Caledonia*. She was built at the Pusey & Jones Company of Wilmington, Delaware in 1854. The *Caledonia* operated out of Edenton, North Carolina. (Lytle 1975: 28) In 1856 her home port changed from Edenton to Plymouth. At the outbreak of the American Civil War, the *Caledonia*, now renamed *Beaufort*, was put in commission at Norfolk, Virginia on July 9, 1861 by Lieutenant Robert C. Duvall, North Carolina Navy, and sailed immediately for New Bern, North Carolina. While en route she engaged the large steamer USS *Albatross* in an inconclusive battle off Oregon Inlet. (ORN 6: 21, 790ff)

After North Carolina seceded, *Beaufort* was turned over to the Confederate States Navy, and on September 9 Lieutenant William Harwar Parker, CSN, was placed in command. Thereafter she participated in the battles of Roanoke Island on February 7-8, 1862, and Elizabeth City, North Carolina 2 days later. Right before the battle of Elizabeth City *Beaufort* had to supply most of her crew to man Cobb's Point Battery on the south shore of the Pasquotank River. Thus deprived, Parker ordered *Beaufort* to escape via the Dismal Swamp Canal to Norfolk. (ORN 6: 596f)

In March the *Beaufort* was tender to CSS *Virginia* off Hampton Roads on March 8-9, 1862. In that battle *Beaufort* moved alongside the US frigate *Congress* to accept its surrender. Heavy rifle fire from the shoreline drove her away with several casualties. The *Beaufort* also caused heavy damage to the *Minnesota* before nightfall. (Parker 1985: 276ff)

From May 1862, *Beaufort* operated on the James River, her commander in November 1863 being Lieutenant William Sharp, CSN. *Beaufort* served until the evacuation of Richmond, Virginia on April 3, 1865 when she was taken into the United States Navy. She was sold September 15, 1865. On October 31, 1865 she was redocumented as the *Roanoke*, and in 1878 converted into a barge. Her ultimate fate is unknown.

Commanders

The commanders of the CSS Beaufort were:
- Lieutenant Robert C. Duvall (1861-1862), North Carolina Navy
- Lieutenant William Harwar Parker (1862) CSN
- Lieutenant William Sharp (October 1863) CSN
- Lieutenant Edward J. Means (November 1863-June 1864) CSN
- Lieutenant J. M. Gardner (June

1864) CSN
- Lieutenant William Pinckney Mason (October 1864) CSN
- Lieutenant Joseph W. Alexander (December 19, 1864-February 1865) CSN
- Lieutenant George Henry Arledge (in charge February 12, 1865-) CSN

Source (edited): "http://en.wikipedia.org/wiki/CSS_Beaufort"

CSS Black Warrior

Black Warrior is the name of a Confederate two-masted schooner that participated in the defense of Roanoke Island in North Carolina during the Civil War. Its brief wartime career ended with its burning at Elizabeth City, North Carolina.

History

The *Black Warrior* was originally named the *M.C. Etheridge*. Built in Plymouth, North Carolina, in 1859, she was owned and operated by J. Brown. Initially registered for overseas trade, the *Etheridge* was enroled for interstate trade in 1860. In October of that year her documentation was changed back for overseas trade. (Enrollment abstracts, NA)

The *Black Warrior* was acquired by the Confederate Navy in 1862 and armed with two guns. Under the command of Lieutenant F. M. Harris, the schooner was part of a nine-gunboat naval squadron tasked with the defense of the northeastern North Carolina sounds. She was at anchor in Croatan Sound under the guns of Fort Forrest when a Union army/navy force under the command of General Ambrose Burnside arrived on February 6, 1862 to invade Roanoke Island. Because of her limited mobility and the fact that the Union landing site was well to the south of the schooner, she took no action against the invasion force. The other gunboats of the Confederate squadron engaged in a futile attempt to disrupt the landings on February 7. Late in the day the *Black Warrior* was detailed to salvage what guns and ammunition she could from the partially sunk gunboat *Curlew*. That evening the squadron retreated to Elizabeth City to obtain more ammunition. One of the gunboats, the *Ellis*, took the *Black Warrior* in tow while the remainder of the squadron made their way overnight to Elizabeth City (Parker 1883: 247ff)

Two of the Confederates gunboats steamed back to assist the garrison at Roanoke Island but turned around when it became obvious that the island had fallen. However, gunboats were sighted by the Union fleet and pursued back to Elizabeth City. It was decided to anchor *Black Warrior* near the fort that guarded the approaches to Elizabeth City while the rest of the gunboat squadron formed a line abreast across the channel opposite the fort. On February 10 the Union gunboat squadron, consisting of 14 vessels, simply bypassed the fort and *Black Warrior* to attack the other Confederate gunboats. Two Confederate gunboats escaped; the rest were either captured or sunk.(Parker 1883: 258)

The *Black Warrior* was initially ignored by the Union fleet, but when she opened fire the USS *Whitehead* turned and closed in to attack. The crew abandoned ship, setting fire to the *Black Warrior* and escaping ashore to avoid capture. The crew of the *Whitehead* attempted to extinguish the fire, but found it was too far advanced and had to withdraw. (ORN 1922: 617)

In 2000 the wreck site was mapped and in 2001 a gun carriage was retrieved for display at the Museum of the Albermarle.

Source (edited): "http://en.wikipedia.org/wiki/CSS_Black_Warrior"

CSS Bombshell

CSS *Bombshell* — believed to have been an Erie Canal steamer — was a U.S. Army transport. *Bombshell* was sunk by the Confederate batteries in Albemarle Sound, North Carolina on April 18, 1864. She was raised by the Confederate forces and taken into the Confederate States Navy under the command of Lieutenant Albert Gallatin Hudgins, CSN. *Bombshell* was recaptured in Albemarle Sound by USS *Mattabesett* and USS *Sassacus* on May 5, 1864 and sent to New York.

This article includes text from the public domain Dictionary of American Naval Fighting Ships.

Source (edited): "http://en.wikipedia.org/wiki/CSS_Bombshell"

CSS Charleston

The **CSS *Charleston*** was a Confederate Navy ironclad ram during the American Civil War. Construction at Charleston, South Carolina was authorized in fall 1862 and the ship was laid down in December 1862, entering service nine months later. The *Charleston* served as the Charleston Squadron's flagship alongside CSS *Palmetto State* and CSS *Chicora* during the defence of that city. Captained by Cdr. Isaac N. Brown. Set on fire and abandoned in Charleston harbor on February 18, 1865 to prevent capture, along with its sister ships, as the city was evacuated by the Confederates.

The *Charleston* was larger and stronger than the other two Charleston ironclads, but was underpowered with unreliable engines.

Source (edited): "http://en.wikipedia.org/wiki/CSS_Charleston"

CSS Chattahoochee

CSS *Chattahoochee* was a twin-screw steam gunboat built at Saffold, Georgia, entered service in February 1863 for the Confederate States and was named after the river it was built on.

Career

Chattahoochee was plagued by machinery failures, one of which, a boiler explosion which killed 18, occurred on May 27, 1863 as she prepared to sail from her anchorage at Blountstown, Florida, to attempt retaking the Confederate schooner CSS *Fashion*, captured by the Union. On June 10, 1864 she was moved to Columbus, Georgia, for repairs and installation of engines and a new boiler.

While she was undergoing repairs at Columbus, 11 of her officers and 50 crewmen tried unsuccessfully to capture *Adela* blockading Apalachicola, Florida. USS *Somerset* drove off the raiders, capturing much of their equipment.

When the Confederates abandoned the Apalachicola River in December 1864, the *Chattahoochee* was moved up the Chattahoochee River, and then scuttled near Columbus as Union troops approached the city. The remains of the Chattahoochee were found in the river within the boundaries of Fort Benning in 1963, and raised and placed at the National Civil War Naval Museum in Columbus.

Officers and crew

- Lt. Catesby ap Roger Jones, commander (late July 1862 - February 4, 1863)
- Lt. John Julius Guthrie, commander (February 4, 1863 - March 1864)
- Lt. George Washington Gift, commander (March 1864 - July 1864)
- ? , commander (July 1864 - December 1864)

Personnel killed

Those killed in the explosion, along with those who later died of their wounds were:
- Fred W. Arents, Third Assistant Engineer, of Richmond, Virginia
- Charles H. Berry, Quartermaster, of Tampa, Florida
- William B. Bilbro, Pilot, of Columbus, Georgia
- Edward Conn, Coal Heaver, of Apalachicola, Florida
- Charles Douglas, Second Class Fireman
- Henry Fagan, Second Assistant Engineer, of Key West, Florida
- Manassa Faircloth, Landsman, of Hardaway, Florida
- Eugene Henderson, Paymaster's Clerk, of Tuskegee, Alabama
- Joseph Hicks, First Class Fireman, of Georgia
- Euclid P. Hodges, Third Assistant Engineer, of Maryland
- John Joliff, Seaman
- James H. Jones, Landsman, of Florida
- Enoch C. Lanpher, Second Class Fireman, of Columbus, Georgia
- Charles K. Mallory, Midshipman, of Virginia
- William Moore, Landsman, of Florida
- John S. Spear, Landsman, of Florida
- James Thomas, Landsman, of Florida
- Lewis C. Wild, Landsman, of Florida

Several other members of the crew were wounded.

"Poor Mallory! I shall never forget his appearance. I would not have known him had he not spoken. His face, hands, and feet were scalded in the most terrible manner; he plead piteously to have his wounds attended to. I urged the doctor, who, by the way, was almost used up himself, to pay Mallory some attention. He then told me that he would have to wait for some assistance. He then said that Mallory could not live. You would have thought differently had you seen him. I could not make up my mind that he would die. When they first commenced to remove the cloths he was talking cheerfully, but the nervous system could not stand the shock. He commenced sinking and was a corpse before they had gotten half through. Duffy, the fireman, expired on the next day."

Source (edited): "http://en.wikipedia.org/wiki/CSS_Chattahoochee"

CSS Chickamauga

CSS *Chickamauga*, originally the blockade runner *Edith*, was purchased by the Confederate States Navy at Wilmington, North Carolina in September 1864. In September, when she was nearly ready for sea, the Confederate Army sought unsuccessfully to retain her at that place for use as a troop and supply transport. On October 28, 1864, she put to sea under Lieutenant John Wilkinson, CSN, for a cruise north to the entrance of Long Island Sound, thence to St. George, Bermuda, for repairs and coal. She took several prizes before returning to Wilmington on November 19.

During the bombardment of Fort Fisher, December 24-25, 1864, a portion of *Chickamauga'*s crew served the guns at the fort. Although not immediately engaged in defense of Fort Fisher, the ship rendered further aid in transporting ammunition. She lent support to the fort when it was bombarded again on January 15, 1865.

After the evacuation of Wilmington, *Chickamauga* went up the Cape Fear River where she was burned to prevent capture on February 25, 1865.

This article includes text from the public domain Dictionary of American Naval Fighting Ships.

Source (edited): "http://en.wikipedia.org/wiki/CSS_Chickamauga"

CSS Chicora

CSS *Chicora* was a Confederate ironclad ram that fought in the American Civil War. She was built under contract at Charleston, South Carolina in 1862. James M. Eason built her to John L. Porter's plans, using up most of a $300,000 State appropriation for construction of marine batteries; Eason received a bonus for "skill and promptitude." Her iron shield was 4" thick, backed by 22" of oak and pine, with 2-inch armor at her ends. Keeled in March, she was commissioned in November, Commander John Randolph Tucker, CSN assuming command.

In thick, predawn haze on January 31, 1863, *Chicora* and CSS *Palmetto State* raided the Federal blockading force of unarmored ships lying just outside the entrance to Charleston Harbor. With ram and gun, *Palmetto State* forced USS *Mercedita* to surrender, then disabled USS *Keystone State*, who had to be towed to safety. *Chicora* meanwhile engaged other Union ships in a long-range gun duel, from which she emerged unscathed to withdraw victoriously to shelter inside the harbor.

CSS *Chicora* and *Palmetto State* at anchor in Charleston Harbor

She took part in the defense of the forts at Charleston on April 7 when they were attacked by a squadron of ironclad monitors under Rear Admiral Samuel Francis du Pont, USN. The Federal ships were forced to retire for repairs and did not resume the action.

Chicora was actively employed in the fighting around Charleston during 1863 and 1864. Her valuable services included the transporting of troops during the evacuation of Morris Island, and the bombardment of Forts Sumter, Gregg, and Wagner. In August 1863 she had the distinction of furnishing the first volunteer officer and crew for the Confederate Submarine Torpedo Boat *H. L. Hunley*.

"A Lieutenant's commission in the Confederate States Navy was conferred on me with orders to report for duty on the ironclad Chicora at Charleston. My duties were those of a deck officer, and I had charge of the first division. On the occasion of the attack upon the blockading squadron ... It was my part, on the memorable morning, to aim and fire one effective shell into the Keystone State while running down to attack us, which (according to Captain LeRoy's report), killing twenty-one men and severely wounding fifteen, caused him to haul down his flag in token of surrender. The enemy now kept at a respectful distance while preparing their ironclad vessels to sail up more closely. Our Navy Department continued slowly to construct more of these rams, all on the same general plan, fit for little else than harbor defense." -- William T. Glassell, Lt. CSN

She was destroyed by the Confederates when Charleston was evacuated on February 18, 1865.

Source (edited): "http://en.wikipedia.org/wiki/CSS_Chicora"

CSS Clarence

CSS *Clarence*, also known as *Coquette*, was originally a brig from Baltimore captured by the Confederate cruiser CSS *Florida* during the American Civil War and converted into a Confederate cruiser for commerce raiding.

Built in 1857 for Baltimore, Maryland fruit dealer J. Crosby, it was transporting a cargo of coffee from Rio de Janeiro, Brazil, to Baltimore when the CSS *Florida* captured the *Clarence* off the coast of Brazil. Lt. Charles W. Read was appointed commander and a sufficient number of the *Florida*'s crew were transferred to the new cruiser to man the ship.

Lieutenant Read had requested that, rather than burn *Clarence*, he might try, with the ship's papers, to sail into Hampton Roads, Virginia, and if possible destroy or capture a Union gunboat and burn Union merchant vessels congregated at Fortress Monroe. *Florida*'s Commander John Newland Maffitt armed *Clarence* with one gun so that Read might capture prizes on his way to Hampton Roads.

In its brief career as a Confederate cruiser it captured a number of ships: The *Whistling Wind*, *Kate Stewart*, *Mary Alvina*, *Mary Schindler* were burned, and the *Alfred H. Partridge* was bonded. Its final capture was the bark *Tacony* on June 12, 1863, which being a better ship suited for commerce raiding, the crew and armaments were transferred to it and the *Clarence* was destroyed.

Officers and crew

- Lt. Charles W. Read, commander
- Billups, Matthewson, and Pride,

master's mates
- Brown, engineer

16 men

Source (edited): "http://en.wikipedia.org/wiki/CSS_Clarence"

CSS Colonel Lovell

CSS *Colonel Lovell* was a cotton-clad ram of the Confederate States Navy during the American Civil War

Service history

The ship was built in Cincinnati, Ohio, in 1843, as *Hercules*, and was owned by the Ocean Towing Co. of New Orleans. She was taken over in 1861 by General Mansfield Lovell, commanding the New Orleans military district, and converted to a cottonclad ram by installation of double pine bulwarks filled with compressed cotton and one-inch iron plates on each bow. She operated under the direction of the Confederate War Department and was attached to the Mississippi River Defense Fleet, commanded by Commodore J. E. Montgomery, a former river steamboat captain.

Battle of Plum Point Bend

On 10 May 1862, while operating off Fort Pillow, Tennessee, in defense of the river approaches to Memphis, *Colonel Lovell*, in company with seven of Montgomery's vessels, attacked the ironclad gunboats of the Federal Mississippi Flotilla. The action of Plum Point Bend which followed witnessed successful ramming tactics by the Confederates, though each of their vessels mounted at least four 8-inch guns. The Federal gunboats USS *Cincinnati* and USS *Mound City* were run on the banks in sinking condition. Later, Montgomery's force held off the Federal rams and gunboats until Fort Pillow was successfully evacuated on 1 June, and the Confederate rams fell back on Memphis to take on coal.

Battle of Memphis

Following the Federal capture of Fort Pillow Flag Officer Charles Henry Davis, USN, commanding the Mississippi Flotilla, pressed on without delay and appeared off Memphis with superior force on 6 June 1862. Included in his force were two of the Federal Army's rams, commanded by Colonel Charles Ellet, Jr. Montgomery, unwilling to retreat to Vicksburg because of his shortage of fuel and unwilling to destroy his boats, determined to fight against heavy odds. In the engagement that followed, one of *Colonel Lovell*'s engines malfunctioned and she became unmanageable. She was then rammed amidships by USS *Queen of the West*, and immediately struck again by USS *Monarch*, both of the Ellett fleet. *Colonel Lovell* sank in deep water in the middle of the river. Capt. J. C. Delancy and a number of his crew were able to swim ashore.

Source (edited): "http://en.wikipedia.org/wiki/CSS_Colonel_Lovell"

CSS Columbia

CSS *Columbia* was an ironclad ram in the Confederate States Navy and later in the United States Navy.

As CSS *Columbia*

Columbia was constructed under contract at Charleston, South Carolina in 1864, of yellow pine and white oak with iron fastenings and 6 inch (150 mm) iron plating. Hull work was done by F. M. Jones to John L. Porter's plans, plating and machinery by James M. Eason; her casemate was shortened to conserve precious metal and clad with 6" iron.

Columbia was launched in March 1864 and entered service later in that year.

When the Union forces took possession of Charleston on February 18, 1865, they found the greatly prized *Columbia* in jeopardy near Fort Moultrie; while on duty as part of the defenses of Charleston, she had run on a sunken wreck and been damaged on January 12, 1865. *Columbia* was found to have had her guns and some armor plating removed and ship-worms already at work.

As USS *Columbia*

She was raised on April 26 and placed under the command of Lieutenant G. W. Hayward, USN. *Columbia* was towed by USS *Vanderbilt* to Hampton Roads, Virginia, where she arrived May 25, 1865. *Columbia* was drydocked on June 5 and repairs were begun, but on June 15, she was decommissioned and placed in ordinary. Her hulk was sold October 10, 1867.

Source (edited): "http://en.wikipedia.org/wiki/CSS_Columbia"

CSS Cotton Plant

CSS *Cotton Plant*, sometimes referred to as *Cotton Planter*, was built at Philadelphia, Pennsylvania in 1860 and reportedly carried troops in the Pamlico River as early as September 1861. She sailed with CSS *Albemarle* when that ironclad ram attacked Union forces at Plymouth, North Carolina, sank USS *Southfield* and drove off USS *Miami*, USS *Ceres* and USS *Whitehead* on April 18-19 1864. On May 5, 1864 she steamed as convoy to *Albemarle* from the Roanoke River en route to the Alligator River. The convoy was engaged by ships of the North Atlantic Blockading Squadron, but both the ram and *Cotton Plant* with several launches in tow escaped into the Roanoke River.

In May 1865, *Cotton Plant* was surrendered to Union officials near Halifax, North Carolina by parties claiming that she had been appropriated by Confederate authorities. Ownership was adjudicated at Plymouth and she was turned over to the U.S. Treasury purchasing agent to transport cotton and provisions. She was later delivered to the U.S. Navy at Norfolk, Virginia.

This article includes text from the public domain Dictionary of American Naval Fighting Ships.
Source (edited): "http://en.wikipedia.org/wiki/CSS_Cotton_Plant"

CSS David

The wreck of the CSS *David*

Photograph of a captured *David*-class torpedo boat (possibly CSS *David* herself), taken after the fall of Charleston in 1865

CSS *David* was built as a private venture by T. Stoney at Charleston, South Carolina in 1863, and put under the control of the Confederate States Navy. The cigar-shaped boat carried a 60- or 70-pound explosive charge on the end of a spar projecting forward from her bow. Designed to operate very low in the water, *David* resembled in general a submarine; she was, however, strictly a surface vessel. Operating on dark nights, and using anthracite coal which burns without smoke, "David" was nearly as hard to see as a true submarine.

On the night of October 5, 1863, *David*, commanded by Lieutenant William T. Glassell, CSN, slipped down Charleston Harbor to attack the casemated ironclad steamer USS *New Ironsides* The torpedo boat approached undetected until she was within 50 yards of the blockader. Hailed by the watch on board *New Ironsides*, Glassell replied with a blast from a shotgun and *David* plunged ahead to strike. Her spar torpedo detonated under the starboard quarter of the ironclad, throwing high a column of water which rained back upon the Confederate vessel and put out her boiler fires. Her engine dead, *David* hung under the quarter of *New Ironsides* while small arms fire from the Federal ship spattered the water around the torpedo boat.

Believing that their vessel was sinking, Glassell and two others abandoned her; the pilot, Walker Cannon, who could not swim, remained on board. A short time later, Assistant Engineer J. H. Tomb swam back to the craft and climbed on board. Rebuilding the fires, Tomb succeeded in getting David's engine working again, and with Cannon at the wheel, the torpedo boat steamed up the channel to safety. Glassell and Seaman James Sullivan, *David*'s fireman, were captured. *New Ironsides*, though not sunk, was seriously damaged by the explosion. US Navy casualites were Acting Ensign C.W.Howard (died of gunshot wound), Seaman William L. Knox (legs broken) and Master at Arms Thomas Little (contusions). See

The next 4 months of *David*'s existence are obscure. She or other torpedo boats tried more attacks on Union blockaders; reports from different ships claim three such attempts, all unsuccessful, during the remainder of October 1863. On March 6, 1864, *David* attacked USS *Memphis* in the North Edisto River. The torpedo boat struck the blockader first on the port quarter, but the torpedo did not explode. *Memphis* slipped her chain, at the same time firing ineffectively at *David* with small arms. Putting about, the torpedo boat struck *Memphis* again, this time a glancing blow on the starboard quarter; once more the torpedo misfired. Since *Memphis* had now opened up with her heavy guns, *David*, having lost part of her stack when rammed, retreated up the river out of range. *Memphis*, uninjured, resumed her blockading station.

David's last confirmed action came on April 18, 1864 when she tried to sink the screw frigate USS *Wabash*. Alert lookouts on board the blockader sighted *David* in time to permit the frigate to slip her chain, avoid the attack, and open fire on the torpedo boat. Neither side suffered any damage.

The ultimate fate of *David* is uncertain. Several torpedo boats of this type fell into Union hands when Charleston was captured in February 1865. *David* may well have been among them.
Source (edited): "http://en.wikipedia.org/wiki/CSS_David"

CSS Drewry

CSS *Drewry* was a wooden gunboat with foredeck protected by an iron V-shaped shield. Classed as a tender, she was attached to Flag Officer French Forrest's James River Squadron sometime in 1863 with Master Lewis Parrish, CSN, in command.

In addition to transporting troops and other routine service, she took part in several engagements along the river prior to January 24, 1865, when, in Trent's Reach, she was destroyed by two shots from a 100-pounder rifle in a battery of the 1st Connecticut Artillery. The second hit exploded her magazine as she assisted CSS *Richmond* to get afloat; all but two of her crew had reached safety before the explosion.

Commanders

The commanders of the CSS *Drewry* were:
- William Harwar Parker (May-fall 1862)
- Master Lewis Parrish (around October 1863-May 1864)
- Lieutenant William B. Hall (May 19-May 21, 1864)
- Lieutenant William H. Wall (June 1864-January 23, 1865)

Source (edited): "http://en.wikipedia.org/wiki/CSS_Drewry"

CSS Ellis

CSS *Ellis* (later **USS *Ellis***) was a gunboat in the Confederate States Navy and the United States Navy during the American Civil War. It was lost during a raid while under command of famed Navy officer Lieutenant William B. Cushing.

Confederate Service

The *Ellis* was purchased at Norfolk, Virginia in 1861 by the State of North Carolina and turned over to the Confederacy when that State became a member. With Commander W. T. Muse, CSN, in command, she played an important part in the defense of Fort Hatteras and Fort Clark in Hatteras Inlet, North Carolina on August 28–29, 1861, of Roanoke Island on February 7–8, 1862, and of Elizabeth City, North Carolina on February 10, 1862; that day she was captured by the Union Army after a desperate struggle in which her commander, Lieutenant James W. Cooke, CSN, was badly wounded.

U.S. Navy Service

Ellis was taken into the U.S. Navy and assigned to the North Atlantic Blockading Squadron. She was placed under the command of Lieutenant C. L. Franklin, USN, and spent her entire U.S. Navy service in the sounds and rivers of North Carolina.

Ellis took part in a combined expedition which captured Fort Macon, near Beaufort, North Carolina, on April 25, 1862. She had a brief engagement with Confederate cavalry off Winton, North Carolina on June 27, and from August 15 to 19 she made an expedition to Swansboro, North Carolina to destroy salt works and a battery. On October 14, she was detailed to the blockade of Bogue Inlet, and a week later, captured and burned the schooner *Adelaide* with a valuable cargo of turpentine, cotton, and tobacco.

Final Action

In November 1862, *Ellis*, under command of Lieutenant William B. Cushing, sailed up New River Inlet to capture Jacksonville, North Carolina. The steamer captured two schooners, some arms and mail. On her way down river, *Ellis* ran aground on November 24 and could not be refloated. After dark her commanding officer, with great coolness, moved all the crew except six and all her equipment and supplies except her pivot gun, some ammunition, 2 tons of coal, and a few small arms to one of the captured schooners. While the schooners slipped down the river to wait, Cushing and five of his men remained to fight it out. Early on the morning of November 25, the Confederates opened fire on *Ellis*, and in a short time, Cushing was forced to decide between surrender and a pull of a mile and a half to a waiting schooner. Cushing chose not to surrender, and before leaving his ship, set fire to her in five places, leaving the gun trained on the enemy to let the ship herself carry on the fight when flames would fire the cannon. Cushing and his men reached the schooner and made for the sea, getting the vessel over the bar just in time to escape several companies of cavalry trying to cut off the schooner at the mouth of the inlet. *Ellis* was blown to pieces by the explosion of her magazine on the morning of November 25, 1862.

Source (edited): "http://en.wikipedia.org/wiki/CSS_Ellis"

CSS Fanny

CSS *Fanny* was a small propellor-driven steamer used by the Confederate Navy to defend the sounds of northeastern North Carolina. Originally operated by the Union, she was captured early in the war by the Confederate Navy, and later lost at the battle for Elizabeth City. *Fanny* is sometimes credited with being the first self-propelled aircraft carrier.

Union Service

The *Fanny* was originally operated by the United States Army Quartermaster Corps. On August 3, 1861, while on the James River, ballonist John La Mountain made an ascent from the deck of the *Fanny* to observe Confederate positions, making the *Fanny* a balloon carrier. Previous water-launched balloon flights had taken place on barges.

Capture & Confederate Service

After the Federals captured Hatteras Inlet the *Fanny* was used to supply a Union army outpost at Chicamacomico, an Outer Banks settlement north of the Cape Hatteras Lighthouse. While at anchor there it was surprised by a Confederate gunboat squadron on 1 October 1861. This squadron consisted of the CSS *Curlew*, CSS *Raleigh*, and CSS *Youngalaska*. The *Curlew* closed first while the other two gunboats circled around to cut off any escape attempt. After a brisk half-hour engagement the *Fanny* was run aground and surrendered. A large quantity of commissary and quartermaster's stores was captured with the steamer. Also captured were members of Twentieth Indiana and the New York Zouaves. However, the *Fanny's* captain, J. H. Morrison, and his crew escaped, having essentially abandoned ship once the Confederate steamers approached. Refloated and taken into the Confederate Navy, it was placed in command of Midshipman J. L. Tayloe, CSN.

Chicamacomico Incident

Four days later the *Fanny* participated in a relatively large Confederate naval and army effort to 1) encircle and attack the Union encampment at Chicamacomico, 2) take and destroy the Cape Hatteras lighthouse, and 3) attempt to recapture the forts at Hatteras Inlet. The initial landing effort was successful, and the Union encampment at Chicamacomico was abandoned. However, the encirclement effort failed, and the Union troops were able to retreat back to the Hatteras Lighthouse. The next day Union reinforcements came up from Hatteras Inlet and chased the Confederate troops back to their transports. Both sides then retreated back to their base camps, the Union troops to Hatteras Inlet and the Confederate troops to Roanoke Island.

Battles at Roanoke Island and Elizabeth City

The *Fanny* spent the next four months patrolling Pamlico Sound, reconnoitering Hatteras Inlet, and towing supply schooners to Roanoke Island. On 7-8 of February 1862 the *Fanny* engaged the Union invasion force in the battle of Roanoke Island. The *Fanny* eventually retreated to Elizabeth City with the other surviving members of its gunboat squadron when ammunition supplies ran low. On February 10 the *Fanny* and the other gunboats were attacked by Federal gunboats advancing from Roanoke Island. In the ensuing battle it was run aground and blown up by her captain who escaped with his crew to shore.

Works Cited

Source (edited): "http://en.wikipedia.org/wiki/CSS_Fanny"

CSS Florida

At least three ships of the Confederate States Navy were named **CSS Florida** *in honor of the third Confederate state:*
- The blockade runner CSS *Florida* was commissioned in January 1862, captured by the U.S. Navy in April 1862, and became USS *Hendrick Hudson*
- The cruiser CSS *Florida* was commissioned in August 1862 and captured by the U.S. Navy while in port in Bahia, Brazil in October 1864
- The gunboat CSS *Selma* was named CSS *Florida* prior to July 1862.

Source (edited): "http://en.wikipedia.org/wiki/CSS_Florida"

CSS Florida (blockade runner)

For other ships named Florida, *see CSS Florida.*

The Confederate blockade runner **CSS Florida**, built at Greenpoint, New York in 1859, was thrice considered for a gunboat before she became one. Contrary to previous interpretation of the official records, closer comparison of entries reveals that she did not serve the Mississippi River Defense Fleet as originally intended but became a Government-owned blockade runner; most authors have confused her with the Mobilian CSS *Florida* who did not receive her name CSS *Selma* until July 1862. CSS *Florida* of New Orleans was one of 14 steamers of Charles Morgan's Southern Steamship Co. which Major General Mansfield Lovell "impressed for public service" at New Orleans, January 15, 1862, acting on Confederate Secretary of War Judah P. Benjamin's orders.

The colorful Lieutenant Beverly Kennon, CSN, had sought *Florida's* command but had to be content with CSS *Governor Moore*. He nostalgically described *Florida* to a court of inquiry as "a very fast and a very handsome vessel indeed .. A direct-acting screw of about 100 horsepower [75 kW] …about the same size in all respects as the U.S. steam sloop *Pocahontas*."

Of the several ships of the same name, she apparently is the *Florida* who arrived at Havana, Cuba on March 23, 1862 with 1,000 bales of cotton. Attempting to repeat her success, she had loaded 211 bales in St. Joseph Bay near Pensacola, Florida when captured by Acting Master Elnathan Lewis, USN, with armed boats from the bark USS *Pursuit* on April 6. The boarders had just captured a sloop, *Lafayette*, at St. Andrew's, Florida, 20 miles below, and the latter's Captain Harrison volunteered to pilot Lewis' party on up to capture *Florida*. Surprised at 4 o'clock Sunday morning, *Florida's* crew were unable to fire their ship.

It later appeared that the pilot, chief mate, first and second engineers were Union sympathizers. Mr. Lewis, after running *Florida* aground twice and jettisoning 30 bales of cargo, found "it was impossible to bring her out without the assistance of the engineers, pilot, and mate; so rather than burn her he considered it prudent to bargain with them, and gave his word that they would receive $500.00 each. They were faithful."

In the 30 mile (50 km) passage to the bar, *Florida* and *Lafayette* were almost recaptured by the Confederates on April 8 after Captain R. L. Smith, CSA, and his company of dragoons had galloped 24 hours from Marianna, Florida to intercept them off St. Andrew's. A ship's boat was ambushed with four casualties, one dead, but the prizes continued on to Key West. There, on April 19, 1862, Commodore William McKean reporting to United States Secretary of the Navy Gideon Welles confirmed that *Florida* had never been converted: "I have examined her, and find that her upper deck is too light to carry guns of any weight. I have not the means to strengthen her sufficiently, or I should retain and convert her into a gunboat." Despite this rejection, the U.S. Navy bought *Florida* from the Philadelphia prize court on September 20, 1862, changed her name to USS *Hendrick Hudson* and placed 4, later 5, guns on board.
Source (edited): "http://en.wikipedia.org/wiki/CSS_Florida_(blockade_runner)"

CSS Florida (cruiser)

For other ships named Florida*, see CSS* Florida*.*
CSS *Florida* was a cruiser in the Confederate States Navy.

Florida was built by the British firm of William C. Miller & Sons of Toxteth, Liverpool, and purchased by the Confederacy from Fawcett, Preston & Co., also of Liverpool, who engined her. Known in the shipyard as *Oreto* and initially called by the Confederates *Manassas*, the first of the foreign-built commerce raiders was commissioned *Florida*. Union records long continued to refer to her as *Oreto* or to confuse her with CSS *Alabama* although, fitted with two funnels, she was readily distinguishable from single-stacked *Alabama*.

Florida departed England on March 22, 1862 for Nassau, Bahamas, to coal and contrived to fill her bunkers, although entitled only to enough to make the nearest Confederate port. The governor drew the line, however, at an attempted rendezvous with her tender in Nassau harbor; so she transferred stores and arms at isolated Green Cay. There she commissioned as *Florida* on August 17, with veteran Lieutenant John Newland Maffitt, CSN, in command. During her outfit, yellow fever raged among her crew, in 5 days reducing her effective force to one fireman and four deckhands. In desperate plight, she ran across to Cuba. There in Cárdenas, Maffitt too was stricken with the dreaded disease.

In this condition, against all probability, the intrepid Maffitt sailed her from Cárdenas to Mobile, Alabama. In an audacious dash the "Prince of Privateers" braved a hail of projectiles from the Union blockaders and raced through them to anchor beneath the guns of Fort Morgan for a hero's welcome by Mobile. *Florida* had been unable to fight back not only because of sickness but because rammers, sights, beds, locks and quoins had, inadvertently, not been loaded in the Bahamas. Having taken stores and gun accessories she lacked, along with added crew members, *Florida* escaped to sea on January 16, 1863.

After coaling at Nassau, she spent 6 months off North and South America and in the West Indies, with calls at neutral ports, all the while making captures and eluding the large Federal squadron pursuing her.

Florida sailed 27 July from Bermuda for Brest, France where she lay in the French government dock from August 23, 1863 to February 12, 1864. There, broken in health, Maffitt relinquished command to Lieutenant Charles Manigault Morris. Departing for the West Indies, *Florida* bunkered at Barbados, although the 3 months specified by British law had not elapsed since last coaling at a British Empire port. She then skirted the U.S. coast, sailed east to Tenerife in the Canaries and thence to Bahia, Brazil, arriving October 4, 1864.

Anchored in the Brazilian haven, on October 7 *Florida*, while her captain was ashore with half his crew, was caught defenseless in an illegal night attack by Commander Napoleon Collins of USS *Wachusett*. Towed to sea, she was sent to the United States as a prize despite Brazil's protests at this clear violation of their sovereignty. Commander Collins was court-martialed and was convicted of violating Brazilian territorial rights, but the verdict was set aside by Secretary of the Navy Gideon Welles; Collins won fame and eventual promotion for his daring.

At Newport News, Virginia on November 28, 1864, *Florida* reached the end of her strange career when she sank under dubious circumstances after a collision with the USAT *Alliance*, a troop ferry. The sinking was most likely done at Admiral David Dixon Porter's encouragement, if not his orders. The Florida could therefore not be delivered to Brazil in satisfaction of the final court order, and could not rejoin the ranks of the Confederate Navy.

Florida captured 37 prizes during her impressive career; her prizes CSS *Tacony* and CSS *Clarence* in turn took 23 more.

Today, many of the artifacts from CSS *Florida* are at the Hampton Roads Naval Museum .

This article includes text from the public domain Dictionary of American Naval Fighting Ships*.*
Source (edited): "http://en.wikipedia.org/wiki/CSS_Florida_(cruiser)"

CSS Forrest

The CSS *Forrest* was a wood hull Confederate gunboat that saw action in the North Carolina sounds in 1861 to 1862. Despite being considered "worn out", she saw continuous service until destroyed after the Battle for Elizabeth City in February 1862.

Ship History

The *Forrest* was originally named the *J. A. Smith* when launched in 1855. Designed as a canal boat, she was converted to steam in 1856. The *Smith* was bought at Norfolk in 1861 and renamed *Weldon N. Edwards* in honor of the President of the North Carolina Secession Convention. She was ordered to Hatteras Inlet by Flag Officer Samuel Barron on July 27, 1861:

from which place you will make every exertion to defend the coasts of that State and harass and annoy the commerce of the enemy. Should you make prizes you will send them either to Norfolk, Va., or some port in North Carolina, as your judgment may determine to be most proper, proceeding in accordance with the law of the Confederate States on the subject of prizes. You will ship any seamen that may offer. (ORN 6: 715)

The *Edwards* patrolled Hatteras Inlet in North Carolina under the command of Lt. J. Cooke. In August 1861 Cooke would report to Flag Officer Barron that his ship was "entirely worthless, the boilers worn out and the timbers of his vessel rotten." (ORN 6: 795f)

By early October the tug was back in Norfolk, where on the 3rd she received orders from Flag Officer French Forrest to return quickly to Roanoke Island and place the gunboat at the service of local CSN commander William Lynch. (ORN 6:736f)

At some point in late 1861 the *Edwards* name was changed to *Forrest*. She was part of a 5 gunboat fleet that attempted to provoke the Union forces at anchor at Hatteras Inlet on November 3, 1861. The Union gunboats did not reply to the Confederate challenge, so the Confederate gunboats retreated with the *Curlew* towing the *Forrest* back home. (ORN 6:784)

On December 30, 1861 the *Forrest* had to be towed by the *Curlew* to Edenton for repairs. By January 3, 1862 she was back with the rest of the Mosquito Fleet at Roanoke Island. For the rest of the month the *Forrest* was involved in towing schooners and performing patrolling duties.(ORN 6:784ff)

The *Forrest* participated in the battle of Roanoke Island on February 7, 1862 during which her commanding officer, Lt. J. L. Hoole, CSN, was seriously wounded. Furthermore, *Forrest* was disabled late in the action "by the displacement of her propellor" and towed to Elizabeth City, N.C., for repairs. (ORN 6: 595ff) There, 3 days later, while out of water on the marine railway, she was burned to prevent capture by Union forces.

Source (edited): "http://en.wikipedia.org/wiki/CSS_Forrest"

CSS Fredericksburg

CSS *Fredericksburg* was an ironclad gunboat of the Confederate States Navy during the American Civil War.

Fredericksburg was built at Richmond, Virginia in 1862-63. The CSS *Fredericksburg* was the second ironclad to be completed in Richmond. On November 30, 1863 she was reported completed and awaiting armament. In March 1864 she was taken down to Drewry's Bluff to be fitted out, and placed in command of Commander Thomas R. Rootes, CSN.

Fredericksburg, one of the ships of the James River Squadron commanded by Commodore John K. Mitchell, CSN, was actively engaged in the James River from mid-1864 until the end of the war. Accompanied by the CSS *Virginia II*, she participated in an engagement with the Union ship USS *Onondaga* at Trent's Reach on June 21, 1864, but little damage was inflicted on either side due to the distance between them. Similar inconclusive encounters took place in August, October, December, and the following January. With the evacuation of Richmond on April 3, 1865, the Confederates blew up *Fredericksburg* and other ships in the vicinity the following day. The Confederate Fleet was found in the James River. Her remains lie about fifty yards up river from her sister ship. The ship lies parallel with the river under the mud, which might be between six to fifteen feet deep.

Commanders

The commanders of the CSS *Fredericksburg* were:
- Commander Thomas R. Rootes (March 1864-December 1864)
- Lieutenant Francis E. Shepperd (?-December 28, 1864; January 14-January 25, 1865)
- Lieutenant Alphonse Barbot, Executive Officer in Charge (February 1865)

Source (edited): "http://en.wikipedia.org/wiki/CSS_Fredericksburg"

CSS Gaines

CSS *Gaines* was hastily constructed by the Confederates at Mobile, Alabama during 1861-62, from unseasoned wood which was partially covered with 2-inch iron plating. *Gaines* resembled CSS *Morgan* except that she had high pressure boilers. Operating in the waters of Mobile Bay, under the command of Lieutenant John W. Bennett, CSN, she fought gallantly during the Battle of Mobile Bay on August 5, 1864 until finally run aground near Fort Morgan and destroyed by her own officers to avoid surrender to the Union forces.

This article includes text from the public domain Dictionary of American Naval Fighting Ships.

Source (edited): "http://en.wikipedia.org/wiki/CSS_Gaines"

CSS General Beauregard

CSS *General Beauregard* was a cotton-clad sidewheel ram of the Confederate Navy during the American Civil War.

Built in Algiers, Louisiana in 1847 as a towboat, the paddle steamer *Ocean* was selected in January 1862 by Capt. James E. Montgomery, former river steamboat master, for his River Defense Fleet. At New Orleans, on 25 January, Captain Montgomery began her conversion to a cotton-clad ram, installing 4-inch (100 mm) oak and 1-inch (25 mm) iron sheathing over her bow, with cotton bales sandwiched between double pine bulkheads to protect her boilers.

Service history

Battle of Plum Point Bend

Conversion completed on 5 April, and now renamed CSS *General Beauregard*, the ship steamed to Fort Pillow, Tennessee, to defend the approaches to Memphis. On 10 May 1862, *General Beauregard*, Capt. J. H. Hart, and seven more of Montgomery's fleet, attacked the Federal Mississippi ironclad flotilla. The Battle of Plum Point Bend witnessed effective ramming tactics by the Confederates, although *General Beauregard* succeeded only in keeping her four 8-inch guns bravely firing in the face of a withering hail of Union shells. Montgomery's force held off the Federal rams until Fort Pillow was safely evacuated, 4 June, then fell back on Memphis to coal, on the fifth.

Battle of Memphis

After Fort Pillow fell, Flag Officer Charles Henry Davis, USN, commanding the Mississippi River Squadron, lost no time in appearing off Memphis, on 6 June 1862. Montgomery, with a smaller squadron short of fuel, was unable to retreat to Vicksburg; unwilling to destroy his boats, he fought against heavy odds. In the ensuing Battle of Memphis, "witnessed by thousands on the bluff," *Beauregard* unluckily missed ramming USS *Monarch* and "cut away entirely the port wheel and wheel-house" of her partner, CSS *General Sterling Price*, also engaging *Monarch*. *General Beauregard*, backing out, gave Union flagship USS *Benton* a close broadside with a 42-pounder, and *Benton* replied with a shot into the Confederate's boiler, killing or scalding many of her crew, 14 of whom, in agony, were rescued by *Benton*. *General Beauregard* exploded and was sinking fast as *Monarch* captured the rest of her complement and took her in tow towards the Arkansas shore, where the wreck remained for a short time partially visible in shoal water.

Source (edited): "http://en.wikipedia.org/wiki/CSS_General_Beauregard"

CSS General Earl Van Dorn

The **CSS *General Earl Van Dorn***, a side-wheel river steamer, was fitted out in early 1862 at New Orleans, Louisiana as a River Defense Fleet "cottonclad" ram.

In late March, she steamed up the Mississippi River to Memphis, Tennessee, where her outfitting was completed. In the naval action off Fort Pillow on May 10, she attacked a Union mortar boat with gunfire and rammed the ironclad USS *Mound City*.

On June 1, she helped cover the Confederate evacuation of Fort Pillow, then retreated to Memphis, where, on June 6 she was the only survivor of the River Defense Fleet's final battle. After escaping to Yazoo City, Mississippi, *General Earl Van Dorn* was burned on June 26, 1862 to avoid capture by Federal warships.

Source (edited): "http://en.wikipedia.org/wiki/CSS_General_Earl_Van_Dorn"

CSS General M. Jeff Thompson

CSS *General M. Jeff Thompson* was a cotton-clad sidewheel ram of the Confederate Navy during the American Civil War.

The ship was selected in January 1862 by Captain James E. Montgomery to be part of his River Defense Fleet. At New Orleans on 25 January, Capt. Montgomery began to convert her into a cottonclad ram by placing a 4-inch (100 mm) oak sheath with a 1-inch (25 mm) iron covering on her bow, and by installing double pine bulkheads filled with compressed cotton bales.

Service history

Battle of Plum Point Bend

When *General M. Jeff Thompson*'s conversion was completed on 11 April, she steamed to Fort Pillow, Tennessee, where she operated in defense of the river approaches to Memphis. On 10

May 1862, *General M. Jeff Thompson*, in company with seven other vessels of Montgomery's fleet, attacked the ironclad gunboats of the Federal Mississippi Flotilla. The Battle of Plum Point Bend which followed witnessed successful ramming tactics by the Confederates, but *General M. Jeff Thompson*, under Captain J. H. Burke, was not able to get into the battle except with her guns. These she manned coolly and effectively despite the discouraging effect of heavy Union fire. Montgomery's force held off the Federal rams and gunboats until Fort Pillow was successfully evacuated on 1 June. Then the Confederate vessels fell back on Memphis to take on coal.

Battle of Memphis

Following the Federal capture of Fort Pillow, Flag Officer Charles Henry Davis, USN, commanding the Mississippi River Squadron pressed on without delay and appeared off Memphis with a superior force on 6 June 1862. Montgomery, unable to retreat to Vicksburg, Mississippi, because of his fuel shortage, and unwilling to destroy his boats, determined to fight against heavy odds. In the ensuing Battle of Memphis, *General M. Jeff Thompson* was heavily hit and set on fire by Union shells. She ran aground and was abandoned by her crew. She burned to the water's edge and her magazine blew up violently, strewing the shore with iron braces and fastenings, with charred remains of broken timbers, and leaving her wrecked remains half buried and half sunk.

Source (edited): "http://en.wikipedia.org/wiki/CSS_General_M._Jeff_Thompson"

CSS George Page

CSS *George Page*, a 410-ton sidewheel steamship, was originally built as a transport at Washington, D.C. in 1853.

She was attached to the Quartermaster's Department of the United States Army, until captured by the Confederates at nearby Aquia Creek, Virginia in May 1861, when she became a part of the Virginia State Navy. Acquired by the Confederate States Navy, *George Page*, commanded by Lieutenant Charles Carroll Simms, CSN, was fitted out for river defense service, and sometime later renamed *City of Richmond*. Her upper works may have been removed at this time.

She operated in the Potomac River in the vicinity of Quantico Creek. On July 7, 1861, she was damaged by gunfire from USS *Pocahontas*. *George Page* was destroyed by her crew upon abandonment of the Evansport batteries on March 9, 1862.

This article includes text from the public domain Dictionary of American Naval Fighting Ships.

Source (edited): "http://en.wikipedia.org/wiki/CSS_George_Page"

CSS Georgia (battery)

CSS *Georgia*, also known as *State of Georgia* and *Ladies' Ram*, was an ironclad floating battery built at Savannah, Georgia in 1862–1863. Funding in the amount of $115,000 for her construction was provided by the Ladies' Gunboat Association.

Placed under command of Lieutenant Washington Gwathmey, CSN, she was employed in defending the river channels below Savannah, training her batteries against the Union advance. Since she lacked effective locomotive power, the Confederates found it necessary to burn and destroy her during the evacuation of Savannah on December 21, 1864.

After settling to the bottom of Savannah Harbor, the wreck was noted as an obstruction, and several years later a survey of the wreck was completed. This survey found that the *Georgia* had settled slightly into the bottom, was covered by 11 feet of water at low tide. A sandbar was rapidly building up around the wreck, which ensured that the Georgia would be buried relatively quickly.

Unfortunately, the Army Corps of Engineers undertook a dredging and expansion of the channel several times since the Civil War, with the effect that the wreck was uncovered, and gradually destroyed over the years. Today all that remains are a portion of the forward and after casemate, along with remnants of the ship's engines including boilers, shafts, propellers, and condensers. Several cannon were found near the wreck as well, along with assorted ordinance.

A survey completed in 2006-2007 confirmed that by and large, the bulk of the CSS *Georgia* had been destroyed by a combination of manmade and natural forces since the ship's sinking. The remains have been scoured repeatedly over time by dredging and anchored ships, to the effect that scattered remains extending into the channel are the only remnants of the ironclad.

Source (edited): "http://en.wikipedia.org/wiki/CSS_Georgia_(battery)"

CSS Georgia (cruiser)

For other ships named Georgia*, see* USS Georgia.

CSS *Georgia* was built in 1862 as the fast merchantman *Japan*. The Confederate States Government purchased her at Dumbarton, Scotland, in March 1863

On April 1, she departed Greenock, reputedly bound for the East Indies and carrying a crew of fifty who had shipped for a voyage to Singapore. She rendezvoused with the steamer *Alar* off Ushant, France, and took on guns, ordnance and other stores.

On April 9, 1863 the Confederate flag was hoisted and she was placed in commission as CSS *Georgia*, Commander William Lewis Maury, CSN, in command. Her orders read to prey against United States shipping wherever found.

Georgia had a round stern, iron frame, fiddle-bow figurehead, short, thick funnel and full poop. Being an iron hull, she was clearly unsuited to long cruises without drydocking during a period when antifouling under-body coatings were yet unknown. Commander James Dunwoody Bulloch, a key Confederate procurement agent overseas, would have nothing to do with iron bottoms, but Commander Maury settled for *Japan* because wood (which could be coppered) was being superseded in Great Britain by the new metal; consequently wooden newbuilding contracts were not easy to buy up in British shipyards.

Calling at Bahia, Brazil and at Trinidad, *Georgia* recrossed the Atlantic to Simon's Bay, Cape Colony, Africa, where she arrived on August 16. She sailed next to Santa Cruz, Tenerife in the Canary Islands, thence up to Cherbourg, arriving October 28. During this short cruise she captured nine prizes.

While she was undergoing repair at Cherbourg in late January 1864, it was decided to shift her armament to CSS *Rappahannock*. The transfer was never effected, and *Georgia* was moved to an anchorage 3 miles below Bordeaux. On May 2, 1864 she was taken to Liverpool and sold on June 1 to a merchant of that city over the protest of Charles Francis Adams, Sr., United States Minister to Great Britain. The steamer again put to sea on August 11, and 4 days later was captured by the frigate USS *Niagara* off Portugal. She was sent into Boston, Massachusetts, where she was condemned and sold as a lawful prize of the United States.

She was documented as the U.S. merchant vessel SS *Georgia* in New Bedford, Massachusetts on August 5, 1865. She was reregistered in Canada in 1870 and was wrecked on the Maine coast in January 1875.

This article includes text from the public domain Dictionary of American Naval Fighting Ships.
Source (edited): "http://en.wikipedia.org/wiki/CSS_Georgia_(cruiser)"

CSS Governor Moore

LSNS *Governor Moore* was a schooner-rigged steamer in the Confederate States Navy.

Governor Moore had been Southern S. S. Company's **Charles Morgan**, named for the firm's founder and built at New York in 1854 as a schooner-rigged, low pressure, walking beam-engined, seagoing steamer. She was seized at New Orleans, Louisiana by Brigadier General Mansfield Lovell, CSA, in mid-January 1862 "for the public service." As a gunboat, renamed for Louisiana's Governor Thomas Overton Moore, her stem was reinforced for ramming by two strips of flat railroad iron at the waterline, strapped and bolted in place, with pine lumber and cotton-bale barricades to protect her boilers, but the *Governor Moore* was never commissioned as a ship in the Confederate States Navy.

The larger of two similar cotton-clads owned and operated by the State of Louisiana, *Governor Moore* was commanded for some time by Lieutenant Beverley Kennon, CSN, then serving as Commander in the Louisiana Provisional Navy without pay. She distinguished herself in the battle of April 24, 1862, when Admiral David Farragut, USN, passed Fort Jackson and Fort St. Philip before dawn en route to capture New Orleans. After a furious exchange of raking fire, *Governor Moore* twice rammed USS *Varuna*, and a third thrust from another cottonclad forced *Varuna* aground. Next attacking USS *Cayuga*, *Governor Moore* exposed herself to fire from most of the Union flotilla. With practically her whole upper hamper shot away and 64 men dead or dying, she went out of command, drifting helplessly to shore, where her captain, pilot, and a seaman set her afire. *Governor Moore* blew up while they and three other survivors were being captured by USS *Oneida*'s boats to be imprisoned on board USS *Colorado*; two-thirds of the two dozen or more crew members escaped into the marshes, the rest being captured by other ships' launches; no one drowned.

"The pennant and remains of the ensign were never hauled down," wrote Kennon from *Colorado*. "The flames that lit our decks stood faithful sentinels over their halyards until they, like the ship, were entirely consumed. I burned the bodies of the slain. Our colors were shot away three times. I hoisted them myself twice; finally every stripe was taken out of the flag, leaving a small constellation of four little stars only, which showed to our enemy how bravely we had defended them." The ship sank with the Louisiana's colors flying.(It is unclear if the flag referred to was the Confederate Stars and Bars or Louisiana State banner of January 1861; the *Dictionary of American Naval Fighting Ships* claims the latter.)
Source (edited): "http://en.wikipedia.org/wiki/CSS_Governor_Moore"

CSS Grampus

CSS *Grampus* was a stern-wheel river steamer built in 1856 at McKeesport, Pennsylvania, for civilian employment. Taken by the Confederate Army in early 1862, she served as a scout boat and transport on the Mississippi River. Late in March 1862, Captain Marsh Miller in command, she took an active part in the defense of Island No. 10 where the Confederates finally sank her to prevent capture, on 7 April. The Union Gunboat Flotilla set out to raise her during May 1862 and did so, but she is believed to be the *Grampus No. 2* which burned the following 11 January.

Source (edited): "http://en.wikipedia.org/wiki/CSS_Grampus"

CSS Grand Duke

CSS *Grand Duke*, a steamer built at Jeffersonville, Indiana in 1859, was outfitted as a cotton-clad gunboat for service with the Confederate States Army in February 1863.

Grand Duke transported troops to Fort Taylor, Louisiana late in February 1863. On April 14, 1863 she was in company with the steamer *Mary T.* and ram CSS *Queen of the West* when they were taken under attack on the Atchafalaya River by Union vessels USS *Estrella*, USS *Calhoun* and USS *Arizona*. Her speed, turning power, and superior piloting allowed *Grand Duke* to escape up river.

On May 4, 1863 *Grand Duke* and *Mary T.* were taking on guns, ordnance stores, and other public property prior to the evacuation of Fort De Russy when a Union reconnaissance force that included USS *Albatross*, *Estrella* and *Arizona* hove into view. In the ensuing hour-long engagement, each of the principal contestants sustained damage, but the Union ships withdrew, allowing the Confederates to remove their materiel further up the Red River and to delay the Federal advance by obstructing the river. *Grand Duke* was ordered to Shreveport, Louisiana where she burned late in 1863.

Source (edited): "http://en.wikipedia.org/wiki/CSS_Grand_Duke"

CSS Hampton

CSS *Hampton* was a wooden gunboat of the Confederate States Navy, one of the few *Hampton* class gunboats to be built.

Hampton was built at Norfolk Navy Yard in 1862 and based there until May 1862, when the yard was abandoned and the fleet moved up the James River. With Lieutenant John Herndon Maury, CSN, in command, *Hampton* participated in significant river actions including the battle at Dutch Gap on August 13, 1864; operations against Fort Harrison on September 29-October 1; and the engagement at Chaffin's Bluff on October 22.

Hampton was burned by the Confederates as they evacuated Richmond, Virginia on April 3, 1865.

Commanders

The commanders of the CSS *Hampton* were:

- Lieutenant George W. Harrison (as of May 1862)
- Lieutenant Hunter Davidson (1862)
- Lieutenant John S. Maury (1863-July 6, 1864; October 26-29, 1864)
- Lieutenant John W. Murdaugh (July 6-October 26, 1864)
- Lieutenant Ivey Foreman (October 29-November 18, 1864)
- Lieutenant Walter Raleigh Butt (November 18, 1864-)
- Lieutenant Francis E. Shepperd (December 28, 1864-January 14, 1865; briefly in February 1865)
- Lieutenant Joseph David Wilson (January-February 1865)

Source (edited): "http://en.wikipedia.org/wiki/CSS_Hampton"

CSS Isondiga

CSS *Isondiga* was a small wooden gunboat without masts that served in the Confederate States Navy during the American Civil War.

Isondiga operated in waters around Savannah, Georgia, and in Saint Augustine Creek, Florida, from April 1863 to December 1864, Lieutenant Joel S. Kennard commanding. She accompanied ironclad ram CSS *Atlanta* in the engagement in which *Atlanta* was captured on June 17, 1863.

She escaped from Savannah on December 21, 1864 before the city fell to the forces of U.S. General William T. Sherman. She was later burned by her commanding officer and crew to prevent seizure by the Union.

Source (edited): "http://en.wikipedia.org/wiki/CSS_Isondiga"

CSS Ivy

CSS Ivy was a sidewheel steamer and privateer purchased by Commodore Lawrence Rousseau for service with the Confederate Navy, and chosen by Commodore George Hollins for his Mosquito Fleet. The Mosquito Fleet was a group of riverboats converted to gunboats, and used to defend the Mississippi river in the area of New Orleans during the American Civil War.

As a privately owned commercial vessel, the Ivy had been known as the *Roger Williams* and the *El-Paraguay*. The *CSS Ivy* began her Civil War career as a New Orleans based privateer *V.H. Ivy*, sent out to capture Union commercial vessels after Jefferson Davis authorized the distribution of letters of marque and reprisal to private citizens after hostilities began in April of 1861. The *Ivy* did well at this, capturing four northern registered vessels, one of which was the ice breaker *Enoch Train*, which was purchased by private investors and rebuilt as the privateer ironclad ram *Manassas*. This vessel in turn was commandeered by Commodore Hollins as the CSS Manassas.

The Union Blockade arrived at the mouth of the Mississippi on May 27, 1861, when the USS Brooklyn took up position. This event energized defense efforts in New Orleans and led to the replacement of Rousseau with Commodore Hollins in July of 1861 to command the river defense. By August Hollins had established his mosquito fleet for defense of the river in the area of New Orleans. The fleet consisted of the CSS McRae, the flagship CSS Tuscarora, CSS Livingston, CSS Calhoun, CSS Jackson, and the *Ivy*.

6.4 inch banded rifle, the weapon type used as the bow pivot gun on the CSS Ivy. Note the 100-pound conical projectile at the right rear of the gun carriage. This image is from the Library of Congress.

The *Ivy*, due to her large, sophisticated walking beam engine and multiple boiler propulsion system, was the fastest ship of the fleet. Because of this, Hollins made her the reconnaissance vessel of the fleet, and increased her firepower. As a privateer the *Ivy* was armed with two brass 24-pounder smoothbore howitzers. Hollins increased her armament to an eight inch smoothbore mounted aft, and a 32-pounder rifled gun mounted on a forward pivot position on the bow. The conventional description of "rifled 32-pounder" is misleading, however. This gun was a former 32-pounder smoothbore that had been "modernized" by rifling the barrel, and machining and shrinking a single layer of red hot bands of wrought iron onto the breech of the barrel to allow it to operate at much greater breech pressures. This rifling and banding allowed the gun to fire a 100-pound (6.4 inch diameter) conical shot or shell at much greater ranges than would be possible with 32-pound round shot fired out of a smoothbore barrel. This modification was similar to the James rifle process used to produce siege guns, and the resulting gun tube resembled a Parrott rifle. This gun could be much more accurately described as a 6.4-inch (162 mm) banded rifle, and was the most powerful, long range weapon in the mosquito fleet.

Map of Louisiana during the Civil War. The CSS Ivy was based in New Orleans and helped defend the lower Mississippi.

The *Ivy* began patrolling the Mississippi south of Forts Jackson and St. Phillip beginning in September of 1861, captained by Lieutenant Fry of the CSN. On September 19, she encountered the USS Water Witch. The Water Witch was scouting the Head of Passes for the blockade fleet, which was planning to occupy the Head of Passes and set up a shore battery to control this strategic point. On October 5th Ivy reported the Head of Passes occupied by three vessels of the Union fleet, and shelled them with her bow pivot gun. Returning to the forts, Fry warned Hollins the Union fleet was establishing a base at the Head of Passes. Hollins decided the advance of the Blockade Fleet was a significant threat to New Orleans and moved to attack with the entire mosquito fleet. This attack resulted in the Battle of the Head of Passes a Confederate victory that routed the Blockade Fleet and sent it back to the mouth of the Southwest Passage.

This victory reinforced the idea in the Confederate War Department that Flag Officer Foote's Union Mississippi River Squadron at the north end of the Mississippi was the greatest threat to the Confederacy. The Battle of Fort Henry, the Battle of Fort Donelson, and the Battle of Shiloh lent a lot of credibility to this idea. As a result the mosquito fleet and the *Ivy* were ordered to the upper Mississippi and took part in the Battle of Island Number 10.

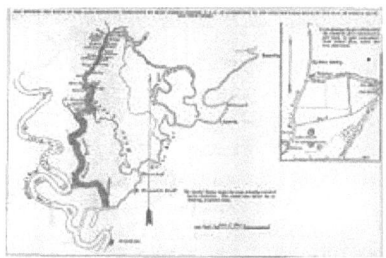

Porter's Yazoo River expedition against the last Confederate Naval base in western waters at Yazoo City. This image is from the Library of Congress.

Island Number 10 was a defeat for the Confederate forces involved. The mosquito fleet could not match the USS *Pittsburgh* and *Carondelet* after these ships successfully ran the Confederate batteries, and were forced to retreat. Commander McBlair CSN at Memphis, being informed that New Orleans had fallen after the Battle of Forts Jackson and St. Philip, ordered remaining Confederate vessels on the Mississippi to concentrate at Yazoo City, Mississippi, on the Yazoo River. He regarded this harbor as the only safe place remaining on the Mississippi River network for the Confederate Navy to maintain a base.

This remaining refuge did not prove safe for long. In May of 1863, Rear Admiral David Dixon Porter ordered a fleet under the command of Lieutenant-commander Walker to destroy Confederate commerce on the Yazoo River. This force consisted of the USS *Baron De Kalb*, *Forest Rose*, *Linden*, *Signal* and *Petrel*. With the *Forest Rose* acting as a mine sweeper, this force advanced steadily up the Yazoo river, from May 24th-31. Fearing the capture of their vessels on the Yazoo, Confederate forces destroyed the CSS *Ivy*, Star of the West, and the transports *Arcadia* and *Magenta*.

Source (edited): "http://en.wikipedia.org/wiki/CSS_Ivy"

CSS Jackson

CSS *Jackson* was a gunboat of the Confederate Navy during the American Civil War.

Built at Cincinnati, Ohio, in 1849 as *Yankee*, the fast side-wheel river tug was purchased at New Orleans on 9 May 1861 by Capt. L. Rousseau, CSN, then strengthened and fitted for service in the Confederate Navy, and renamed *Jackson*.

Service history

On 6 June Lt. W. Gwathmey, CSN, was ordered to her command, and after shipping a crew, took her up the Mississippi River to Columbus, Kentucky, to join the squadron under Capt. G. N. Hollins charged with the defense of the river.

On 4 September 1861 *Jackson* supported by shore batteries briefly and inconclusively engaged the gunboats USS *Lexington* and *Tyler* off Hickman, Kentucky. The Federal ships finding the current fast setting them down upon the Confederate batteries returned to their former position. Six days later the little gunboat took part in a spirited engagement at Lucas Bend, Missouri, between Confederate artillery and cavalry and Union gunboats *Lexington* and *Conestoga* during which she received an 8-inch shell in her wheel house and side which forced her to retire on one engine.

Jackson sailed with Hollins' squadron to attack five of the Federal blockaders at the Head of Passes, Mississippi River, on 12 October 1861. They successfully routed the Union forces and proceeded to the defense of Forts Jackson and St. Philip which the United States Mortar Flotilla under Commodore David Dixon Porter bombarded from 18 to 24 April 1862. On 23 April *Jackson* was despatched to make the canals above the fort inaccessible to Union ships.

When the commanding officer, Lt. F. B. Renshaw, CSN, found it impossible to stem the Federal advance he retired to New Orleans. After the surrender of that city, *Jackson* was destroyed by the Confederates.

Source (edited): "http://en.wikipedia.org/wiki/CSS_Jackson"

CSS Jamestown

CSS *Jamestown*, originally a sidewheel, passenger steamer, was built at New York City in 1853, and seized at Richmond, Virginia in 1861 for the Commonwealth of Virginia Navy. She was commissioned by the Confederate States Navy the following July, and renamed CSS *Thomas Jefferson* but was generally referred to as *Jamestown*, after Jamestown, Virginia.

Brigantine-rigged *Jamestown* was designed and constructed by the well-known shipbuilder William H. Webb for the New York and Old Dominion Line as a sister to *Yorktown*, which became CSS *Patrick Henry*.

Career

With Lt. Joseph Nicholson Barney, CSN, in command, she was actively employed until the end of her career in May 1862. Her service was highlighted by the Battle of Hampton Roads on March 8–9 1862, during which she assisted CSS *Virginia* in attacking USS *Congress* and USS *Cumberland* and stood by during the battle between USS *Monitor* and *Virginia*. The Confederate Congress tendered special thanks to the officers and crew of *Jamestown* for their "gallant conduct and bearing" in combat.

Wreckage of CSS *Jamestown* in the James River. *(Photograph by Mathew Brady)*

Some 4 weeks later, on April 11, 1862, *Jamestown*, *Virginia* and five other Confederate ships sailed from Norfolk, Virginia, into Hampton Roads in full view of the Union squadron there. When it became clear that the Federal ships were not going to attack, *Jamestown*, covered by *Virginia* and the others, moved in, captured three merchant ships, and helped by CSS *Raleigh*, towed them to Norfolk. The merchant ships were the brigs *Marcus of Stockton, NJ* and *Sabout of Providence, RI* and the schooner *Catherine T. Dix* of Accomac County, VA. Their flags were hoisted "Union-side down" to taunt the Federals into fighting. Later that month *Jamestown* was despatched from Norfolk to cooperate with Major General John Bankhead Magruder, CSA, in the James River, and early in May she was used to transport army sick and wounded to Richmond, Virginia.

On the night of May 5, *Jamestown* and *Patrick Henry* proceeded to Norfolk and returned the following night with CSS *Richmond*, CSS *Hampton* and ordnance store boats, passing the Federal battery at Newport News, Virginia unobserved on both occasions. A second attempt to return to Norfolk met with failure.

On May 8, *Jamestown* was ordered to notify Stephen Mallory, Secretary of the Confederate States Navy, of the continuing engagement of two Federal gunboats and ironclad USS *Galena* with the Confederate batteries at Day's Point. Unable to carry out her assignment, *Jamestown* retired up the James River as far as Drewry's Bluff, where on May 15, 1862, she was sunk to obstruct the channel.

Commanders

The commanders of the CSS *Jamestown* were:
- Lt. Joseph Nicholson Barney (1861-1862)
- Lt. George W. Harrison (May 1862, temporarily)

Source (edited): "http://en.wikipedia.org/wiki/CSS_Jamestown"

CSS Lady Davis

CSS *Lady Davis* was a gunboat in the Confederate States Navy during the American Civil War.

Originally the Richmond iron steam tug *James Gray*, built at Philadelphia, Pennsylvania in 1858, *Lady Davis* was purchased in March 1861 by Governor Francis Wilkinson Pickens of South Carolina, who armed her and placed in command Lieutenant William Gaillard Dozier, South Carolina Navy, with orders to thwart reinforcement of Fort Sumter by Union troops.

On May 7, 1861 *Lady Davis* was purchased by the Confederacy for $32,000 and commissioned in the Confederate Navy, operating thereafter along the Georgia and South Carolina coasts. Lieutenant Thomas P. Pelot, CSN, took command about 5 days later, relieving Lieutenant Edward Cantey Stockton, South Carolina Navy. At that time, the little gunboat served as flagship of Commodore Josiah Tattnall's Savannah Defense Squadron, consisting of CSS *Savannah*, CSS *Sampson* and CSS *Resolute*.

On May 19, *Lady Davis* began her career with distinction by capturing and taking into Beaufort, South Carolina the *A. B. Thompson*, a full-rigged ship of 980 tons and a crew of 23 out of Brunswick, Maine, whom she encountered off Savannah while on an expedition seeking the U.S. armed brig Perry. The exploit culminated in acrimonious litigation to decide whether an Army captain and a dozen of his soldiers should share in the prize money. Captain Stephen Elliott, Jr., CSA, happened to be on board and acted as pilot during the capture and afterward, while his men claimed to have helped bring in the prize.

On the following day, the crew were reenlisted into the Confederate States Navy, the State officers being replaced by regulars between then and June 1. *Lady Davis*'s rifled gun remained the property of South Carolina, on loan, while the other, a 24-pounder howitzer, was a gift outright to the Confederacy. By November, Lieutenant John Rutledge commanded her.

She joined in the battle of Port Royal, South Carolina on November 7, 1861. Although her engines were transferred to CSS *Palmetto State* late in 1862, well built iron hulls were in great demand and she was able to continue her successful career as a privately owned blockade runner out of Charleston, South Carolina. With the occupation of Charleston in 1865 by Federal forces, *Lady Davis* was captured and turned over to the Light House Board by Admiral John A. Dahlgren, who praised her hull, while noting that she was, again, minus her machinery, whose disposition is not recorded.

Source (edited): "http://en.wikipedia.org/wiki/CSS_Lady_Davis"

CSS Lark

The ***Lark*** was a paddle steamer employed by the Confederate States of America during the American Civil

War. She was the last blockade runner to successfully escape from a Southern port before the Union blockade completely closed off this vital source of supplies.

Lark was designed and built by John Laird & Sons. The ship made four successful round trips through the blockade between Galveston, Texas, and Havana, Cuba. In April 1865, she ran aground near the entrance to Galveston harbor. Two launches dispatched from the Union blockading squadron attacked the *Lark*, which managed to fend off the assault with help from Confederate ground forces. On May 24, she dashed into Galveston again and managed to slip through the blockade back out to open sea, the last Confederate blockade runner to do so.

Source (edited): "http://en.wikipedia.org/wiki/CSS_Lark"

CSS Louisiana

CSS *Louisiana* was an ironclad ship of the Confederate States Navy built to aid in defending the lower Mississippi River from invasion by the Union Navy during the American Civil War. She took part in one major action of the war, the Battle of Forts Jackson and St. Philip, and when that ended disastrously for the Confederacy, she was destroyed by her crew.

Construction

Louisiana was laid down in mid-October 1861 by E.C. Murray in a new shipyard just north of New Orleans. The ship had two paddlewheels and two screws, each driven by its own engine. The paddlewheels were mounted one abaft the other in a center well. The screws were not intended for propulsion, but were to aid the two rudders in steering in the confined waters and unpredictable currents of the Mississippi. The engines were taken from steamer *Ingomar*, but two months were needed for their transfer. The casemate extended her full length, less 25 feet at each end. It was covered by T-rail iron in two courses, while its top was encompassed by sheet iron bulwarks nearly four feet high.

Construction was delayed by several circumstances. First was the lack of materials, particularly iron. Always in short supply in the Confederacy, its procurement was made even more difficult by the blockade and by Army demands on the overstrained railroads of the South. The blockade also negated efforts to bring in needed light oak from Florida, forcing the builders to find alternative sources. Labor troubles led to a strike that lost about a week. Even more time was lost to demands of the local militia, which called out the workers for drills, including parades. Competition for skilled workmen with the builders of CSS *Mississippi*, an ironclad being built in an adjacent shipyard by Nelson and Asa Tift, also slowed down construction, until Murray and the Tifts agreed to let *Louisiana* have first call on the labor force; *Mississippi* would go forward only when work on *Louisiana* was halted for some other reason. She was not ready to launch until 6 February 1862, nearly four months after the keel was laid.

In battle

Shortly after *Louisiana* was launched, the Federal West Gulf Blockading Squadron, under Flag Officer (later Admiral) David G. Farragut had moved into the lower Mississippi River, threatening the Confederate-held Forts Jackson and St. Philip, about 120 kilometers or 75 miles below New Orleans. A portion of the squadron, a division of mortar boats led by Commander (later Admiral) David Dixon Porter, had on 16 April 1862 taken position downstream, and on 18 April they began their bombardment. Brigadier General Johnson K. Duncan, commanding the forts, and his immediate superior officer, Major General Mansfield Lovell, importuned Commander William C. Whittle, in charge of Confederate naval forces in the vicinity, to bring the ship down to the forts, even though she was not yet complete, and for that reason was still in the hands of her builders. Whittle yielded to their pleas, and on 20 April commissioned the vessel in the CS Navy, with Commander Charles F. McIntosh commanding.

At this time, the main engines of *Louisiana* had been installed, but those for the screws, needed for steering, had not Furthermore, the main engines were found to be inadequate; even at dangerously high boiler pressure, she could barely make headway against the river current. Unable to move on her own, she had to be towed down to the forts, with workmen still aboard. There she was tied to the left bank (here, the north side of the river) a short distance above Fort St. Philip. This did not completely mollify General Duncan, who wanted the ship to be positioned below the forts, but Commander Whittle would not risk his vessel, with unarmored deck, against the plunging fire of the Union mortars. She remained at this position throughout the ensuing battle.

In assessing the battle-readiness of the ship, the engines are not alone in deserving attention. Many of her gun carriages were found to be either too high or too low, and had to be modified. Because the workmen and their tools occupied much of the gun deck, the gun crews were unable to practice. In addition, the crew was incomplete, as a result of the hasty commissioning; to handle the guns, soldiers had to be transferred from the forts.

After nearly a week of bombardment, Farragut concluded that it was ineffective, so he moved his fleet past the forts on the night of 24 April. Because of her position on the river bank, *Louisiana* could use neither her stern guns nor those on her port side. The magnitude of her contribution to the ensuing firefight between the forts and the Federal fleet is not known; General Duncan stated that she may have fired as few as twelve shots. On the other hand, testimony from her enemies indicates that she exchanged shots with at least one attacking ship, USS *Brooklyn* (misidentified as *Hartford* in the Confederate reports). Three shots from *Louisiana* went all the way through the Federal vessel, while the return broadside bounced harmlessly off the Rebel's armor. Indeed, the armor was effective; only three men were killed on *Louisiana,* all of them in exposed positions. One of them was her captain, Commander McIntosh.

Destruction

Once the Federal fleet had passed out of range, *Louisiana* had no further part in the action. Her fate was henceforth tied to that of the forts, which prepared for an expected attack by the Union army accompanying the fleet, led by Major General Benjamin Butler. However, on the night of 28 April, the enlisted men in Fort Jackson mutinied and forced the surrender of both forts to Commander Porter. The naval officers on *Louisiana* were not consulted at any time during the negotiations between Porter and General Duncan, so they considered themselves not bound to respect the truce declared by the two sides. While discussions of terms were going on, they decided not to let their ship fall into enemy hands. *Louisiana* was set afire, and her crew went ashore. The flames soon parted the lines that held her to the bank, and she drifted down the river. When she was nearly abreast of Fort St. Philip, the fire reached her magazine, and she blew up with a blast that killed a soldier there.

Assessment

Perhaps to counter charges that the Confederate Navy was responsible, by its inaction, for the failure of the forts to turn back Farragut's fleet, Commander John K. Mitchell, second in command under Commodore Whittle, pointed out several shortcomings of *Louisiana,* any one of which would have seriously compromised her fighting ability.
1. The arrangement of the paddlewheels meant that the after wheel was always in the wash of the other, with the result that its power was wasted.
2. The wash also created an eddy at the rudders, making it impossible to steer.
3. The gun ports were too small to allow either elevation or traverse. Consequently, she would have to fight at close range, and furthermore her guns covered only 40 degrees of azimuth.
4. The gun deck was uninhabitable in summer, particularly when the boilers were in use.

Today

The wreckage of the *Louisiana* lay at the bottom of the Mississippi River until November 1981, when it was magnetically located by NUMA. The official website of the search is here.
Source (edited): "http://en.wikipedia.org/wiki/CSS_Louisiana"

CSS Manassas

Map of Louisiana during the Civil War. The *CSS Manassas* was based in New Orleans and helped defend the lower Mississippi.

CSS *Manassas*, formerly the steam icebreaker *Enoch Train*, was built as a twin-screw towboat at Medford, Massachusetts, by James O. Curtis in 1855. A New Orleans commission merchant, Captain John A. Stevenson, acquired her for use as a privateer after she was captured by the privateer, later gunboat, CSS Ivy and fitted her out at Algiers, Louisiana as an ironclad ram of radically modern design. Covered with 1½-inch iron plating, her above-water hull was reshaped to a "turtle-back" form and projected only 2½ feet above the water. The convex shape of her plated top caused cannon shot to glance off harmlessly. She was one hundred and twenty-eight feet over all, and had twenty-six feet beam and eleven feet draught. She was given a pointed iron ram at the bow and carried a single gun that fired forward through a small opening. The iron ram was designed to stave holes through enemy vessels. Her low profile made her a difficult target, while her armor protected her against all but the most well-directed enemy gunfire. Fast moving, lying low in the water, she looked like a floating cigar or egg shell and was described by Union intelligence as a "hellish machine."

Commissioned as a Confederate privateer on September 12, 1861, *Manassas was* seized soon afterwards by Flag Officer G. N. Rollins, CSN, for use in the lower Mississippi River. With Lieutenant A. F. Warley, CSN, in command she participated in Flag Officer Rollins' surprise attack on the Federal blockading squadron at Head of Passes, the action being known as the Battle of the Head of Passes, on October 12, 1861. In the action *Manassas* violently rammed USS *Richmond*, damaging her severely below the water line. *Manassas*, however, suffered the loss of her prow and smokestack and had her engines temporarily thrown out of gear from the impact. She managed to retire under heavy fire from USS *Preble* and *Richmond* whose shells glanced off her armor. Two months after this engagement, *Manassas* was purchased for direct ownership by the Confederate Government.

Under Lieutenant Warley, *Manassas* joined the force of Captain John K. Mitchell, CSN, commanding Confederate naval forces in the lower Mississippi. She participated in the Battle of Forts Jackson and St. Philip, during which Commodore David Farragut, USN, on his way to New Orleans, ran his fleet past the Confederate forts of Fort Jackson and Fort St. Philip. In the action *Manassas* attempted to ram USS *Pensacola*, which turned in time to avoid the blow and deliver a broadside at close range. *Manassas* then ran into murderous fire from the whole line of the Union fleet. She then charged USS *Mississippi* and delivered a long glancing blow on her hull, firing her only gun as she rammed. Next she rammed USS *Brooklyn*, again firing her gun, and injuring her rather deeply, but not quite enough to be fatal.

After this action *Manassas* followed the Union fleet quietly for a while, but as she drew closer *Mississippi* furiously turned on her. *Manassas* managed to dodge the blow but was run aground. Her crew escaped as *Mississippi* poured her heavy broadsides into the stranded Confederate vessel. Later *Manassas* slipped off the bank and drifted down the river in flames past the Union mortar flotilla. Commander David Dixon Porter, USN, in command of the mortar boats, tried to save her as an engineering curiosity, but *Manassas* exploded and immediately plunged under water.

Years after the war In "Battles and Leaders of the Civil War" there was a claim that a *Manassas* crewman was knocked off the ironclad by a Union sailor; however the *CSS Manassas* Captain Lt. A. F. Warley reported no casualties among his crew in an official report of August 13, 1863
Source (edited): "http://en.wikipedia.org/wiki/CSS_Manassas"

CSS McRae

The **CSS *McRae*** was a Confederate gunboat that saw service during the American Civil War. Displacing around 680 tons, she was armed with one 9-inch smoothbore and six 32-pound smoothbore cannon.

Originally rebel Mexican-flagged (under the name of *Marqués de la Havana*), the wooden sloop was captured as a pirate ship by the United States Navy ship, USS *Saratoga* during the Battle of Anton Lizardo in 1860. A construction plan authorizing the building of ten fast gunboats was funded by the Confederate Legislature on March 15, 1861. Recognizing that no yard could turn out the vessels fast enough, Stephen R. Mallory, Secretary of the Navy, sent a commission to New Orleans to convert existing steamers to commerce raiders. The Mexican vessel was purchased by the Confederate States Navy at New Orleans on 17 March 1861, and duly fitted out as the CSS *McRae* as part of this plan. Extensive engine repairs prevented the McRae from going to sea before the arrival of the Union Fleet.

Placed under the command of Lieutenant Thomas B. Huger, the *McRae* served as part of Flag Officer G. N. Hollins' defense of the lower reaches of the Mississippi River, and provided cover for blockade-runners. This led to the *McRae* seeing combat with the Union blockading fleet on 12 October 1861. The McRae took part in the Battle of the Head of Passes as part of Hollin's mosquito fleet, driving the Union blockading forces from the Head of Passes in the Mississippi Delta.

The *McRae* again saw action on 24 April 1862 as the Union fleet attempted to pass Fort Jackson and Fort Saint Philip and reach New Orleans. The McRae suffered little damage in the beginning due to its resemblance to the Union Unadilla class gunboats. The leading union ships passed by her without firing. The USS Iroquois was an exception, and replied to the McRae's fire with an 11-inch shell that set fire to the McRae's sail room and threatened her magazines. The officers and crew fought hard in this latter engagement but suffered severe casualties (Huger being amongst those mortally wounded), and the *McRae* itself was severely damaged. She was run against the shore to put out her fires, and remained there till dawn, after which she returned to the forts. Loaded with wounded from the forts McRae was allowed to return to New Orleans on 27 April under a flag of truce. After landing the wounded at the city, her crew scuttled and abandoned her at Algiers, after cutting all her steam pipes.
Source (edited): "http://en.wikipedia.org/wiki/CSS_McRae"

CSS Mississippi

CSS *Mississippi* was a projected ironclad warship of the Confederate States Navy, intended to be used on the Mississippi River in the vicinity of New Orleans during the American Civil War. Her design was unusual, as she was built according to house-building techniques. Whether this would have proved to be feasible cannot be known, as she was not complete when New Orleans fell to the Union Fleet under Flag Officer David G. Farragut on 25 April 1862. Rather than let her fall into enemy hands, Captain Arthur Sinclair, CSN, ordered her to be hastily launched and burned. Despite the delays in construction that left her unfinished and untried, her mere existence, together with that of CSS *Louisiana*, raised thwarted hopes in the defenders of New Orleans, and unfounded fears in Union circles, that affected the strategy of both sides in the campaign on the lower Mississippi. *Mississippi* is significant to the Civil War therefore not so much as a warship as in the way her reputation influenced events, and as an example of the difficulties the South had in the contest with the industrial North.

Origin of the river ironclads

At the start of the Civil War, Confederate Secretary of the Navy Stephen R. Mallory had promptly urged the building of armored warships, to counter by the inherent quality of ships in his Navy the superior numbers the Federal Navy would be able to use. At his prodding, the Confederacy embarked on a construction program that included several armored vessels intended for use on the Mississippi River and other inland waters. The initial plans, prepared after US President Abraham Lincoln had proclaimed the blockade of Southern ports but before the North had taken any major steps to subjugate the South, called for five ironclads to be built in the interior: CSS *Eastport* on the Tennessee River, *Arkansas* and *Tennessee* on the Mississippi at Memphis, and *Louisiana* and *Mississippi* at New Orleans. In the end, only *Arkansas* of these five ever engaged the Union fleet in the intended manner; here we are concerned with why *Mississippi* was unable to do so.

Concept, contract, and construction

Nelson Tift had been raised in Florida, but moved to Georgia as a young man and there became locally prominent. (The town of Tifton, in Tift County, is named for him.) At the outbreak of the Civil War, he realized some of the difficulties faced by the South in its need to confront the Northern navy. Secretary Mallory had called for building a navy essentially from scratch, but not only were there no shipyards, there were also no skilled shipwrights to work in them. Reasoning that too much time would be lost training men in traditional techniques, Tift hit on the idea of constructing ships on house-building principles. He thought of making a ship with flat sides, with square corners except where the pointed ends join with the rest of the hull. He made a model to illustrate his idea, and used it to further his proposal. (See accompanying figure.)

Nelson's brother Asa F. Tift agreed to work with him. Asa's support was important, as he had remained in Florida when Nelson moved to Georgia. He had become a successful businessman in Key West, where he came to know Stephen Mallory before he became a United States Senator and then Confederate Secretary of the Navy. No evidence exists that Asa Tift and Mallory were ever formally associated in any of their businesses, but their friendship opened doors. The Tifts showed the model to Mallory, who in turn showed it to a naval review board. When the board pronounced the idea to be feasible, Mallory authorized the brothers to go to New Orleans and there put their idea into concrete form. They were to supervise the construction of an as yet unnamed armored ship carrying 18 guns, driven by three screws.

The contract, such as it was, was unusual. The Tifts were not paid for their labors, aside from expenses. They were encouraged to alter the planned construction if they thought that doing so would improve it. No completion date and no cost limit were set. All depended upon the skill and integrity of the Tifts. In the words of Secretary Mallory,
The Department trusts to your patriotism, judgment, and discretion to produce the ship designed in the shortest time at the lowest price and to act in the premises generally as if you were building for yourselves and had to pay the money out of your own pockets.
Among the first tasks confronting the brothers was that of finding a shipyard capable of handling a job as big as the one envisioned. None in or near New Orleans was suitable, so they established their own at Jefferson City, on the river just north of the city line. As the builders of CSS *Louisiana* had the same experience and solved it the same way, the two monsters came to be built side by side. *Mississippi*'s name was henceforth forever linked with that of *Louisiana*.

The first plank —it would be incorrect to refer to it as the keel— was laid down on 14 October 1861. Already it had been found that the engines of the original design could not drive the finished vessel at the desired speed, so more boiler space had to be added. This increased the overall length to 252 feet (76.8 meters). The extra length allowed positions for two more guns, for a total of twenty. For comparison, CSS *Virginia* (ex-USS *Merrimack*) carried only 12 guns, while *Louisiana* had 16.

From the first, construction was delayed by a combination of circumstances. Acquisition of parts and materials was most obvious, but the builders also encountered labor troubles, plus interference from the local military authorities. Consider these in turn.

Iron for the armor was in short supply throughout the Confederacy, and was not to be found near New Orleans. Eventually the Tifts were able to find a foundry in Atlanta that would produce plate iron of sufficient thickness, but delivery by way of the already overtaxed railroad system was often sporadic. Plates awaiting shipment sometimes lay in Atlanta for weeks. The final armor arrived in New Orleans on the day the ship was burned.

The engines and shafts added to the problems. The increased size of boilers, already alluded to, caused some delay. The contract that was let for the engines called for the job to be done by the end of January, but they were not installed until April. The greatest mechanical problem, however, was fabrication of the three shafts that were to connect the engines to the screws. The two outboard shafts could be handled by New Orleans shops, but the long central shaft could not be manufactured anyplace in the Confederacy. A satisfactory shaft was found in a wrecked ship in October, but only the Tredegar Iron Works or the Gosport (Norfolk) Navy Yard in Virginia could handle the needed modifications. When they were completed, the shaft then had to be transported over the rails. It was shipped out on 26 March. Although all three shafts were put into the hull, they were not hooked up with the engines, and the two outboard screws were still on the wharf at the end.

Labor troubles of the traditional sort arose in November, shortly after work commenced. The workers in all the shipyards struck, demanding that their wages be increased from $3 to $4 per day. The other owners wanted to wait out the strikers, but after a week the Tifts gave in. The others were forced to follow suit. Trouble of a different sort was found shortly thereafter, when the Tifts found that they were competing with E. C. Murray, who was building *Louisiana*, for the same skilled workmen. To solve this problem, the Tifts and Murray agreed to share labor, with *Louisiana* having first call.

Another set of delays was caused by the local military policies, which insisted that all men of appropriate ages participate in militia activities, including parades. A protest to the governor was rejected. Murray and the Tifts requested of Major General Mansfield Lovell that their men be exempted. Although Lovell agreed and issued the needed order, the practice continued.

Although all the delays cannot be simply added to find how much time was lost, clearly the loss was critical. Long after *Mississippi* was torched and New Orleans was surrendered, Nelson Tift stated that he believed his ship would have been completed in another two or three weeks. (This estimate was contradicted by Captain Sinclair, who thought she was more like ten weeks away from completion.)

The final days

In mid-March 1862, the Union fleet under Flag Officer Farragut began to enter the Mississippi from the Gulf of Mexico, with the obvious ultimate purpose of attacking New Orleans. Farragut was already under some time pressure from Secretary of the Navy Gideon Welles, who feared that if the two ironclad "monsters" (a term widely used at the time to characterize CSS *Louisiana* and *Mississippi*) were to be successfully completed, they would be able to shatter the blockade.

The Confederate government in Richmond was not so much concerned with the blockade as with the threat posed by the Union Western Gunboat Flotilla, then approaching Memphis. Even as Farragut was moving his ships across the bar, President Davis and Navy Secretary Mallory were promising Flag Officer George N. Hollins, commanding the Confederate States Navy forces on the Mississippi, that *Louisiana* would be sent up to Memphis as soon as she could be finished (expected to be within days), and *Mississippi* would follow shortly thereafter. At about this time, the Navy Department ordered Commander Arthur Sinclair to report to New Orleans to take command of *Mississippi*. Sinclair arrived on 3 April.

The Tift brothers about this time came under increasing public pressure to hasten the completion of their ship. A self-appointed group of citizens, calling themselves the Committee of Public Safety, tried to force them to launch *Mississippi* prematurely, against the advice of Sinclair and the engineers working on the ship. The Tifts refused, arguing that to do so would delay completion by several weeks.

All arguments were rendered moot on 24 April, when the Union fleet passed the forts defending New Orleans from the south. Trying to move the ship to a safe place where she could be finished, Sinclair had her hastily launched—with approval of the Tifts—, and tried to have her towed upriver. The tow boats he initially hired were inadequate, however, so next day he tried to find others. While he was so engaged, the Union fleet came in sight, so *Mississippi* was ordered burned.

Source (edited): "http://en.wikipedia.org/wiki/CSS_Mississippi"

CSS Morgan

CSS *Morgan* was a partially armored gunboat of the Confederate States Navy in the American Civil War.

Morgan was built at Mobile, Alabama in 1861-62. She operated in the waters around Mobile from the time of her completion early in 1862 to the close of hostilities. One reference of October 1862 gave her name as *Admiral*.

Morgan, commanded by Commander George W. Harrison, CSN, took an active part in the Battle of Mobile Bay on August 5, 1864. Situated well to the right of the Confederate line of battle as the enemy proceeded up the channel, she was able to deliver a telling broadside raking fire against USS *Hartford* and others. Toward the end of the engagement, she was pursued by USS *Metacomet* but succeeded in driving her off. *Morgan*, attempting to avoid capture, then turned toward shallow water, grounded briefly, but continued on her perilous route and reached the guns at Fort Morgan. She dispatched a boat which effected the destruction of the Union gunboat USS *Philippi* below the fort. When the Union victory was apparent, Captain Harrison initially wanted to scuttle the ship, but was persuaded by his second in command, Lieutenant Thomas Locke Harrison (no relation) that she could be saved by boldly running the gauntlet up to Mobile. Although hotly pursued and shelled by cruisers for a large part of the 25-mile starlight voyage, she reached the outer obstructions near Mobile at daybreak, and that afternoon was permitted to pass through.

Morgan continued to serve in the Mobile area. In April 1865 she participated in the battle off Blakely Island in the last days of the Civil War. Blakely Island is located just off the docks of Mobile between the city and Old Spanish Fort located on the eastern shore of Mobile Bay. It was commanded by Captain Fry and sustained considerable damage in her final battle, but survived the war. CSS Morgan stood alone between the City of Mobile and the invading Union troops. On May 4, 1865, Commodore Ebenezer Farrand, commanding Confederate Naval Forces in the State of Alabama, ordered the surrender of *Morgan* to the United States Navy. She was sold the following December.

Source (edited): "http://en.wikipedia.org/wiki/CSS_Morgan"

CSS Muscogee

This article is about the ironclad ram that operated on the Chattahoochee River. For the converted tugboat named CSS Jackson *that operated on the Mississippi River, see CSS Jackson.*

CSS *Muscogee* also known as **CSS Jackson** was a Confederate States Navy ironclad ram, powered by a steam driven screw and deployed on the Chattahoochee River during the American Civil War.

She was built at Columbus, Georgia, and launched in December 1864. In April 1865, the still incomplete CSS *Muscogee* (or CSS *Jackson*, as she was also called) was burned and scuttled in order to avoid capture by Wilson's Raiders after the Battle of Columbus, Georgia on April 16. Her remains were recovered during the 1960s from the portion of the river inside the boundaries of Fort Benning and placed on exhibit at the National Civil War Naval Museum in Columbus.

Source (edited): "http://en.wikipedia.org/wiki/CSS_Muscogee"

CSS Nashville (1853)

CSS *Nashville* was a brig-rigged passenger steamer built at Greenpoint, Brooklyn in 1853. Between 1853 and 1861 she was engaged in running between New York City and Charleston, South Carolina. After the fall of Fort Sumter, the Confederates seized her at Charleston and fitted her out as a cruiser. Under the command of Lieutenant Robert B. Pegram, CSN, she braved the blockade on October 21, 1861, and headed across the Atlantic to Southampton, England, the first ship of war to fly the Confederate flag in English waters. *Nashville* returned to Beaufort, North Carolina on February 28, 1862, having captured two prizes worth US$66,000 during the cruise. In this interval she was sold for use as a blockade runner and renamed *Thomas L. Wragg*.

On November 5, 1862, she was commissioned as the privateer *Rattlesnake*. After running fast aground on the Ogeechee River, Georgia, the monitor USS *Montauk* destroyed her with shell fire from 11" and 15" turret guns on February 28, 1863.

Source (edited): "http://en.wikipedia.org/wiki/CSS_Nashville_(1853)"

CSS Nashville (1864)

CSS *Nashville* was a large side-wheel steam ironclad built by the Confederates at Montgomery, Alabama intended to exploit the availability of riverboat engines. Launched in mid-1863, *Nashville* was taken to Mobile, Alabama for completion in 1864. Part of her armor came from the CSS *Baltic*. Her first commander was Lieutenant Charles Carroll Simms, CSN.

Still fitting out, she took no part in the Battle of Mobile Bay on August 5, 1864. She helped fend off attacks on Spanish Fort, Alabama on 27 March 1865, supported Confederate commander Randall L. Gibson until driven away by Federal batteries, and shelled Federal troops near Fort Blakely on 2 April 1865. The ships retreated up the Tombigbee River on 12 April 1865 when Mobile surrendered. She was one of the vessels formally surrendered by Commodore Ebenezer Farrand, CSN, at Nanna Hubba, Alabama on May 10, 1865.

Although never quite finished, she had been heavily armored with triple 2-inch plating forward and around her pilot house, only a single thickness aft and there had been some doubts expressed that her builders might have overestimated her structural strength. Rear Admiral Henry K. Thatcher, USN, wrote on June 30, 1865, after survey, "She was hogged when surrendered and is not strong enough to bear the weight of her full armor." He was certain "she could not live in a seaway."

Nashville was purchased by the Navy Department and sold to breakers at New Orleans, Louisiana on November 22, 1867, her iron sheathing having been removed for naval use.

Commanders

- Lieutenant Charles Carroll Simms (1864)
- Lieutenant John W. Bennett (late 1864 - May 1865)

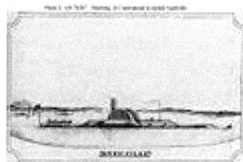

Rebel Ram CSS Nashville

Sketch Ram CSS Nashville

Source (edited): "http://en.wikipedia.org/wiki/CSS_Nashville_(1864)"

CSS Neuse

The **CSS** *Neuse* was an ironclad warship of the Confederate States Navy during the American Civil War. The remains of the ship can now be seen at an exhibit in Kinston, North Carolina as the **CSS Neuse State Historic Site** and **Governor Caswell Memorial**. The ship is listed on the National Register of Historic Places.

Construction

A contract for the construction on the CSS *Neuse* was signed on 17 October 1862 by the shipbuilding company of Thomas Howard and Elijah Ellis and the Confederate Navy. Work began in October on the bank across the Neuse River (her namesake) in North Carolina from the small village of Whitehall (present day Seven Springs). She was designed similarly to the CSS *Albemarle*. Her hull structure was 158 feet (48 m) long by 34 feet (10 m) wide made of mostly pine wood, abundant in the region. Many delays were incurred due to the lack of materials, mostly wrought iron for her deck plating. The Confederate Army exercised priority over the Navy on use of the railroads.

Armament

She was fitted with two 6.4-inch (160 mm) Brooke rifled cannon (similar to a Parrott rifle). Each weighed more than 12,000 pounds.

Service history

Launched in November 1863, *Neuse* sailed in April 1864 for duty on the inland waters of North Carolina as part of the force under Comdr. R. F. Pinkney, CSN. Shortly thereafter she grounded off Kinston and remained fast for almost a month. She never left the river, and in March 1865 she was burned by the Confederates to escape capture by the Union Army under Maj. Gen. William Tecumseh Sherman.

Recovery

Nearly a century later the remains of the ship were discovered. It was raised in 1963. Later the ship was installed beside the river at the Governor Caswell Memorial in Kinston. Bids are being place on the final resting site of the CSS Neuse in a climate controlled site in downtown Kinston. As there are only 3 surviving civil war era ironclads in existence, CSS Neuse, USS Cairo, CSS Jackson soon *Cairo* will be the only one out doors in the brutal Southern climate.

Replica

A full-size replica called the CSS Neuse II is on display at a separate site in Kinston. Constructed by volunteers from 2002 to 2009, it is reportedly the only full-size replica of a Confederate ironclad gunboat.

Source (edited): "http://en.wikipedia.org/wiki/CSS_Neuse"

CSS New Orleans

CSS *New Orleans* was a floating battery fitted out at New Orleans, Louisiana in 1861. The craft featured two small boilers with pump connections for repelling boarders by drenching them with scalding water from her hoses. She was deployed under Lt. S. W. Averett, CSN, in the Mississippi River in time to assist joint army-navy operations at Island Number 10. and New Madrid, Missouri, from 12 March to 7 April 1862. On the final day of the Battle of Island Number Ten, the Confederates, sank the *New Orleans*.

Source (edited): "http://en.wikipedia.org/wiki/CSS_New_Orleans"

CSS North Carolina

For other ships named North Carolina, *see USS* North Carolina.

CSS *North Carolina*, an ironclad gunboat, was built by Berry & Brothers at Wilmington, North Carolina, in 1863 at a cost of $76,000. The ship's bulkheads above the waterline were sloped inward and armored with railroad iron, similar to the CSS *Virginia*. She had two gun ports on each of her four sides and carried six 8-inch guns that could be moved from one port to another, and mounted one pivot gun on her bow. She was placed in commission during the latter part of the year with Commander W. T. Muse, CSN, in command.

North Carolina was discovered to be structurally unsound, and unsuitable for use on the open ocean. She remained in the Cape Fear River until September 27, 1864 when she developed a leak and sank, her hull riddled by shipworms, off Smithville (modern Southport), where she had been serving as a guard ship.

This article includes text from the public domain Dictionary of American Naval Fighting Ships.

Source (edited): "http://en.wikipedia.org/wiki/CSS_North_Carolina"

CSS Oregon

CSS *Oregon*, a wooden steam gunboat was the only ship of the Confederate States Navy to be named for the 33rd state. A wooden steamer similar to *California*, she was built at New York City in 1846 for the Mobile Mail Line, 60 percent owned at the end of April 1861 by the Geddes family of New Orleans, Louisiana, and Cincinnati, Ohio, the remainder by R. A. Heirn and Samuel Wolff of Mobile, Alabama. Described as having "one deck, one mast, no galleries and a billethead," she was permanently enrolled (coastwise) at New Orleans on 20 June 1858. Seized by Louisiana's Governor Moore sometime in 1861, she was an early and successful blockade runner, apparently only in the Gulf of Mexico. Under Captain A. P. Boardman she had somehow contrived to make 92 "entrances and clearances" at blockaded ports before being picked for arming as a man-of-war; how much of this coastal service was under Confederate Army auspices is not altogether clear. Captain A. L. Myers succeeded to her command.

After being converted into a gunboat, *Oregon* operated in Mississippi Sound on various assignments. On 13 July 1861 she steamed in company with *Arrow* to the vicinity of Ship Island Light where they vainly attempted to lure USS *Massachusetts* within range of shore batteries. During September 1861 she evacuated Confederate property and troops from Ship Island, Mississippi. When Confederate forces evacuated New Orleans in April 1862, *Oregon* was destroyed to prevent capture.

Source (edited): "http://en.wikipedia.org/wiki/CSS_Oregon"

CSS Owl

CSS *Owl* was a blockade runner in the Confederate States Navy during the American Civil War. It was built by Jones Quiggen, a ship builder in Liverpool, England and launched on June 21, 1864.

Owl, sister to CSS *Bat*, was more fortunate than her twin which followed her closely. *Owl* succeeded in running into Wilmington, North Carolina sometime in September 1864, although United States Consul Mortimer Melville Jackson telegraphed Washington, D.C. that *Owl* had "a large, valuable cargo" cleared August 31—officially for Nassau, Bahamas. She escaped to sea from Wilmington on October 3; her masts were visible all the while she lay in port loading. The blockaders wounded her captain and several crewmen, but 9 shots failed to stop *Owl*.

She was now commanded by Commander John Newland Maffitt, CSN—the "Prince of Privateers"—detached from CSS *Albemarle* at Plymouth, North Carolina on or about September 9. Confederate Navy Secretary Stephen Mallory, telegraphing on September 19, warned Maffitt: "It is of the first importance that our steamers should not fall into the enemy's hands… these vessels, lightly armed, now constitute the fleetest and most efficient part of his blockading force off Wilmington." Maffitt was to take no passengers, as a rule, and Assistant Paymaster Adam Tredwell, CSN, would deliver "5,000 pounds in sterling bills before sailing," Mallory concluded.

Owl was at Bermuda with cotton October 24–29, as the U.S. Consul faithfully reported. On December 5, Mallory instructed Maffitt to pick up CSS *Florida*'s men in Bermuda. A letter to Mallory captured, along with Assistant Paymaster Talley, CSN, by USS *Forest Rose* on May 7, 1865 bears an endorsement by her commander, Lieutenant A. N. Gould, USN: "It shows that Maffitt has been landing on the Florida coast with the *Owl*." U.S. Consul William Thomas Minor at Havana, Cuba reported on May 20 that Maffitt was to leave there in a day or two for Galveston, Texas. On this last trip *Owl* was almost captured at Wilmington by a Federal cruiser and had to jettison valuable mail as well as sustain 12 casualties. Maffitt then tried Galveston, and grounded on Bird Island Shoals at the entrance within range of 16 enemy cruisers. Captain James H. MacGarvey, CSN, in little CSS *Diana* got *Owl* off barely in time; she not only ran into port but ran out safely too. There is some evidence *Owl's* last two runs through the blockade were made under the name of *Foam*.

Owl was delivered to Fraser, Trenholm & Co. in Liverpool after war's end, and Maffitt took the Board of Trade examinations to command British merchant ships to South America.

Source (edited): "http://en.wikipedia.org/wiki/CSS_Owl"

CSS Palmetto State

CSS *Palmetto State*, an ironclad ram, was built by Cameron and Co., Charleston, South Carolina in January 1862, under the supervision of Flag Officer D. N. Ingraham, CSN. She was readied for service by September 1862 when Lieutenant Commander John Rutledge, CSN, was placed in command. Her armor was 4" thick on the shield, backed by 22" of wood, 2" of iron elsewhere. Her pilothouse was located abaft the stack.

Before dawn on January 31, 1863, *Palmetto State* and her sister ram CSS *Chicora* crept through thick haze to surprise the Union blockading force off Charleston. Taking full advantage of her low silhouette, the ironclad stole in under the guns of USS *Mercedita*, ramming as well as firing into her. Completely disabled, with no guns that would depress enough to fire at *Palmetto State*, the Union ship surrendered. The ram then turned her attention to USS *Keystone State* and put several shells into that blockader. Her steam chests punctured, *Keystone State* lost all power and had to be towed to safety. A long-range gun action between the Confederate rams and other Federal blockaders then took place, but little damage was inflicted by either side before *Palmetto State* and *Chicora* withdrew to safety within Charleston Harbor. The attack of the Confederate rams caused the temporary withdrawal of the blockaders from their inshore positions and led to the claim by the Confederate Government, unsuccessfully advanced, that the blockade of Charleston had been raised.

Palmetto State also joined in the defense of Charleston during Admiral Samuel Francis du Pont's unsuccessful attack on the harbor forts, April 1-7, 1863. Her officers and men were cited for valuable services rendered during the removal of troops from Fort Wagner and Battery Gregg on the night of September 6-7, 1863.

Palmetto State was burned by the Confederates upon the evacuation of Charleston on February 18, 1865.

This article includes text from the public domain Dictionary of American Naval Fighting Ships.
Source (edited): "http://en.wikipedia.org/wiki/CSS_Palmetto_State"

CSS Patrick Henry

CSS *Patrick Henry* was built in New York City in 1853 by the renowned William J. Webb for the Old Dominion Steam Ship Line as the civilian steamer *Yorktown*, a brigantine-rigged sidewheel steamer. She carried passengers and freight between Richmond, Virginia and New York City. *Yorktown* had anchored in the James River when Virginia seceded from the Union on 17 April 1861 and was seized by the Virginia Navy and later turned over to the Confederate Navy on June 8. Commander John Randolph Tucker, who commanded the newly organized James River Squadron, directed that *Yorktown* be converted into a gunboat and renamed *Patrick Henry* in honor of that revolutionary patriot.

Career

Still commonly referred to as *Yorktown*, she was assigned to a position near Mulberry Island in the James to protect the right flank of the Confederate Peninsula Army.

On 13 September 1861 and again on 2 December, Commander Tucker took *Patrick Henry* down the river to a point about a mile and a half above Newport News, Virginia, and opened fire on the Federal squadron at long range hoping to draw out some of the gunboats. The gambit was refused, but Tucker inflicted some minor damage.

During the Battle of Hampton Roads on 8 March 1862 in which *Virginia* destroyed the Federal warships USS *Cumberland* and USS *Congress*, *Patrick Henry* attempted to take the latter's surrender but was fired upon by shore batteries, and took a shell in her steam chest which killed four men. Towed out of action long enough to make repairs, she soon resumed her former position.

During the historic 9 March 1862 action between *Virginia* and USS *Monitor*, *Patrick Henry* fired long range at *Monitor*. The Confederate Congress later accorded special thanks to all officers and men for their gallant conduct during the two-day battle.

A sketch of the CSS Patrick Henry signed by Midshipman J. Thomas Scharf.

Patrick Henry was also present during some of *Virginia's* other actions and, in a daring night operation on 5 May 1862, helped remove Confederate property from the Norfolk Navy Yard before it was abandoned to the Federals.

After the surrender of Norfolk, Virginia on 10 May 1862, the James River Squadron, including *Patrick Henry*, retired up the river to Drewry's Bluff where pursuing Federal ships were repulsed on 15 May.

Patrick Henry was designated an academy ship in May 1862 and underwent appropriate alterations to this end. In October 1863, *Patrick Henry* housed the floating Confederate States Naval Academy at Drewry's Bluff, where instruction for 52 midshipmen began under the superintendency of Lieutenant William Harwar Parker. Numbers later increased to sixty, with thirteen teachers in attendance. Sometimes she took part in action with the midshipmen on board.

When Richmond was evacuated on 3 April 1865, *Patrick Henry* was burned to prevent capture. Her cadets were charged with the delivery of a treasury of some CS$500,000 to the new government seat of Danville, Virginia. Each was rewarded with $40 in gold.

Commanders

The commanders of the CSS *Patrick Henry* were:
- Captain John Randolph Tucker (1861-June 1862)
- Lieutenant William Harwar Parker (1863-end of war)

Source (edited): "http://en.wikipedia.org/wiki/CSS_Patrick_Henry"

CSS Pedee

The **CSS *Pedee***, also known as the **CSS Pee Dee** was a Confederate gunboat launched in January 1865 and scuttled the following month during the American Civil War.

The *Pee Dee* was a Macon-class gunboat that was outfitted with two Brooke rifled cannon and a Union Dahlgren cannon. It was built at the Mars Bluff Navy Yard on the Great Pee Dee River in Marion County, South Carolina.

On December 21, 2010, South

Carolina's state archaeologist announced that a team of researchers believes they have discovered the remains of the *Pee Dee*.

It is believed that in mid-February 1865, after an upriver skirmish with a Union ship, the crew of the *Pee Dee* scuttled the ship so it would not fall into enemy hands.

"They started dismantling the vessel and burning it," *The Associated Press* quoted South Carolina state archaeologist Jonathan Leader as saying. "It's a debris field."

The discovery comes a year and a half after Leader and fellow researcher Chris Amer discovered two cannons belonging to the ship.

Source (edited): "http://en.wikipedia.org/wiki/CSS_Pedee"

CSS Raleigh (1861)

CSS Raleigh was originally a small, iron-hulled, propeller-driven towing steamer operating on the Albemarle and Chesapeake Canal. She was taken over by the State of North Carolina in May 1861, and transferred to the Confederate States the following July. Her commanding officer during 1861-1862 was Lieutenant Joseph W. Alexander. Her entire service was in coastal waters of North Carolina and Virginia and in the James River as part of the James River Squadron.

Raleigh supported Fort Hatteras and Fort Clark on August 28–29, 1861; took part in an expedition on October 1 to capture United States Army steamer *Fanny* with valuable stores on board; and accompanied CSS *Sea Bird* when she reconnoitered Pamlico Sound on January 20, 1862. She was also active in defense of Roanoke Island against an amphibious assault by overwhelming Federal forces on February 7–8, 1862, and at Elizabeth City, North Carolina 2 days later. Thence *Raleigh* escaped through Dismal Swamp Canal to Norfolk, Virginia.

On March 8–9, 1862, *Raleigh* was tender to CSS *Virginia* during the historic Battle of Hampton Roads, for which she received the thanks of the Confederate Congress.

With the Federal recapture of Norfolk Navy Yard in May 1862, *Raleigh* steamed up the James River, but thereafter a shortage of crew members restricted her to flag-of-truce or patrol service.

Raleigh, renamed *Roanoke* near the end of the war, was destroyed by the Confederates on April 4, 1865 upon the evacuation of Richmond, Virginia.

Commanders

The commanders of the CSS *Raleigh* were:
- Lieutenant Joseph W. Alexander (1861–1862)
- Lieutenant Maxwell T. Clarke (1863-June 1864)
- Lieutenant Mortimer Murray Benton (during June 1864)
- Master's Mate A.E. Albertson (July 31, 1864-)
- Acting Master W. Frank Shippey (October–December 1864)
- Lieutenant William Wonder Pollock (January 1865-end of war)

Source (edited): "http://en.wikipedia.org/wiki/CSS_Raleigh_(1861)"

CSS Raleigh (1864)

For other ships named Raleigh, *see CSS* Raleigh.

CSS *Raleigh*, a casemate ironclad, was constructed by the Confederate States Navy at Wilmington, North Carolina in 1863-64, with Lieutenant John Wilkinson, CSN, commanding. She was reported in commission on April 30, 1864 under the command of Lieutenant J. Pembroke Jones, CSN.

Built to Constructor John L. Porter's plans, similar to those of CSS *North Carolina*, she had been laid down and launched at the foot of Church Street, completed at the shipyard of J. L. Cassidey & Sons.

On May 6, she emerged from Cape Fear River accompanied by CSS *Yadkin* and CSS *Equator* and inconclusively engaged six Federal blockaders, including the USS *Britannia* and the USS *Nansemond*, off New Inlet, North Carolina. When the six reappeared the following day, *Raleigh* hastily withdrew up river, struck Wilmington Bar and "broke her back." Her iron plating was salvaged.

In 1994 the wreck was investigated by the North Carolina State Underwater Archaeology Unit with help from students of East Carolina University.

This article includes text from the public domain Dictionary of American Naval Fighting Ships.

Source (edited): "http://en.wikipedia.org/wiki/CSS_Raleigh_(1864)"

CSS Rappahannock

CSS *Rappahannock*, a steam sloop-of-war, was built on the River Thames in 1855 as an *Intrepid*-class gunvessel for the Royal Navy and named HMS *Victor*. Although a handsomely modelled vessel, numerous defects occasioned her sale in 1863. An agent of the Confederate States Government purchased her ostensibly for the China trade, but British authorities suspected she was destined to be a Confederate commerce raider and ordered her detention. Nevertheless, she succeeded in escaping from Sheerness, England, on November 24, with workmen still on board and only a token crew. Her Confederate Naval officers joined in the English Channel.

When he bought her from the Admiralty through his secret agent on November 14, Commander Matthew F. Maury had intended *Rappahannock* to replace the unwanted, iron CSS *Georgia* and was about to transfer *Georgia's* battery to her. She was ideal for a cruiser—wooden hull, bark-rigged, two engines and a lifting screw propeller—but she was doomed to serve the Confederacy no more glamorously than a floating depot.

She was commissioned a Confederate man-of-war underway, but while passing out of the Thames Estuary her bearings burned out and she had to be taken across to Calais for repairs. There Lieutenant C. M. Fauntleroy, CSN, was placed in command.

Detained on various pretexts by the French Government, *Rappahannock* never got to sea and was turned over to the United States at the close of the war.
Source (edited): "http://en.wikipedia.org/wiki/CSS_Rappahannock"

CSS Resolute

CSS *Resolute* was a tugboat built in 1858 at Savannah Georgia as the *Ajax* which served in the Confederate States Navy during the American Civil War.

Resolute entered Confederate service in 1861 and operated as a tow boat, transport, receiving ship, and tender to the sidewheeler CSS *Savannah* on the coastal and inland waters of Georgia and South Carolina.

On 5 -6 November 1861, *Resolute*, under Lieutenant John Pembroke Jones, CSN, in company with CSS *Lady Davis*, CSS *Sampson* and *Savannah*, under the overall command of Flag Officer Josiah Tattnall, CSN, offered harassing resistance to a much larger Union fleet preparing to attack Confederate strongholds at Port Royal Sound, S.C.

During November 7, while *Resolute* had been sent to Savannah with dispatches, the Union fleet under Flag Officer Samuel Francis du Pont, USN, pounded the Confederate Fort Walker and Fort Beauregard until they were abandoned. Upon her return, *Resolute* helped evacuate the garrison of Fort Walker and then returned to spike the Confederate guns at Pope's Landing on Hilton Head Island.

Later that month, on November 26, *Resolute*, in company with *Sampson* and *Savannah*, under Flag Officer Tattnall, weighed anchor from under the guns of Fort Pulaski, S.C., and made a brief attack on Union vessels at the mouth of the Savannah River. On January 28, 1862, accompanied by *Sampson* and *Savannah*, she delivered supplies to the fort despite the spirited opposition of Federal ships.

While on an expedition to destroy the Charleston and Savannah Railway bridge spanning the Savannah River, in cooperation with gunboats CSS *Macon* and *Sampson*, under Flag Officer William W. Hunter, CSN, on December 12, 1864, *Resolute* received heavy fire from battery I, First New York Artillery. Although hit twice, she was not seriously damaged until she was disabled in collision with the two gunboats during their retreat. Although the gunboats escaped, *Resolute* grounded on Argyle Island on the Savannah River. She was captured on the same day by soldiers of the 3rd Wisconsin Veteran Infantry under Colonel W. Hawly, USA, in the army of General William T. Sherman, and destroyed.

Source (edited): "http://en.wikipedia.org/wiki/CSS_Resolute"

CSS Richmond

CSS *Richmond*, an ironclad ram, was built at Gosport (Norfolk) Navy Yard to the design of John L. Porter with money and scrap iron collected by the citizens of Virginia, whose imagination had been captured by the ironclad CSS *Virginia*. Consequently she was sometimes referred to as *Virginia II*, *Virginia No. 2* or *Young Virginia* in the South and as *Merrimack No. 2*, *New Merrimack* or *Young Merrimack* by Union writers, months before the actual CSS *Virginia II* was ever laid down.

Begun in March 1862, *Richmond* was launched May 6 and towed up to the Confederate capital that very night to escape Federal forces again in possession of Norfolk Navy Yard and the lower James River. *Richmond* was thus finished at Richmond, Virginia in July 1862 and placed in commission by Commander Robert B. Pegram, CSN as part of the James River Squadron. Twenty-two inches of yellow pine and oak plus 4 inches of iron protected her roof and "she is ironed 3½ feet below her load lines," wrote Shipyard Superintendent John H. Burroughs.

During 1863 and early 1864 the James front was quiet, but from May 1864 momentous events followed in quick succession. The Confederates had three new ironclads in Captain French Forrest's squadron there and minor actions were frequent.

During 1864 *Richmond*, under Lieutenant William Harwar Parker, CSN, took part in engagements at Dutch Gap on August 13, Fort Harrison on September 29-October 1, and Chaffin's Bluff on October 22. On January 23-24, 1865, she was under heavy fire while aground with *Virginia II* above the obstructions at Trent's Reach — at an angle that caused Federal projectiles to ricochet harmlessly off their casemates. But *Richmond's* tender, CSS *Scorpion*, not thus armored, was severely damaged by the explosion of CSS *Drewry*'s magazine as *Drewry* ended her life, lashed alongside *Richmond*. The ironclads withdrew under their Chaffin's Bluff batteries for a few weeks but *Richmond* had to be destroyed by Rear Admiral Raphael Semmes, CSN, squadron commander, prior to evacuation of the capital on April 3.

Commanders

The commanders of the CSS *Richmond* were:
- Commander Robert B. Pegram (November 1862-May 1864)
- Commander William Harwar Parker (May-June 1864)
- Lieutenant John S. Maury (July-October 26, 1864)
- Commander William A. Webb (October-November 1864)
- John McIntosh Kell (December 30, 1864-February 1865)
- Lieutenant Hamilton Henderson Dalton (February 1865-)
- Passed Midshipman J.A. Peters (during February 1865)

Source (edited): "http://en.wikipedia.org/wiki/CSS_Richmond"

CSS Robert E. Lee

CSS *Robert E. Lee* was a blockade runner for the Confederate States during the American Civil War that later served in the United States Navy as **USS *Fort Donelson*** and in the Chilean Navy as ***Concepción***.

CSS *Robert E. Lee*

Robert E. Lee was originally the merchant ship *Giraffe*, a schooner-rigged, iron-hulled, oscillating-engined paddle-steamer with two stacks, built on the River Clyde in Scotland during the autumn of 1862 as a fast Glasgow-Belfast packet. Alexander Collie & Co. of Manchester acquired her for their blockade-running fleet, but were persuaded by renowned blockade-runner Lieutenant John Wilkinson, CSN, to sell her to the Confederate States Navy for the same £32,000 just paid.

Her first voyage was into Old Inlet, Wilmington, North Carolina in January 1863 with valuable munitions and 26 Scottish lithographers, eagerly awaited by the Confederate Government bureau of engraving and printing. On January 26, Union intelligence maintained she "could be captured easily" at anchor in Ossabaw Sound, but this was not to be for another 10 months. Running out again, *Robert E. Lee* started to establish a nearly legendary reputation for blockade running by leaving astern blockader USS *Iroquois*.

Lieutenant Richard H. Gayle, CSN, assumed command in May 1863, relieving Lieutenant John Wilkinson; but Wilkinson was conning the ship again out of the Cape Fear River from Smithville, North Carolina on October 7, 1863, as recounted by Lieutenant Robert D. Minor, CSN, in a letter to Admiral Franklin Buchanan dated February 2, 1864, detailing the first venture to capture USS *Michigan* and liberate 2,000 Confederate prisoners at Johnson's Island, Sandusky, Ohio. *Robert E. Lee* transported Wilkinson, Minor, Lieutenant Benjamin P. Loyall and 19 other naval officers to Halifax, Nova Scotia with $35,000 in gold and a cotton cargo "subsequently sold at Halifax for $76,000 (gold) by the War Department — in all some $111,000 in gold, as the sinews of the expedition."

Thus Wilkinson was in Canada and Gayle commanding when *Robert E. Lee's* luck ran out on November 9, 1863, after 21 voyages in 10 months carrying out over 7,000 bales of cotton, returning with munitions invaluable to the Confederacy. She left Bermuda five hours after her consort, CSS *Cornubia*, only to be run down a few hours after her by the same blockader, USS *James Adger*. The two runners were conceded to be easily "the most noted that ply between Bermuda and Wilmington."

USS *Fort Donelson*

CSS *Robert E. Lee*

USS *Fort Donelson*, December 1864

Robert E. Lee was condemned as a prize at Boston, Massachusetts, acquired by the United States Navy and placed in commission on June 29, 1864 as USS *Fort Donelson*, with Acting Volunteer Lieutenant Thomas Pickering in command.

Fort Donelson was assigned to the North Atlantic Blockading Squadron, cruising in blockade of the North Carolina coast through the remainder of 1864 with brief periods of repair at Norfolk, Virginia. From January 13 to January 22, 1865 she aided in the bombardment of Fort Fisher's batteries and landed ammunition supplies for the Union forces. *Fort Donelson* joined the fleet in attacking Fort Anderson on February 17–February 18. During March she cruised in company with USS *Pequot* to Bermuda, was present at City Point, Virginia when U.S. President Abraham Lincoln arrived on board *River Queen* on March 20, and acted as guardship at Fort Fisher. She operated with the South Atlantic Blockading Squadron until June, but when ordered to the West Gulf squadron was found to be in such poor condition that she returned to Norfolk.

Fort Donelson was decommissioned

on August 17, 1865 at Philadelphia, Pennsylvania and sold in October 1865. She subsequently returned to civilian employment under the name *Isabella*.

Concepción
In 1866 the ship was purchased for $85,000 by the Chilean Navy and commissioned as *Concepción*, arriving at Valparaíso on August 22. On September 3, Commander José Galvarino Riveros Cárdenas was placed in command of *Concepción*, which saw service in southern Chile during that nation's war against Spain. The Chilean Navy sold *Concepción* on May 1, 1868; her subsequent history is unknown.
Source (edited): "http://en.wikipedia.org/wiki/CSS_Robert_E._Lee"

CSS Savannah (gunboat)

CSS *Savannah*, later called *Old Savannah*, was a gunboat in the Confederate States Navy during the American Civil War.

Savannah was formerly the steamer *Everglade*, built in 1856 at New York City. She was purchased early in 1861 by the State of Georgia and converted into a gunboat for coast defense. With Georgia's admission to the Confederacy, *Savannah*, under Lieutenant John Newland Maffitt, CSN, was commissioned by the Confederate States Navy. She was attached to the squadron of Flag Officer Josiah Tattnall, CSN, charged with the naval defense of South Carolina and Georgia.

On November 5-6, 1861, *Savannah*, flying Tattnall's flag, in company with CSS *Resolute*, CSS *Sampson*, and CSS *Lady Davis*, offered harassing resistance to a much larger Union fleet, under Flag Officer Samuel Francis Du Pont, USN, preparing to attack Confederate strongholds at Port Royal Sound, S.C. On November 7, *Savannah* fired on the heavy Union ships as they bombarded Fort Walker and Fort Beauregard. Driven finally by the Federal gunboats into Skull Creek, Ga., Tattnall disembarked with a landing party in an abortive attempt to support the fort's garrison, and *Savannah* returned to Savannah, Georgia to repair damages.

On November 26, 1861, *Savannah*, in company with *Resolute* and *Sampson*, all under Flag Officer Tattnall, weighed anchor from under the guns of Fort Pulaski S.C., and made a brave but brief attack on Union vessels at the mouth of the Savannah River. On January 28, 1862, the same three vessels delivered supplies to the fort despite the spirited opposition of Federal ships. *Savannah* later assisted in the unsuccessful defense of Fort Pulaski on April 10-11, 1862, and for the remainder of the year served as a receiving ship at the city of Savannah.

Her name was changed to *Oconee* on April 28, 1863, and in June she was loaded with cotton and dispatched to England to pay for much-needed supplies. After some delay she escaped to sea—only to founder on August 18 during bad weather. A boat with four officers and eleven men was captured two days later; the remainder of her crew escaped.

See also CSS *Savannah* (ironclad).
Source (edited): "http://en.wikipedia.org/wiki/CSS_Savannah_(gunboat)"

CSS Savannah (ironclad)

CSS *Savannah* was a *Richmond*-class casemate ironclad in the Confederate States Navy during the American Civil War.

Savannah was built by H. F. Willink for the Confederacy at Savannah, Georgia in 1863. On June 30, 1863 she was transferred to naval forces in the Savannah River under the command of Flag Officer William W. Hunter, CSN. Under Commander Robert F. Pinkney, CSN, she maintained her reputation as the most efficient vessel of the squadron and was kept ready for service. She remained on the river and was burned by the Confederates on December 21, 1864 when the city of Savannah was threatened by the approach of General William T. Sherman, USA.
Source (edited): "http://en.wikipedia.org/wiki/CSS_Savannah_(ironclad)"

CSS Scorpion

CSS *Scorpion* was a *Squib*-class torpedo boat procured late in 1864 by the Confederate States Navy and armed with a spar torpedo fitted to her stem. She performed picket duty in the James River under command of Lieutenant E. Lakin, CSN.

On January 23 to January 25, 1865, torpedo boats *Scorpion*, CSS *Hornet*, and CSS *Wasp*, under overall command of Lieutenant Charles W. Read, CSN, joined Flag Officer J.K. Mitchell's James River Squadron in the abortive attack on General Ulysses S. Grant's main supply base at City Point, Virginia. Attempting to rejoin her consort, the ironclad CSS *Richmond*, aground above Trent's Reach, *Scorpion* ended up fast ashore also and was severely damaged by the magazine explosion which destroyed nearby gunboat CSS *Drewry*, January 24. Abandoned, she fell into Federal hands.

See also USS *Scorpion* and HMS *Scorpion*.
Source (edited): "http://en.wikipedia.org/wiki/CSS_Scorpion"

CSS Sea Bird

CSS *Sea Bird* was a sidewheel steamer in the Confederate States Navy.

Sea Bird was built at Keyport, New Jersey in 1854, was purchased by North Carolina at Norfolk, Virginia in 1861 and fitted for service with the Confederate States Navy. She was assigned to duty along the Virginia and North Carolina coasts with Lieutenant Patrick McCarrick, CSN, in command. *Sea Bird* served as the flagship of Confederate Flag Officer William F. Lynch's "mosquito fleet" during the hard-fought battles in defense of Roanoke Island on February 7–8, 1862, and Elizabeth City, North Carolina, on February 10 when she was rammed and sunk by USS *Commodore Perry*. Her casualties were two killed, four wounded, and the rest captured.

Source (edited): "http://en.wikipedia.org/wiki/CSS_Sea_Bird"

CSS Selma (1856)

CSS *Selma* was a steamship in the Confederate States Navy during the American Civil War.

Selma was a coastwise packet built at Mobile, Alabama for the Mobile Mail Line in 1856. Little doubt now remains that she was originally named *Florida*. As the latter, she was inspected and accepted by Captain Lawrence Rousseau, CSN, on April 22, 1861, acquired by the Confederacy in June, cut down and strengthened by hog frames and armed as a gunboat — all, apparently, in the Lake Pontchartrain area. Her upper deck was plated at this time with ⅜ inch iron, partially protecting her boilers, of the low pressure type preferred for fuel economy and greater safety in battle. CSS *Florida* is cited on November 12, 1861 as already in commission and serving Commodore G. N. Rollins' New Orleans defense flotilla under command of Lieutenant Charles W. Hays, CSN.

The *Mobile Evening News* editorialized early in December on the startling change "from her former gay, first-class hotel appearance, having been relieved of her upper works and painted as black as the inside of her smokestack. She carries a jib forward and, we suppose, some steering sail aft, when requisite."

Service as *Florida*

Although much of *Florida's* time was spent blockaded in Mobile, she made some forays into Mississippi Sound, two of which alarmed the United States Navy's entire Gulf command. On October 19, *Florida* convoyed a merchantman outside. Fortunately for her, the coast was clear of Union ships and batteries, for *Florida* fouled the area's main military telegraph line with her anchor, and had no sooner repaired the damage than she went aground for 36 hours. Luck returning, she tried out her guns on USS *Massachusetts*, "a large three-masted propeller" she mistook for the faster *R. R. Cuyler*. Being of shallower draft and greater speed, she successfully dodged *Massachusetts* in shoal water off Ship Island. The havoc caused by one well-placed shot with her rifled pivot gun is described by Commander Melancton Smith, USN, commanding *Massachusetts*;

"It entered the starboard side abaft the engine five feet above the water line, cutting entirely through 18 planks of the main deck, carried away the table, sofas, eight sections of iron steam pipe, and exploded in the stateroom on the port side, stripping the bulkheads of four rooms, and setting fire to the vessel ... 12 pieces of the fragments have been collected and weigh 58 pounds." The first sortie by *Florida* caused consternation. Captain L. M. Powell, USN, in command at Ship Island — soon to be main advance base for the New Orleans campaign — wrote to Flag Officer William McKean, October 22;

"The first of the reported gun steamers made her experimental trial trip on the Massachusetts, and, if she be a sample of the rest, you may perhaps consider that Ship Island and the adjacent waters will require a force of a special kind in order to hold them to our use. The caliber and long range of the rifled cannon from which the shell that exploded in the Massachusetts was fired established the ability of these fast steam gunboats to keep out of the range of all broadside guns, and enables them to disregard the armament or magnitude of all ships thus armed, or indeed any number of them, when sheltered by shoal water." Protecting CSS *Pamlico*, in contrasting white dress and laden with some 400 troops, "the black rebel steamer" *Florida* on December 4 had a brush with USS *Montgomery* in Horn Island Pass that caused jubilation in the Southern press. Commander T. Darrah Shaw of *Montgomery*, finding his 10-inch shell gun no match for *Florida's* long-range rifles, signaled Commander Melancton Smith for assistance, and when it was not forthcoming, ran back to safety under the guns of Ship Island. Shaw saved *Montgomery* and lost his command for fleeing from the enemy. Commodore McKean promptly sent Lieutenant James Edward Jouett to relieve him and forwarded Shaw's action report to United States Secretary of the Navy Gideon Welles, noting, "It needs no comment." Crowed *Richmond Dispatch* on December 14, quoting *Mobile Evening News*, "The *Florida* fought at great disadvantage in one respect, owing to her steering apparatus being out of order, but showed a decided superiority in the effectiveness of her armament. That gun which scared the *Massachusetts* so badly, and had nearly proved fatal to her, is evidently a better piece or must be better handled than any which the enemy have."

Service as *Selma*

With the advent of cruiser CSS *Florida*,

she was renamed *Selma* in July 1862, Lieutenant Peter U. Murphey, CSN, assuming command.

On February 5, 1863, while steaming down Mobile Bay with 100 extra men in search of a blockader to carry by boarding, *Selma* was bilged by a snag in crossing Dog River Bar, entrance to Mobile, and sank in 8 feet of water. Pumped out hastily, she was back in service February 13.

By the following year, *Selma*, CSS *Morgan* and CSS *Gaines*, the only ships capable of defending lower Mobile Bay, were having a serious problem with deserting seamen, and intelligence reported *Selma*'s crew as having fallen as low as 15 men about mid-February.

At the crucial Battle of Mobile Bay on August 5, 1864, *Selma* particularly annoyed Rear Admiral David Farragut, USN by a steady, raking fire as she stood off USS *Hartford*'s bow. After passing the forts, Farragut ordered gunboat USS *Metacomet* cast loose from *Hartford* to pursue *Selma*. After an hour-long running fight, Murphey, unable to escape to shallows out of reach, had to surrender to faster, more heavily armed *Metacomet*. *Selma* lost 7 killed and 8 wounded, including her captain.

That evening, Admiral Farragut commissioned the prize gunboat as USS *Selma* and placed her under the command of Lieutenant Arthur R. Yates, USN. Five days later, *Selma* joined in the Union Navy's bombardment of Fort Morgan. On August 16, she participated in a reconnaissance expedition up the Dog River.

In January 1865, *Selma* was transferred to New Orleans where she served until decommissioned on July 16, 1865. Sold at auction the same day to G. A. Hall, *Selma* was redocumented for merchant service on August 17, 1865 and foundered on June 24, 1868 south of Galveston, Texas, off the mouth of the Brazos River.

Source (edited): "http://en.wikipedia.org/wiki/CSS_Selma_(1856)"

CSS Shenandoah

CSS *Shenandoah*, formerly *Sea King*, was an iron-framed, teak-planked, full rigged ship, with auxiliary steam power, captained by Commander James Waddell, Confederate States Navy, a North Carolinian with twenty years' service in the United States Navy.

During 12½ months of 1864–1865 the ship undertook commerce raiding resulting in the capture and sinking or bonding of thirty-eight Union merchant vessels, mostly New Bedford whaleships. This ship is notable for firing the last shot of the American Civil War, at a whaler in waters off the Aleutian Islands.

History and mission

A pencil sketch of CSS Shenandoah, from the inside cover of a notebook kept by her Commanding Officer, James I. Waddell

She was designed as a British commercial transport vessel for the East Asia tea trade and troop transport. She was built on the River Clyde in Scotland. The Confederate Government purchased her in September 1864 for use as an armed cruiser to capture and destroy Union merchant ships.

On October 8, she sailed from London ostensibly for Bombay, India, on a trading voyage. She rendezvoused at Funchal, Madeira, with the steamer *Laurel*, bearing officers and the nucleus of a crew for *Sea King*, together with naval guns, ammunition, and stores. Commanding officer Lieutenant James Iredell Waddell supervised her conversion to a ship-of-war in nearby waters. Waddell was barely able, however, to bring his crew to half strength even with additional volunteers from *Sea King* and *Laurel*.

The new cruiser was commissioned on October 19 and her name changed to *Shenandoah*. The ship, commanded by Captain Waddell, then sailed around the Cape of Good Hope of Africa to Australia. While at Melbourne, Victoria, in January 1865, Waddell obtained additional men and supplies.

In accord with operation concepts originated in the Confederate Navy Department and developed by its agents in Europe, *Shenandoah* was assigned to "seek out and utterly destroy" commerce in areas as yet undisturbed (i.e., attack Union ships), and thereafter her course lay in pursuit of merchantmen on the Cape of Good Hope–Australia route and of the Pacific whaling fleet.

En route to the Cape she picked up six prizes. Five of these were put to the torch or scuttled, after Captain Waddell had safely rescued crew and passengers; the other was bonded and employed for transport of prisoners to Bahia, Brazil.

Australia stopover

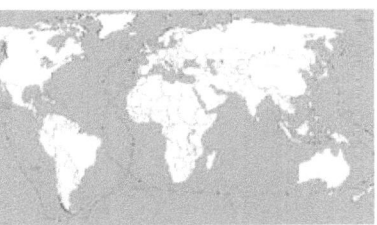

Map of *Shenandoah*'s 12½ month voyage around the world.

Still short-handed, though her crew had been increased by voluntary enlistments from prizes, *Shenandoah* arrived at Melbourne, Victoria, on January 25, 1865, where she filled her complement and her storerooms.

She also took on 40 crew members who were stowaways from Melbourne. However, they were not enlisted until the ship was outside the legal limits of Australian waters. The Shipping Articles show that all these 40 crew members enlisted on the day of her departure from Melbourne, February 18, 1865. Nineteen of her crew deserted at Melbourne, some of whom gave statements of their service to the United States Consul there. An 1871 hearing at the International Court in Geneva awarded damages of £820,000 against Britain to the US government for use of the port facilities at Williamstown by the CSS *Shenandoah*.

Vessels captured

Shenandoah destroying whale ships

Sea King departed Liverpool October 8, 1864, and on October 19, off the coast of France, was surreptitiously re-commissioned as the warship CSS *Shenandoah*. En route to Cape Horn, she captured and disposed of eight prizes in the Atlantic Ocean.

Shenandoah took only one prize in the Indian Ocean, but hunting became more profitable after refitting in Melbourne. Enroute to the North Pacific whaling grounds, on April 3–4, Waddell burned four whalers in the Caroline Islands. After a 3-week cruise to the ice and fog of the Sea of Okhotsk yielded only a single prize, due to a warning which had preceded him, Waddell headed north past the Aleutian Islands into the Bering Sea and the Arctic Ocean. *Shenandoah* then proceeded to capture 11 more prizes.

On June 27, 1865, he learned, from a prize *Susan & Abigail*, of General Robert E. Lee's surrender when her captain produced a San Francisco newspaper reporting the flight from Richmond, Virginia, of the Confederate Government 10 weeks previously. The same paper contained Confederate President Jefferson Davis's proclamation, after Lee's surrender, that the "war would be carried on with re-newed vigor." He then proceeded to capture 10 more whalers in the space of 7 hours in the waters just below the Arctic Circle. It was not until August 2 that *Shenandoah* learned of the final Confederate collapse when she encountered the British barque *Barracouta*. Among the devastating news was surrender of General Johnston's, Smith's, and Magruder's armies and, crucially, the capture of Mr. Davis and a part of his cabinet. Captain Waddell then disarmed the ship and proceeded back to surrender at Liverpool.

Surrender of CSS *Shenandoah*

Editorial cartoon satirizing James Waddell still engaging in combat after the American Civil War was regarded over.

Regardless of Davis's proclamation and knowing the unreliability of newspapers at the time, Captain Waddell and the crew knew returning to a US port would mean facing a Union court with a Northern perspective of the war. They correctly predicted the risk of being tried in a US court and hanged as pirates. This later showed to be accurate. Commerce Raiders were not included in the reconciliation and amnesty that Confederate soldiers were given. Captain Raphael Semmes of CSS *Alabama* escaped charges of piracy by surrendering May 1, 1865 as a Ground General under General Johnston. Semmes's former sailors surrendered as artillerymen.

After the surrender of *Shenandoah* to the British, the British had to decide what to do with the Confederate crew, knowing the consequences of piracy charges.

After a full investigation by law officers of the crown, it was decided that the officers and crew had done nothing against the rules of war or the laws of nations to justify being held as prisoners, so they were unconditionally released. But the authorities of the United States considered them pirates and in their hatred of that time would have treated them as such if they had fallen into their hands.

S. S. Lee, Orris M. Brown, John T. Mason and W. C. Whittle sometime in December 1865 sailed from Liverpool to Buenos Aires, via Bahia, Rio de Janeiro and Montevideo. After prospecting for a while, they went to Rosario, upon Parana River, and near there bought a small place and began farming.

As the animosity of the United States Government began to soften towards them, Brown and Mason returned home, Lee and Whittle returned sometime later.

On returning home, Mason took a law course at the University of Virginia, graduated, and was brilliantly successful at his profession. He settled in Baltimore, and married Miss Helen Jackson, of New York, daughter of the late Lieutenant Alonzo Jackson of the U. S. Navy.

Barracouta had come from San Francisco; Waddell was heading to the city to attack it, believing it weakly defended. Immediately *Shenandoah* underwent physical alteration. She was dismantled as a man-of-war; her battery was dismounted and struck below, and her hull repainted to resemble an ordinary merchant vessel. The Captain of HMS *Donegal* took the last surrender of the American Civil War on November 6, 1865, when CSS *Shenandoah* under Captain Waddell surrendered after travelling 9,000 miles (14,500 km) to Liverpool to do so.

She was then turned over to the United States government. *Shenandoah* had been in the Pacific Ocean when news reached her of the end of the Civil War, necessitating such a long voyage.

Extracts from the United States Naval War Records published by the United States Printing Office *The Official Records of the Union and Confederate Navies in the War of Rebellion* of 1894 says, "November 5 - Arrived in the Mersey, off Liverpool, and on Monday, the 6th, surrendered the Shenandoah to the British nation, by letter to Lord John Russell, premier of Great Britain. (signed) JAMES I WADDELL."

Conclusions

Nineteenth Century artwork, depicting *Shenandoah* under sail

Shenandoah remained at sea for 12 months and 17 days, traversed 58,000 miles (carrying the Confederate flag around the globe for the only time) and sank or captured 38 ships, mostly whalers. Waddell took close to one thousand prisoners, without a single war casualty among his crew: two men died of disease. The reason the vessel did not have any war casualties was because it was never involved in a battle against any Union Naval vessel, as was the CSS *Alabama*, but instead took United States merchant vessels.

In 1866 the US, having taken possession of *Shenandoah*, sold her to the first Sultan of Zanzibar, who renamed her after himself (*El Majidi*). On April 15, 1872 a hurricane hit Zanzibar. *Shenandoah* (*El Majid*) was one of 6 ships owned by Seyed Burgash which were blown on shore and seriously damaged.

Repercussions

During her year-long service as a commerce raider, *Shenandoah* caused disorder and devastation across the globe for Union merchant shipping. The Confederate cruiser claimed more than 20 prizes valued at nearly $1,400,000 ($20 million in today's dollars). In an important development in international law, the U.S. Government pursued claims (collectively called the Alabama Claims) against the British Government and following a court of arbitration, won heavy damages.

Battle ensign

The Second Confederate Navy Ensign, 1863–1865 (photo:#0985.03.0193)

The battle ensign of CSS *Shenandoah* is unique amongst all of the flags of the Confederate States of America as it was the only Confederate flag to circumnavigate the Earth during the Confederacy, and it was the last Confederate flag to be lowered by a combatant unit in the Civil War (Liverpool, UK, on November 5, 1865).

The Shenandoah's battle ensign has been in the Museum of the Confederacy's collection since 1907 and is currently on display. Lieutenant Dabney Scales CSN, gave the flag to a cousin, Eliza Hull Maury, for safekeeping. Eliza Hull Maury was a daughter of and Richard Launcelot Maury was the eldest son of Commodore Matthew Fontaine Maury. Colonel Richard Launcelot Maury CSA, Eliza's brother, brought the flag from England in 1873, and donated it to the Museum in 1907. The flag itself measures 88" x 136."
Source (edited): "http://en.wikipedia.org/wiki/CSS_Shenandoah"

CSS Spray

The **CSS *Spray*** was a steam-powered, side-paddle wheel tugboat built in New Albany, Indiana originally fitted as a mercantile ship before becoming a gunboat in the Confederate States Navy and used in the St. Marks, Newport, Florida area.

History

As the civilian *Spray*

In 1850, Daniel Ladd, a Newport, Florida cotton and general mercantile businessman, purchased the *Spray* for $15,000. The *Spray* operated as far south as Cedar Key, Florida, up the Apalachicola River to Columbus, Georgia, up the Suwannee River and west to New Orleans transporting cotton, naval stores, hides, tobacco, beeswax. It first sailed into St. Marks, Florida in 1850.

As CSS *Spray*

As a confederate vessel and refitted, the *Spray* operated in the vicinity of the naval station at St. Marks during 1863-1865, and was the object of much attention by the Federal forces in that vicinity. On September 12, 1863, the captain of the USS *Stars and Stripes* reported an unsuccessful attack on the *Spray* up river on the St. Marks River. The CSS *Spray* was said to be the only Confederate States Navy vessel to operate exclusively in Florida waters.

In February 1864, Federal troops in two naval expeditions of 14 ships landed at St. Marks. Their mission was to capture Fort Ward, Port Leon, and burn the nuisance gunboat CSS *Spray*. The mission failed.

March 6, 1865, the *Spray* participated in the Battle of Natural Bridge with a complement of 25 men.

The *Spray*'s fate is specious in that it was reported as sunk by Confederates on St. Marks River in a few accounts and yet survived into the early 20th century by the accounts of the Ladd family.

Commanders
- Lt. Charles W. Hays, CSN (1863)
- Lt. Henry. L. Lewis, CSN (1864).

Henry Lewis was born in Virginia and appointed to the CSN from Virginia. He was formerly a lieutenant with the U.S. Navy. Lewis also commanded the CSS *Rappahannock* from 1862 to 1863 before taking command of the *Spray* in 1864.

Source (edited): "http://en.wikipedia.org/wiki/CSS_Spray"

CSS Stonewall Jackson

CSS *Stonewall Jackson* was a cottonclad sidewheel ram of the Confederate Navy during the American Civil War.

Stonewall Jackson was selected in January 1862, by Capt. James E. Montgomery to be part of his River Defense Fleet at New Orleans. On 25 January Montgomery began to convert her into a cottonclad ram by placing a 4-inch (100 mm) oak sheath with 1-inch (25 mm) iron covering on her bow, and by installing double pine bulkheads fitted with compressed cotton bales.

Service history

Stonewall Jackson's conversion was completed on 16 March 1862. Under Capt. G. M. Phillips she was detached from Montgomery's main force and sent to Forts Jackson and St. Philip on the lower Mississippi to cooperate in the Confederate defense of New Orleans. There, with five other vessels of Montgomery's fleet, all under Capt. J. A. Stevenson, she joined the force under Capt. J. K. Mitchell, CSN, commanding Confederate naval forces in the lower Mississippi.

On 24 April 1862 a Union fleet under Flag Officer David Farragut, USN, ran past Forts Jackson and St. Philip on its way to capture New Orleans. In the engagement *Stonewall Jackson* rammed USS *Varuna*, which had already been struck by CSS *Governor Moore*. With *Varuna's* shot glancing off her bow, *Stonewall Jackson* backed off for another blow and struck again in the same place, crushing *Varuna*'s side. The shock of the blow turned the Confederate vessel, and she received five 8-inch shells from *Varuna*, abaft her armor. *Varuna* ran aground in a sinking condition, and *Stonewall Jackson*, chased by USS *Oneida* coming to *Varuna*'s rescue, was driven ashore and burned.

Source (edited): "http://en.wikipedia.org/wiki/CSS_Stonewall_Jackson"

CSS Sumter

CSS *Sumter*, a 473-ton bark-rigged screw steam cruiser, was built as the merchant steamship *Habana* at Philadelphia in 1859 for McConnell's New Orleans & Havana Line. Purchased by the Confederate Government at New Orleans in April 1861, she was converted to a cruiser and placed under the command of Raphael Semmes. Renamed *Sumter*, she was commissioned in the Confederate Navy on 3 June 1861 and broke through the Federal blockade of the Mississippi River mouth late in that month.

Eluding the sloop-of-war USS *Brooklyn* in hot pursuit, early in July, the pioneering Confederate Navy commerce raider captured eight U.S. flag merchant ships in waters near Cuba, then moved to the south to Maranhão, Brazil coast where she took two more. Two additional merchantman fell to *Sumter* in September and October 1861. While coaling at Martinique in mid-November, she was blockaded by the Federal sloop of war *Iroquois*, but was able to escape to sea at night and resume her activities. *Sumter* captured another six ships from late November into January 1862, while cruising from the western hemisphere to European waters. Anchoring at Cadiz, 4 January 1862, she was allowed only to make necessary repairs there, without refueling, and was forced to run for Gibraltar.

Unable to obtain needed repairs, she was laid up in April and remained inactive, watched through the year by a succession of U.S. Navy warships, among them the sloop of war USS *Kearsarge* and gunboat *Chippewa*. Semmes and many of her officers were reemployed in the new cruiser CSS *Alabama*.

Disarmed and sold at auction 19 December 1862 to the Fraser-Trenholm interests, *Sumter* quietly continued her service to the Confederacy under British colors as the blockade runner *Gibraltar* of Liverpool.

Though her career as a warship had lasted barely six months, *Sumter* had taken 18 prizes, of which she burned 8, released or bonded 9; only one was recaptured. The diversion of Federal blockade ships to hunt her down had been in itself of significant service to the Confederate cause.

As *Gibraltar*, she ran at least once into Wilmington, NC, under Capt. E. C. Reid, a Southerner. He sailed from Liverpool 3 July 1863 with a pair of 22-ton Blakely guns and other particularly valuable munitions, returning with a full load of cotton. The beginning of this voyage is recorded only because the U.S. Consul at the British port passionately protested *Gibraltar's* being allowed to sail — ostensibly for Nassau, days before formal customs clearance:

"She is one of the privileged class and not held down like other vessels to strict rules and made to conform to regulations." The arrival at Wilmington is also accidental matter of record today because of the troop transport *Sumter* tragedy at Charleston the same summer, which, until November, Admiral Dahlgren's intelligence understandably confused with the former cruiser *Sumter*, now *Gibraltar*.

Mr. Trenholm's son-in-law long maintained *Sumter* finally "went down in a gale near the spot where the *Alabama* was sunk," but supplied no date; one source suggests 1867. The last official report of her seems to have been by the U.S. Consul at Liverpool, 10 July 1864: "The pirate Sumter (called Gibraltar) is laid up at Birkenhead."

Source (edited): "http://en.wikipedia.org/wiki/CSS_Sumter"

CSS Tacony

CSS *Tacony* was originally a bark captured by the Confederate cruiser CSS *Clarence* during the American Civil War and converted into a Confederate cruiser for commerce raiding.

The CSS *Clarence*, commanded by Lt. Charles W. Read, captured the *Tacony* on June 12, 1863, and since it was a better ship suited for commerce raiding, the crew and armaments were transferred to it and the *Clarence* was destroyed.

In its brief career as a Confederate cruiser it captured a number of ships: The *Whistling Ada, Arabella, Byzantium, Elizabeth Ann, Florence, Goodspeed, Isaac Webb, Z.A. Macomber, Marengo, Ripple, Rufus Choate, Shattemuc, Umpire* and *Wanderer*. Its final capture was the schooner *Archer* on June 25, 1863, which being a better ship suited for commerce raiding, the crew and armaments were transferred to it and the *Tacony* was destroyed.

Officers and crew

- Lt. Charles W. Read, commander
- Billups, Matthewson, and Pride, master's mates
- Brown, engineer
- 16 men

Source (edited): "http://en.wikipedia.org/wiki/CSS_Tacony"

CSS Tallahassee

The **CSS** *Tallahassee* was a twin-screw steamer and *cruiser* in the Confederate States Navy, purchased in 1864, and used for commerce raiding off the Atlantic coast.

History

The iron Confederate cruiser *Tallahassee* was named after the Confederate state capital of Tallahassee in Florida and was built on the River Thames by J. & W. Dudgeon of Millwall, London for London, Chatham & Dover Rly. Co. to the design of Capt. T. E. Symonds, Royal Navy, ostensibly for the Chinese opium trade. She was previously the blockade runner *Atalanta* and made the Dover-Calais crossing in 77 minutes on an even keel. She had made several blockade runs between Bermuda and Wilmington, N.C. before the Confederates bought her.

John Taylor Wood

After the *Tallahassee* was commissioned and prepared for sea she was placed under Commander John Taylor Wood, CSN. Wood was a grandson of President Zachary Taylor and a nephew of Jefferson Davis, who at the time was President of the Confederate States of America. The officers and crew were all volunteers from the Confederate gunboats on the James River and North Carolina waters.

The *Tallahassee* went through the blockade on August 6, 1864 from her home port of Wilmington, North Carolina. Her first day out, four cruisers chased the *Tallahassee* without incident.

She made a spectacular 19-day raid off the Atlantic coast as far north as Halifax, Nova Scotia. The *Tallahassee* destroyed 26 vessels and captured 7 others that were bonded or released. Wood sailed the *Tallahassee* into Halifax Harbour on August 18 to take on bunker coal and water. Neutrality laws limited her stay in Halifax to 24 hours. *Tallahassee* was granted an extra 12 hours to fix a broken mast but was only allowed to load enough coal to take her to the nearest Confederate port. Two Federal war ships, the USS *Nansemond* and USS *Huron*, had chased her north and were believed to be waiting for the *Tallahassee* at the harbour entrance. Wood hired a legendary Halifax pilot John "Jock" Flemming, who is believed to have guided the warship through the narrow and shallow Eastern Passage between Dartmouth and McNabs Island, a route only suited for small fishing vessels. *Tallahassee* succeeded in negotiating the passage out of the harbour, although no Northern warships were in fact waiting. The first Northern warship, the gunboat USS Pontoosuc, arrived at the harbour entrance several hours after the Confederate cruiser departed.

Being unable to procure enough coal to continue, Wood was forced to return to Wilmington where he arrived safely on August 26.

Victims

- The schooner *Sarah A. Boice* of Boston, Mass. Her crew and their personal effects were brought on board, and she was scuttled.
- The pilot-boat schooner *James Funk*, No. 22 of New York. Was turned into a tender of the *Tallahassee* using 20 of the *Tallahassee's* crew.
- The bark *Bay State*
- The brigantine *Carrie Estelle*.
- The brigantine *A. Richards*.
- The schooner *Carroll* by the *Tallahassee's* tender *James Funk*.
- The pilot-boat schooner *William Bell,* No. 24 of New York burned.
- The packet ship *Adriatic* (1000 tons) from London, England was burned. During the seizure, the *Tallahassee* collided with her losing her main mast.
- The bark *Glenarvoz* from Thomaston, Maine was scuttled.
- The *James Littlefield* of Bangor, Maine loaded with coal was scuttled.
- The *Atlantic* burned.
- The *Spokane* burned.
- The schooner *Billow* scuttled.
- The bark *Suilote* bonded.
- The *Robert E. Packer*, a 222 ton packet, burned.
- The *Glenarvon*, a 789 ton schooner from Scotland, burned.
- The schooner *Lamont Du Pont* from Wilmington was sunk
- The *P.C. Alexander*, a 283 ton bark, burned.
- The *Neva*, at 286 tons, bonded for $17,500 and loaded with prisoners.
- The *Roan*, a 127 ton brigantine.
- 14 small schooners ranging from 39 tons to 148 tons, sunk.

Renaming

CSS Olustee

The *Tallahassee* was renamed CSS *Olustee* after the Battle of Olustee in northern Florida and placed under the command of Lt. W. H. Ward, CSN. The *Olustee* ran through the blockade off Wilmington again on October 29, 1864 but suffered some damage from Federal guns. She captured and destroyed six ships off the Cape of Delaware before having to return for coal. She stopped attempts by USS *Sassacus* to capture her on November 6, 1864 and by four other United States ships on November 7, 1864 finally passing into the safety of Wilmington harbor.

CSS Chameleon

The *Olustee* was renamed the CSS *Chameleon* with Lt. J. Wilkinson, CSN, commanding. The battery had been removed and she ran through the Union blockade on December 24, 1864 while the United States fleet was preoccupied with bombarding Fort Fisher. The *Chameleon* proceeded to Bermuda to obtain provisions for the Confederate army.

Wilkinson made two attempts to enter one of the southern ports, but finding it impossible, he took Chameleon to Liverpool, England, and turned her over to Comdr. J. D. Bullock, CSN, financial agent of the Confederate Navy Department.

On her arrival in England on April 9, 1865 the *Chameleon* was seized and sold by the British authorities and was about to enter the merchant service when the United States instituted suit for possession. She was awarded to the United States Government and handed over to the consul at Liverpool on April 26, 1866.

Source (edited): "http://en.wikipedia.org/wiki/CSS_Tallahassee"

CSS Teaser

6.4 inch banded rifle, the stern pivot mount on the CSS Teaser. These guns were made by banding and rifling the 32 pound smoothbore. This image is from the Library of Congress.

12 pounder on the bow

Deck detail

CSS *Teaser* had been the aging Georgetown, D.C. tugboat *York River* until the beginning of the American Civil War, when she was taken into the Confederate States Navy. Later, she was captured by the United States Navy and became the first **USS *Teaser***.

CSS *Teaser*

Teaser was built at Philadelphia, Pennsylvania. Purchased at Richmond, Virginia by the State of Virginia in 1861, she was assigned to the naval forces in the James River with Lieutenant James Henry Rochelle, Virginia State Navy, in command. Upon the secession of Virginia, *Teaser* became a part of the Confederate States Navy and continued to operate in Virginia waters. With Lieutenant William A. Webb, CSN, in command, she took an active part in the Battle of Hampton Roads on March 8–March 9, 1862, acting as tender to CSS *Virginia*. She received the thanks of the Congress of the Confederate States for this action.

Teaser was a pioneer "aircraft carrier", serving as a base for an observation hot air balloon, she also became a pioneer minelayer when ordered on June 17, 1862, to assist General Robert E. Lee's Army of Northern Virginia. Under Lieutenant Hunter Davidson, CSN, she was used by the Confederate Naval Submarine Battery Service to plant and service "torpedoes" (mines) in the James River. While engaging USS *Maratanza* at Haxall's on the James on July 4, 1862, a Union shell blew up *Teaser*'s boiler and forced her crew to abandon ship When seized by *Maratanza*, *Teaser* was carrying on board a balloon for aerial reconnaissance of Union positions at City Point and Harrison's Landing.

Commanders

The commanders of the CSS *Teaser* were:
- Lieutenant James H. Rochelle (May–June 1861)
- Lieutenant Robert Randolph Carter (June–July 1861)
- Boatswain Master William H. Face (June 1861-January 1862)
- Lieutenant William A. Webb (February 1862-)
- Lieutenant Hunter Davidson (June–July 1862)

USS *Teaser*

Later that summer, *Teaser* was taken into the United States Navy and was assigned to the Potomac Flotilla. With the exception of three brief deployments elsewhere, USS *Teaser* plied the waters of the Potomac River from Alexandria, Virginia, south to Point Lookout, Maryland to enforce the blockade by interdicting a thriving trade in contraband between the Maryland and Virginia shores.

On September 22, she captured schooner *Southerner* in the Coan River. On October 19, while operating in the vicinity of Piney Point in St. Mary's County, Maryland, she captured two smugglers and their boat as they were nearing the exit of Herring Creek and preparing to cross the river to Virginia. On November 2, near the mouth of the Rappahannock River, the tug surprised three men attempting to violate the blockade in a canoe. *Teaser* took them prisoner and turned their contraband over to pro-Union Virginians living on Gwynn's Island. Four days later in Chesapeake Bay, *Teaser* took the cargo-less sloop *Grapeshot* and captured her three-man crew.

By December 1862, she had moved to the Rappahannock River with other units of the Potomac Flotilla to support General Ambrose Burnside's thrust toward Richmond. On December 10, she exchanged shots with a Confederate battery located on the southern shore of the river about three miles below Port Royal, Virginia. After Burnside's bloody rebuff at Fredericksburg, Virginia on December 13, *Teaser* and her colleagues returned to their anti-smuggling patrol along the Potomac.

Teaser joined USS *Primrose* to make March 1863 an active month. On March 24, the two ships sent a boat expedition to reconnoiter Pope's Creek, Virginia. The landing party found two boats used for smuggling and collected information from Union sympathizers in the area. Almost a week later, on the night of March 30—March 31, they dispatched a three-boat party to Monroe's Creek, Virginia. The previous day, a Federal cavalry detachment had surprised a smuggler in the area; and, though the troops captured his goods, the man himself escaped. Boats from *Teaser* and *Primrose* succeeded where the Union horsemen had failed, and they gathered some intelligence on other contrabanders as well.

In April 1863, *Teaser* left the Potomac for duty with Acting Rear Admiral Samuel Phillips Lee's North Atlantic Blockading Squadron at Hampton Roads. On April 17, she joined USS *Alert* and USS *Coeur de Lion* in an expedition up the Nansemond River west of Norfolk, Virginia. However, she ran aground, damaged her machinery, and had to retire from the venture.

By mid-summer, *Teaser* was back in action on the Potomac. On the night of July 27, she captured two smugglers with a boatload of tobacco in the mouth of the Mattawoman Creek just south of Indian Head, Maryland. She destroyed the boat and sent the prisoners and contraband north to the Washington Navy Yard. During the night of October 7, *Teaser* and another flotilla ship (extant records do not identify her companion) noticed signalling between Mathias Point, Virginia, and the Maryland shore. The two ships shelled the woods at Mathias Point, but took no action against the signallers on the Maryland shore other than to urge upon the United States Army's district provost marshal the necessity of constant vigilance.

On January 5, 1864, *Teaser* and USS *Yankee* landed a force of men at Nomini, Virginia to investigate a rumor that the Southerners had hidden a large lighter and a skiff capable of boating 80 men there. The force, commanded by *Teaser's* commanding officer, Acting Ensign Sheridan, found both boats, destroyed the lighter, and captured the skiff. During the landing, Confederate soldiers appeared on the heights above Nomini, but the gunboats dampened their curiosity with some well-placed cannon shots.

In April, *Teaser*, *Yankee*, USS *Anacostia*, USS *Fuchsia*, and USS *Resolute* accompanied an Army expedition to Machodoc Creek, Virginia. At 5:00 A.M. on April 13, the five ships cleared the St. Mary's River in company with the Army's steamer USAT *Long Branch* with a battalion of soldiers under the command of General Edward W. Hinks. *Long Branch* landed her troops at about 8:00 A.M. while the five ships covered the operation. A contingent of Confederate cavalry appeared on the southern bank of the Machodoc, but retired when *Teaser* and *Anacostia* sent four armed boat crews ashore. The landing party netted a prisoner, probably a smuggler, and a large quantity of tobacco. By April 14, General Hinks' troops reembarked in *Long Branch* and headed for Point Lookout. *Anacostia* accompanied the Army steamer while the other four warships investigated Currioman Bay and Nomini. They returned to St. Mary's, Virginia that afternoon to resume patrols.

During the summer of 1864, *Teaser* was called upon to leave the Potomac once more. On this occasion, the Union forces needed her guns to help defend strategic bridges across the rivers at the head of Chesapeake Bay near Baltimore, Maryland, against Lieutenant General Jubal A. Early's raiders. On July 10, she departed the lower Potomac, rounded Point Lookout, and headed up the Chesapeake Bay. That night, she had to put into the Patuxent River because of heavy winds and leaks in her hull. Before dawn the following morning, she continued up the bay. During the forenoon, the leaks became progressively worse and, by the time she arrived off Annapolis, Maryland, she had to remove her exhaust pipe for temporary repairs. Early that evening, *Teaser* reached Baltimore where she put in for additional repairs.

The gunboat did not reach her destination, the bridge over the Gunpowder River, until late on July 12. She was too late; the bridge had already been burned. She returned to Baltimore immediately to report on the bridge and to pick up arms and provisions for the vessels stationed in the Gunpowder River. When she arrived back at the bridge, she found orders to return to the Potomac awaiting her. *Teaser* departed the northern reaches of the Chesapeake and reported back to the Potomac Flotilla at St. Inigoes, Virginia on the St. Mary's River in late afternoon on April 14.

For the remainder of the war, *Teaser* and her flotilla-mates plied the Potomac and contributed to the gradual economic strangulation which brought the South to its knees by April 1865. Less than two months after General Robert E. Lee's surrender at Appomattox, Virginia, *Teaser* was decommissioned at the Washington Navy Yard on June 2. Sold at public auction at Washington to Mr. J. Bigler on June 25, the tug was re-documented as *York River* on July 2, 1865, and she served commercially until 1878.

Source (edited): "http://en.wikipedia.org/wiki/CSS_Teaser"

CSS Tennessee (1862)

The first **CSS *Tennessee*** was an ironclad ram, built for the Confederate States Navy.

Tennessee was begun by John T. Shirley and Company, at Memphis, Tennessee, under fixed price contract for $76,920. Chief constructor of the twin-screw ironclad was a Mr. Prime Emerson.

In correspondence with Major General Leonidas Polk, CSA, throughout January 1862, seeking Army workmen from Columbus, Kentucky, Secretary Stephen Mallory promised for *Tennessee* and her sister, *Arkansas*, building at Shirley's yard, that "with such aid as mechanics under your command can afford, they may be completed, I am assured, in 60 days." The desired "shipwrights, carpenters and joiners in the Army" were refused—"on furlough or otherwise" —although the general was reminded that, "One of them at Columbus would have enabled you to complete the annihilation of the enemy . . . Mr. Shirley," Mallory prophesied correctly, "will fail in completing them within the stipulated time entirely from the difficulty of obtaining workmen", although they "would be worth many regiments in defending the river."

Little more is known of the first *Tennessee*, which was never completed. She was burned on the stocks by order of the provost marshal, 5 June 1862, to escape capture.

See CSS *Tennessee* for other ships of this name.

This article includes text from the public domain Dictionary of American Naval Fighting Ships.

Source (edited): "http://en.wikipedia.org/wiki/CSS_Tennessee_(1862)"

CSS Tennessee (1863)

CSS *Tennessee*, an ironclad ram, was built at Selma, Alabama, where she was commissioned on February 16, 1864, Lieutenant James D. Johnston, CSN, in command. CSS *Baltic* towed her to Mobile where she was fitted out for action.

Tennessee was laid down in October 1862, hull and other woodwork turned out by Henry D. Bassett, who launched her the following February, ready for towing to Mobile to be engined and armed. Her steam plant came from the steamer *Alonzo Child*; only casemate design differed materially from CSS *Columbia* and CSS *Texas*. Her iron mail was the same 2 by 10 in (50 by 250 mm) plate used on CSS *Huntsville* and CSS *Tuscaloosa* but triple instead of double thickness. A fearsome detail of her armament was a "hot water attachment to her boilers for repelling boarders, throwing one stream from forward of the casemate and one aft."

The vicissitudes implicit in creating such an ironclad are graphically conveyed by Admiral Franklin Buchanan, writing September 20, 1863 to Confederate Navy Secretary Stephen Mallory: "The work on the *Tennessee* has progressed for some weeks past, under Mr. Pierce, as fast as the means in his power would permit. There is much delay for want of plate and bolt iron. It was impossible to iron both sponsons at the same time, as the vessel had to be careened several feet to enable them to put the iron on. Even then several of the workmen were waist deep in the water to accomplish it — to careen her, large beams 12 feet (3.7 m) square had to be run out of her posts and secured, on which several tons of iron had to be placed, and during the progress of putting on the sponson iron the shield iron could not be put on. The work has been carried on night and day when it could be done advantageously. I visited the *Nashville* and *Tennessee* frequently and, to secure and control the services of the mechanics, I have had them all conscripted and detailed to work under my orders. Previously, they were very independent and stopped working when they pleased."

(Joseph Pierce, referred to above, was Acting Naval Constructor in the Mobile area.)

Lieutenant (later Commander) James D. Johnston, CSN, commander of the CSS *Tennessee*

Tennessee became flagship of Admiral Buchanan, and served gallantly in action in the Battle of Mobile Bay on August 5, 1864. On that morning *Tennessee* and wooden gunboats CSS *Gaines*, CSS *Morgan*, and CSS *Selma*, steamed into combat against Admiral David G. Farragut's powerful fleet of four ironclad monitors and 14 wooden steamers. Unable to ram the Union ships because of their superior speed, *Tennessee* delivered a vigorous fire on the Federals at close range. The Confederate gunboats were sunk or dispersed. Farragut's fleet steamed up into the bay and anchored. Buchanan might have held *Tennessee* under the fort's protection but steamed after the Federal fleet and engaged despite overwhelming odds. The ram became the target for the entire Union fleet. *Tennessee* was rammed by several ships, and her vulnerable steering chains (which, oddly, lay in exposed trenches on the after deck) were carried away by the heavy gunfire. Unable to maneuver, *Tennessee* was battered repeatedly by heavy solid shot from her adversaries. With two of her men killed, Admiral Buchanan and eight others wounded, and increasingly severe damage being inflicted on her, *Tennessee* was forced to surrender.

USS *Tennessee*

Immediately following her capture, *Tennessee* was commissioned in the United States Navy, Acting Volunteer Lieutenant Pierre Giraud in command. The ironclad participated in the Federal assault on Fort Morgan on August 23 which resulted in the fort's capitulation that same day. That autumn, she moved from Mobile, AL to New Orleans, LA for repairs before joining the Mississippi Squadron. She served on the Mississippi river through the end of the war in April 1865 and briefly thereafter. On August 19, 1865, *Tennessee* was placed out of commission and was laid up at New Orleans. There, she remained until November 27, 1867 when she was sold at auction to J. F. Armstrong for scrapping. Though the remainder of the vessel was scrapped, two 7 inch Brooke rifles and two 6.4 inch Brooke rifles were preserved and are still on display in the Old weapons exhibit in East Willard Park at the Washington Navy Yard, Washington, D.C. One of her 6.4-inch (160 mm) double-banded Brooke rifled cannon is on display at the Headquarters of the Commander-in-Chief U. S. Atlantic Command at the Norfolk, Virginia Naval base.

Source (edited): "http://en.wikipedia.org/wiki/CSS_Tennessee_(1863)"

CSS Texas

The **CSS *Texas* (Confederate States Ship *Texas*)**, was a twin propeller casement ironclad ram of the Confederate Navy, named for the state of Texas. She was sister ship to CSS *Columbia*. Since the ship was built so late in the American Civil War, it saw no action before being captured by Union forces.

History

The keel for the CSS *Texas* was laid down at Richmond, Virginia. She was launched in January 1865. At the time of Robert E. Lee's evacuation of Richmond on 3 April 1865, she was left unfinished but intact in an outfitting berth at the Richmond Navy Yard, one of only two vessels which escaped destruction by the departing Confederate forces. Captured when the city fell the following day, the ironclad was taken into the United States Navy, but saw no service. *Texas* was laid up at Norfolk until 15 October 1867 when she was sold to J.N. Leonard & Co. of New Haven, Connecticut.

Design

From a technological view, the CSS *Texas* was one of a series of three 'Tennessee class' ironclads (the other two being the CSS *Tennessee II* and CSS *Columbia*) which embodied the latest developments in Confederate shipbuilding technology. Her casemate was diamond-shaped rather than being a sloped box as on earlier ships and fitted snugly around the front, aft and side cannon placement. Instead of bolted on, the pilot house almost formed a seamless natural extension of the side armor. Details of her armament are sketchy, but her sister ship, the CSS *Tennessee II* carried four 6.4 in. Brooke rifles, two 7 in. Brooke rifles and a bolted-on spar torpedo. Also for the *Tennessee II*, armor was given as 3 layers of 2 in., top speed as 5 knots and crew as 133 men. It is unclear however in how far the CSS *Texas* resembled the *Tennessee II* as other sources give her a (projected) speed of no less than 10 knots and note that both the *Tennessee II* and the *Texas* differed from the original design due to availability of key materials (in particular guns and engines) and due to improvements made during construction from lessons learned in combat.

Plan of a gun and mounting intended for the Confederate ironclad *CSS Texas*.

CSS *Texas* in fiction

- In the 1992 novel *Sahara* by adventure writer Clive Cussler, President Abraham Lincoln is kidnapped by a group that impersonated a Union cavalry detachment and overpowered his military escort in early April 1865 as the Civil War was drawing to a close. Edwin Stanton, Secretary of War, took the lead in arranging a cover-up supposedly employing John Wilkes Booth as a patriot who quickly brought the situation to an abrupt conclusion - supported by Stanton then destroying documentation and concealing the accused conspirators under heavy hoods so no one really knew who they were, but of importance here is that the real Lincoln was supposedly spirited out of the country on the CSS *Texas*. Casting off at night after loading Confederate gold and government files, they initially ran dark down the river but eventually got caught in a running gun battle, suffering some damage but avoiding a pounding and probably sinking by Union batteries at the mouth of the river when the captain of the boat raised a white flag and exposed Lincoln on top of the pilot house as they escaped into a fog bank. The story resumes in modern times with the ship discovered in the sand of the Sahara having gotten grounded up a branch of the Niger River. Evidence includes the dead bodies of fifty men plus the captain and Lincoln, who are preserved in the dry heat. After running aground the ship, the crew had to trade gold with natives for food. Then more natives realized there was gold on board and they essentially blockaded the boat, starving all but one of the crew to death. The single surviving man of initially four in his group escaped in a small boat and was saved by English traders.
- In the 2005 film *Sahara* based on Cussler's novel, the fictional CSS *Texas* more actively figures in the action sequences of the movie as opposed to the book.

Source (edited): "http://en.wikipedia.org/wiki/CSS_Texas"

CSS Virginia

CSS *Virginia* was the first steam-powered ironclad warship of the Confederate States Navy, built during the first year of the American Civil War; she was constructed as a casemate ironclad using the raised and cut down hull of the scuttled USS *Merrimack*. *Virginia* was one of the participants in the Battle of Hampton Roads, opposing the Union's

USS *Monitor* in March, 1862. The battle is chiefly significant in naval history as the first battle between ironclads.

USS *Merrimack* becomes CSS *Virginia*

When the Commonwealth of Virginia seceded from the Union in 1861, one of the important federal military bases threatened was Gosport Navy Yard (now Norfolk Naval Shipyard) in Portsmouth, Virginia. Accordingly, the order was sent to destroy the base rather than allow it to fall into Confederate hands. Unfortunately for the Union, the execution of these orders was bungled on 20 April. The steam frigate USS *Merrimack* sank in shallow water before she completely burned. When the Confederate government took possession of the yard, the base commander, Flag Officer French Forrest, contracted on 18 May to salvage the wreck of the *Merrimack*. This was completed by 30 May and she was moved into the shipyard's only graving dock where the burned structures were removed.

The wreck was surveyed and her lower hull and machinery were undamaged so she was selected for conversion into an ironclad by Stephen Mallory, Secretary of the Navy, as she was the only large ship with intact engines available to the Confederacy in the Chesapeake Bay area. Preliminary sketch designs were submitted by Lieutenants John Brooke and John L. Porter, each of which envisaged the ship as a casemate ironclad. Brooke's design showed the ends of the ship as submerged and was selected, although detailed design work would be done by Porter as he was a trained naval constructor. Porter had overall responsibility for the conversion, but Brooke was responsible for her iron plate and armament while William P. Williamson, Chief Engineer of the Navy, was responsible for the ship's machinery.

Reconstruction

Cut away view showing the 4 inches (10 cm) of iron armor and 24 inches (61 cm) of wood backing it.

The burned hull timbers were cut down past the waterline, and a new deck and armored casemate (fortress) were added. The deck was 4-inch (10 cm) thick iron. The casemate was built up of 24 inches (61 cm) of oak and pine in several layers, topped with two 2-inch (5 cm) layers of iron plating oriented perpendicular to each other, and angled to deflect shot hits. The battery consisted of four single-banded Brooke rifles and six 9-inch (23 cm) Dahlgren smoothbore shell guns. Two of the rifles, bow and stern pivots, were 7-inch (18 cm), of 14,500 pounds; the other two were 6.4-inch (16 cm) (32 pound calibre) of 9000 pounds, one on each broadside. The 9-inch (23 cm) gun on each side nearest the furnaces was fitted for firing hot shot. A few 9-inch (23 cm) shot with extra windage (slightly smaller diameter) were cast for hot shot. No other solid shot were on board during the fight.

As *Virginia*'s designers had heard of plans by the North to build an ironclad, and figuring her guns would be unable to harm such a ship, they equipped her with a ram—at that time an anachronism in a warship. *Merrimack*'s steam engines, now part of *Virginia*, were in poor working order (the ship had been slated for an engine rebuild prior to the decision to abandon the Norfolk naval yard), and the salty Elizabeth River water and addition of tons of iron armor and ballast did not improve the situation. As completed CSS Virginia had a turning radius of about one mile (1.6 km) and required 45 minutes to complete a full circle, which was a major handicap in its battle with the far more nimble USS Monitor.

The commanding officer, Flag Officer Franklin Buchanan, arrived to take command only a few days before sailing. The ship was placed in commission and equipped by the executive officer, Catesby ap R. Jones.

Battle of Hampton Roads

Painting depicting the Battle of Hampton Roads

The Battle of Hampton Roads began on March 8, 1862 when *Virginia* took on the blockading Union fleet. Despite an all-out effort to complete her, the new ironclad still had workmen on board when she sailed into Hampton Roads with her flotilla of five support ships *Raleigh* and *Beaufort*, *Patrick Henry*, *Jamestown*, and *Teaser*.

The first Union ship engaged, the all wood and sail-powered USS *Cumberland*, was sunk after being rammed by *Virginia*. However, as *Cumberland* sank, *Virginia's* iron ram was broken off, causing a bow leak. Seeing what happened to *Cumberland*, the captain of USS *Congress* ordered his ship into shallow water, where she soon grounded. *Congress* and *Virginia* traded fire for an hour, after which the badly-damaged *Congress* surrendered. While the surviving crewmen of *Congress* were being ferried off the ship, a Union battery on the north shore opened fire on *Virginia*. In retaliation, the captain of *Virginia* gave the order to open fire on the surrendered *Congress* with red-hot shot, setting her ablaze; she burned for many hours, well into the night.

Virginia did not emerge from the battle unscathed. Shot from *Cumberland*

Congress, and the shore-based Union troops had riddled her smokestack, reducing her already low speed. Two of her guns were out of order, and a number of armor plates had been loosened. Even so, her captain attacked USS *Minnesota*, which had run aground on a sandbank trying to escape *Virginia*. However, because of her deep draft, *Virginia* was unable to do significant damage. It being late in the day, *Virginia* left with the expectation of returning the next day and completing the destruction of the Union blockaders.

Later that night, USS *Monitor* finally arrived at Union-held Fort Monroe. She had been rushed to Hampton Roads, still not quite completed, all the way from the Brooklyn Navy Yard, in hopes of defending the Union force of wooden ships and preventing "the rebel monster" from further threatening the blockading fleet and nearby Union cities, like Washington, D.C.. While being towed south, she almost foundered in a storm on the way to Hampton Roads. She still had workmen aboard when she arrived by the firelight from the still burning triumph of *Virginia*'s first day of handiwork.

The next day, on March 9, 1862, the world's first battle between ironclads took place. The smaller, nimbler *Monitor* was able to outmaneuver *Virginia*, but neither ship proved able to do significant damage, despite numerous hits. *Monitor* had a much lower freeboard, and thus much harder to hit by the *Virginia's* guns, but vulnerable to ramming and boarding. Finally, *Monitor* retreated. This was because the captain of the *Monitor* was hit by gunpowder in his eyes while looking through the pilothouse's peepholes, which caused *Monitor* to haul off. The *Monitor* had retreated off into the shoals and remained there, and so the battle was a draw. The captain of *Virginia*, Lieutenant Catesby ap Roger Jones, CSN received the advice from his pilots to take the midnight high tide to depart back over the bar toward the CS Navy base at Norfolk until noon of the next day. Lieutenant Jones wanted, instead, to re-attack, but to "turn the ship and fight the starboard gun, was impossible, for heading up stream on a strong flood-tide, she would have been wholly unmanageable." The pilots emphasized that the *Virginia* had "nearly three miles to run to the bar" and that she could not remain and "take the ground on a falling tide." So to prevent getting stuck, Lieutenant Jones called off the battle and moved back toward harbor. After the battle with the *Monitor*, the *Virginia* retired to the Gosport Naval Yard at Portsmouth, Virginia, for repairs and remained in drydock until April 4, 1862.

In the following month, the crew of the *Virginia* were unsuccessful in their attempts to break the Union blockade. The blockade had been bolstered by the hastily ram-fitted *SS Vanderbilt*, and SS Illinois as well as the SS Arago and USS *Minnesota* which had been repaired. The *Virginia* made several sorties back over to Hampton Roads hoping to draw *Monitor* into battle. *Monitor*, however, was under orders not to engage.

On April 11, the Confederate Navy sent Lieutenant Joseph Nicholson Barney in command of the side-paddle CSS *Jamestown*, along with the *Virginia* and five other ships in full view of the Union squadron, enticing them to fight. When it became clear that the US Navy ships were unwilling to fight, the CS Navy squadron moved in and captured three merchant ships, the brigs *Marcus* and *Sabout* and the schooner *Catherine T. Dix*. Their flags were then hoisted "Union-side down" to further taunt the US Navy into a fight, as they were towed back to Norfolk, with the help of the CSS *Raleigh*.

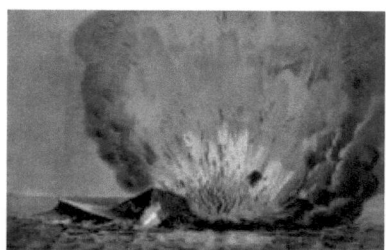

Destruction of the rebel vessel Merrimac *off Craney Island, May 11, 1862,* by Currier and Ives

Neither ironclad was ever to fight again. By late April the new Union ironclads USS Naugatuck/USRC E. A. Stevens and USS Galena had also joined the blockade. On May 8, 1862, *Virginia* and the James River Squadron ventured out when the Union ships began shelling the Confederate fortifications near Norfolk but the Union ships retired under the shore batteries on the north side of the James River and on Rip Raps island.

On May 10, 1862, advancing Union troops occupied Norfolk. Since *Virginia* was a steam-powered battery and not a cruiser, she was not seaworthy enough to enter the ocean even if she was able to pass the Union blockade. *Virginia* was also unable to retreat further up the James River due to her deep 22-foot (6.7 m) draft. In an attempt to reduce her draft, supplies and coal were dumped overboard but this exposed the unclad, wooden hull. Without a home port, *Virginia* was ordered blown up to keep her from being captured. This task fell to Lieutenant Jones, the last man to leave CSS *Virginia* after all of her guns had been safely removed and carried to the CS Marine Corps base and fortifications at Drewy's Bluff to fight again. Early on the morning of May 11, 1862, off Craney Island, fire reached her magazine and she was destroyed by a great explosion. Her thirteen star Stars and Bars battle ensign was saved from destruction and today resides in the collection of the Chicago Historical Society, minus three of its stars.

The USS Monitor was lost on December 31 of the same year, when the vessel was swamped by high waves in a violent storm while under tow by the tug *Rhoad Island* off Cape Hatteras North Carolina. Some of her crew went down with the ironclad but others were saved by lifeboats sent from *Rhoad Island*.

Historical names: *Merrimack, Virginia, Merrimac*

The name of the warship which served the Confederacy in the Battle of Hampton Roads has become a source of confusion, which continues to the present day.

When she was first commissioned into the United States Navy in 1856, her name was *Merrimack*, with the *K*. The name derived from the Merrimack River near where she was built. She was the second ship of the U.S. Navy to be named for the Merrimack River, which is formed by the junction of the Pemigewasset and Winnipesaukee Rivers at Franklin, New Hampshire. The Merrimack flows south across New Hampshire, and then eastward across northeastern Massachusetts before emptying in the Atlantic at Newburyport, Massachusetts.

The Confederacy bestowed the name *Virginia* on her when she was raised, restored, and outfitted as an ironclad warship, but the Union preferred to call the Confederate ironclad warship by either its earlier name, "*Merrimack*", or by the nickname, "The Rebel Monster".

Perhaps because the Union won the Civil War, the history of the United States generally records the Union version. In the aftermath of the battle, the names *Virginia* and *Merrimack* were used equally by both sides, as attested by the newspapers and correspondence of the day. Some Navy reports and pre-1900 historians misspelled the name as "Merrimac," which is actually an unrelated ship. Hence "the Battle of the *Monitor* and the *Merrimac*". Both spellings are still in use in the Hampton Roads area.

Memorial, heritage

- It is said the most popular exhibit at Jamestown Exposition held in 1907 at Sewell's Point was the "Battle of the *Merrimac* and *Monitor*," a diorama that was in a special building.
- The small community in Montgomery County, Virginia near where the coal burned by the Confederate ironclad was mined is now known as Merrimac, Virginia.
- The October 8, 1867 issue of the *Norfolk Virginian* newspaper carried a prominent classified advertisement in the paper's "Private Sales" section for the salvaged iron ram of the CSS *Virginia*. The ad states verbatim "A RELIC OF WAR FOR SALE: The undersigned has had several offers for the IRON PROW! of the first iron-clad ever built, the celebrated Ram and Iron Clad Virginia, formerly the Merrimac. This immense RELIC WEIGHS 1,340 POUNDS, wrought iron, and as a sovereign of the war, and an object of interest as a revolution in naval warfare, would suit a Museum, State Institute, or some great public resort. Those desiring to purchase will please address D. A. UNDERDOWN, Wrecker, care of *Virginian* Office, Norfolk, Va." It is unclear from the above whether this was the first iron ram that broke off and lodged in the starboard bow of the sinking USS *Cumberland* during the first day of the Battle of Hampton Roads or was the second iron ram affixed to *Virginia*'s bow at the time she was run aground and turned to avoid capture by Union forces. No further mention has been found concerning the final disposition of this historic artifact.
- Other pieces of *Virginia* did survive and are on display at the Mariners' Museum in Newport News and the Museum of the Confederacy in Richmond, where one of her anchors has resided on its front lawn for many years.
- In 1907, an armor plate from the ship was melted down and used in the casting of the Pokahuntas Bell for the Jamestown Exposition.
- Starting around 1883, numerous souvenirs, made from recently salvaged iron and wood raised from *Virginia*'s sunken hulk, found a ready and willing market among eastern seaboard residents who remembered the historic first battle between ironclads. Various tokens, medals, medalets, sectional watch fobs, and other similar metal keepsakes are known to have been struck by private mints in limited quantities. Known examples still exist today, being held in both public and private collections, rarely coming up for public auction. Nine examples made from *Virginia*'s iron and copper can be found cataloged in great detail, with front and back photos, in David Schenkman's 1979 numismatic booklet listed in the Reference section (below).
- The name of the Monitor-Merrimac Memorial Bridge-Tunnel, built in Hampton Roads in the general vicinity of the famous engagement, with both Virginia and federal funds, also reflects the more recent version.

Source (edited): "http://en.wikipedia.org/wiki/CSS_Virginia"

CSS Virginia II

CSS *Virginia II* was a Confederate Navy steam-powered ironclad ram laid down in 1862 at the William Graves' shipyard in Richmond, Virginia. Acting Constructor William A. Graves, CSN, was the superintendent in charge of her building. In order to conserve scarce iron plating, he ordered the ship's armored casemate shortened from the specifications given in John L. Porter's original building plans; in addition, the ship's iron-plating, while six-inches thick on the casemate's forward face, was reduced to five-inches on her port, starboard, and aft faces.

The *Virginia II* was named after the more famous Confederate ironclad, the CSS *Virginia*, more popularly known as the *Merrimack*. In fact, the original *Virginia*'s success caused "gunboat associations" to emerge around the South, mainly driven by women, and their efforts helped with the construction of the *Virginia II*.

Construction

Money to help with the construction of this ironclad was largely contributed by the Richmond chapter of the "Ladies Aid and Defense Society" called the

"National Defense Association" which adopted this ironclad in early April 1862 for the defense of Richmond. The chairman was Maria Gaitskell Clopton. It is estimated that the society contributed more than $30,000 towards its construction.

By November 1862, John Mercer Brooke was able to report that she was "pretty well advanced, frames up, clamps in, etc... She will be a strong and fine vessel."

However, after this promising start, significant delays plagued the new ironclad. It was not until more than a year after she was laid down that the *Virginia II* was finally launched without incident on June 29, 1863. "She glided into the water 'like a thing of life' amid the prolonged cheers of the spectators." However, she suffered from further delays in being fitted out and was not fully commissioned until May 18, 1864, almost a year later, and was made the flagship of the James River Squadron (replacing CSS *Richmond* in this role).

Career

Virginia II, Commander Robert B. Pegram, CSN, went into action on 21 June 1864 as flagship of Commodore John K. Mitchell, CSN, during the engagement between the Confederate James River Squadron and Federal ships in Trent's Reach, however she suffered from mechanical trouble and problems with her propeller when the chain of the CSS *Richmond* got caught up in it and so could not participate in this battle.

On August 13, the Virginia II participated in the attack on the Union forces at Dutch Gap. The USS *Maugus* and her gunboats joined in the battle but could not effectively train her guns, though they did manage to get two shots that hit *Virginia II*. On August 17, she participated in the capture of Signal Hill, shelling the Union defenses from 3 PM until 9 PM.

From September 29 through October 1, the *Virginia II* and the rest of the squadron attacked New Market Heights and Fort Harrison in conjunction with the Confederate Army in what was the largest operation north of the James River since Cold Harbor, and would remain so until the end of the war. Once again, though, the Virginia II suffered some difficulty which delayed her entrance into the battle. She had just received a new gun and in the rush to leave the dock, got the supply ship *Gallego* caught in her anchor chain, causing the *Gallego* to sink.

In their routine patrol of the James River, the squadron was surprised on the morning of October 22 to discover that the Union Army had finished fortifying Cox Hill. To cover the retreat of the wooden vessels of the fleet, the Virginia II approached the battery, followed by the other two ironclads, and effected the retreat upstream to Chaffin's Bluff. During this, the *Virginia II*'s smokestack was riddled by shells. Though they were caught by surprise, this small action helped determine the effectiveness of the ironclads' casemates against close rifled fire, and in the case of the *Virginia II* the results were favorable: her armor withstood 7 hits by 100-pound conical bolts, which barely dented its surface.

On December 7, the *Virginia II*, along with the *Fredericksburg* and *Richmond*, came down to Fort Brady near Trent's Reach, and exchanged fire with the fort near sunset until darkness approached.

Battle of Trent's Reach

Her final action took place on January 23-January 24, 1865 when the Confederate squadron in the James River, including ironclads *Virginia II*, CSS *Richmond* and CSS *Fredericksburg*, with five smaller vessels, made a second unsuccessful attempt to circumvent obstructions in Trent's Reach. A reliable report indicated that there was a passage through, as a result of a freshet of melting ice. To avoid the risk of collision, the gunboats and tenders were lashed to the starboard sides of the ironclads - Virginia accreted the gunboats *Nansemond* and *Torpedo*, with the torpedo boat *Scorpion* in tow, to her bulk. After passing the Union batteries at Fort Brady sometime after 8 PM, the *Virginia II* accidentally beached the *Torpedo* by cutting too close to the shore. The captain of the *Nansemond*, untied his ship from Virginia II in an attempt to free the *Torpedo*. The fleet continued on and reached the obstructions at Trent's Reach.

Site of the sinking of the Virginia II and other ships in the James River. The part showing above water is from the CSS *Jamestown*. (Photograph by Mathew Brady)

Again *Virginia II* ran into trouble, this time running aground and the smaller ships tried to free her for three hours. Only two ships made it through, the rest were either running aground or helping the ones who had. Dawn came with most of the squadron in full view of the Union fortifications at Battery Parsons, and they had to suffer the fire until the water was able to rise high enough to allow them to retreat. Just as the water rose high enough to float the *Virginia II* in late morning, the Union fleet arrived and added to the fire, this time more deadly, as the double-turretted monitor USS *Onondaga* was able to pierce her armor. She and the rest of the squadron retreated upstream until they were out of the way and under cover of the Confederate batteries at Battery Dantzler. They attempted to try again that night, but the Union soldiers had erected a huge light illuminating the obstructions, and combined with several other factors, decided to abandon the attempt.

When leaving, the *Hampton* managed to catch her propeller in *Virginia II*'s anchor chain. They suffered more fire on their return upriver from Fort Brady and Virginia II ran aground again before making it to the safety of Chaffin's Bluff. *Virginia II* had at least 6 killed and more than a half dozen wounded from the action, and also suffered damage which required extensive repairs. Her smokestack was destroyed, her engines were faulty and the iron shielding and wooden framework were damaged. Her repairs had just been finished, when the *Virginia II* was one of the ships destroyed in the James River before the evacuation of Richmond on 3 April 1865.

Commanders

The commanders of the CSS *Virginia II* were:
- Commander Robert B. Pegram (May 1864-around August 1864)
- Lieutenant Oscar F. Johnston (August 1864, commanding *pro tem*)
- Lieutenant Francis E. Shepperd (September 24, 1864-around December 1864)
- Lieutenant John W. Dunnington (December 1864-end of war)

Source (edited): "http://en.wikipedia.org/wiki/CSS_Virginia_II"

CSS Webb

CSS *Webb*, a 655-ton side-wheel steam ram, was originally built in New York City in 1856 as the civilian steamship *William H. Webb*. She received a Confederate privateer's commission at New Orleans in May 1861, but was instead employed as a transport until January 1862. Converted to a "cotton clad" ram by the Confederate Army, *Webb* thereafter served on the Mississippi and Red rivers. On February 24, 1863, she participated in the sinking of the Federal ironclad USS *Indianola*. *Webb* was transferred to the Confederate Navy in early 1865.

On April 23-24, 1865, she broke through the Federal blockade at the mouth of the Red River, Louisiana, and made a dramatic run down the Mississippi toward the Gulf of Mexico. After passing New Orleans, she was cornered by United States Navy ships, run ashore and destroyed by her crew.

Source (edited): "http://en.wikipedia.org/wiki/CSS_Webb"

CS Bayou City

C.S. *Bayou City* captures the USS *Harriet Lane* during the Battle of Galveston

C.S. Army Gunboat *Bayou City* (1861-1865) was a 165-foot side-wheel steamboat built for commercial use at Jeffersonville, Indiana, in 1859.

Serving as a mail boat between Galveston and Houston, Texas, the ship was chartered on 26 September 1861 by Comdr. W. Hunter, CSN, commanding the Texas Marine Department, from the Houston Navigation Co.

Military use

The *Bayou City* was clad with pressed cotton for protection, armed with artillery and operated by the State of Texas as a gunboat in the Galveston area. Just over a year after its charter, in October 1862, she was taken over by the Confederate States Army.

The Battle of Galveston

On 1 January 1863, in what would come to be known as the Battle of Galveston, the cotton-clad *Bayou City* and the tugboat *Neptune* were used by Confederate troops in an operation to drive Union warships out of Galveston Bay.

After a brief contest at sea, the USS *Harriet Lane* sank the *Neptune*, and one-half of the two-vessel Confederate fleet was lying on the bottom of the harbor. As the lone surviving Rebel steamer, the *Bayou City* was outnumbered six-to-one among the armed vessels in the harbor.

However, the *Bayou City* circled around and made a second run on the USS *Harriet Lane*. This time, the Confederates hit their target. In short order, the crew of the *Bayou City* succeeded in storming and overpowering the crew of the *Lane*. The men from the *Bayou City* boarded and seized the federal vessel despite the explosion of their own heavy cannon. Ultimately, the attack was a success, with the *Harriet Lane* captured and another Union vessel, the USS *Westfield* destroyed.

Continued service

Following the Battle of Galveston, *Bayou City* served the Confederacy in Texas waters until the conclusion of the American Civil War.

Fate of the Steamer

An advertisement for an Auction Sale in *Flake's Daily Galveston Bulletin* (Galveston, Galveston Co., TX), Sun., 24 Jun 1866, p. 5, c. 5 - Sale of Government Property - Will be sold on Tuesday, the 12th July, at 10 o'clock a.m. at the corner of Strand and Tremont streets, in the city of Galveston, the following property: Stm'r Bayou City, near Lagrange, Neches river. The engines, machinery of these boats are said to be good and can be recovered at little cost. Terms, Cash in U.S. Treasury Notes. By order of Geo. W. Dent, Supervising Agent, Treas. Dept., Alex'r N. Shipley, Government Auctioneer.

Source (edited): "http://en.wikipedia.org/wiki/CS_Bayou_City"

CS Neptune

C.S. Army Tug *Neptune* (circa 1862-1863) was a wooden tugboat taken over by the Confederate Army in about 1862 for the Texas Marine Department. She was employed as a tug, transport and lookout vessel in the vicinity of Galveston.

On 1 January 1863, during the Battle of Galveston, Confederate troops used her and the gunboat *Bayou City* in an effort to board and capture the USS *Harriet Lane*. Though the enterprise was a success, the *Neptune* was badly damaged and sank shortly afterwards.
Source (edited): "http://en.wikipedia.org/wiki/CS_Neptune"

Danish ironclad Danmark

The ***Danmark*** was an armored frigate of the Royal Danish Navy originally ordered by the Confederate States Navy.

The origins of the *Danmark* lie in efforts of the Confederate States of America to purchase warships in Europe, which is to say in the United Kingdom and France, during the American Civil War. These efforts were led by James Dunwoody Bulloch, but the *Danmark* was ordered by another Confederate agent, Lieutenant (later Commander) James H. North.

North was sent to Europe by Confederate Navy secretary Stephen Mallory with the aim of buying a completed sea-going ironclad warship, the French Navy's *Gloire*, and ordering a similar vessel on Confederate account. The French government refused to sell *Gloire*, or to allow a sister ship to be built in French shipyards.

North proceeded to Britain, where the Whig government had adopted a laissez-faire attitude to American arms-buying. Here he met with George Thompson, co-owner of the Clydebank shipbuilders J. & G. Thompson. North signed a contract with Thompson's on 21 May 1862 for an armoured frigate of some 3,000 tons and 80 metres in length, for a contract price of 190,000 pounds sterling—around two million Confederate dollars at the prevailing rate of exchange—paying a deposit of 18,000 pounds. Thompson's contracted to the deliver the ship by 1 June 1863.

Known to the Confederates as "North's ship", or as "Number 61", she was *Santa Maria* to her builders. As finally completed, she displaced 4,750 tons, a slab-sided three-masted barque. Under steam, she would make 8 knots (15 km/h; 9.2 mph).

By the summer of 1863, the Confederate agents in Europe were seeking to sell off North's ship, offering her to the Imperial Russian Navy. The ship was clearly unsuited to Confederate needs, too large a crew, and too large a ship, for their limited resources to support, and her draft of 6 metres was too deep for operations in the shoal waters on the Confederate coasts. Thompson's too were concerned that they would not be allowed to deliver the ship to the Confederates in the changed political climate and cancelled the contract in late 1863.

Work continued slowly on the ship, which was launched on 23 February 1864. The outbreak of the Second War of Schleswig led the Royal Danish Navy to purchase the ship, but delays in fitting out and working up meant that she was not ready for service before the end of the war.

The *Danmark* undertook only one active commission, from June to October 1869. At sea with her armament aboard she rolled violently, and the coal consumption of her engines was extremely high. As a result, she remained in reserve thereafter, becoming a barracks ship in 1893.

As commissioned into Danish service, she was armed with 20 60-pounder (8-inch) smoothbore muzzle-loading guns of 88 hundredweight and 8 18-pounder rifled muzzle-loading guns of 40 hundredweight. In 1865 this was changed to an all-rifled muzzle-loading armament of 12 60-pounder guns and 10 24-pounder guns. Two more 24-pounder guns were added in 1867.
Source (edited): "http://en.wikipedia.org/wiki/Danish_ironclad_Danmark"

Era No. 5

Era No. 5 — a shallow-draft steamer built in 1860 at Pittsburgh, Pennsylvania — was chartered by the Confederates early in 1863 to transport corn from the Red River to Camden, Arkansas.

As the steamer — laden with 4,500 bushels of corn — proceeded to her destination on 14 February 1863, she rounded a sharp bend 15 mi (24 km) above the mouth of the Black River, came upon and was captured by USS *Indianola*. *Era No. 5* was then assigned to Colonel Charles R. Ellet's river fleet, fitted out with protective cotton baling and used by the Union as a dispatch boat and transport in the Mississippi River.
Source (edited): "http://en.wikipedia.org/wiki/Era_No._5"

Japanese ironclad Kōtetsu

Kōtetsu (甲鉄, literally "Ironclad"), later renamed *Azuma* (東, "East") was the first ironclad warship of the Imperial Japanese Navy. Built in France in 1864, and acquired from the United States in February 1869, she was an ironclad ram warship. She had a decisive role in the Naval Battle of Hakodate Bay in May 1869, which marked the end of the Boshin War, and the complete establishment of the Meiji Restoration.

Her sister ship *Cheops* was sold to the Prussian Navy, becoming the *Prinz Adalbert*.

Origins

The *Kōtetsu* was built by shipbuilder L'Arman in Bordeaux, France. Originally named the *Sphynx*, this ship was initially built for the Confederate Navy during the American Civil War.

In June 1863 John Slidell, the Confederate commissioner to France, asked Emperor Napoleon III in a private audience if it would be possible for the Confederate government to build ironclad warships in France. Arming ships of war for a recognized belligerent like the Confederate States would have been illegal under French law, but Slidell and Confederate agent James D. Bulloch were confident that the French emperor would be able to circumvent his own laws more easily than could the British government. Napoleon III agreed to the building of ironclads in France on the condition that their destination remained a secret. The following month Bulloch entered a contract with Lucien Arman, an important French shipbuilder and a personal confidant of Napoleon III, to build a pair of ironclad rams capable of breaking the Union blockade. To avoid suspicion, the ships' guns were manufactured separately in England and they were named *Cheops* and *Sphynx* to encourage rumors that they were intended for the Egyptian navy.

Prior to delivery, however, a shipyard clerk walked into the U.S. foreign minister's office in Paris and produced documents which revealed that L'Arman had fraudulently obtained authorization to arm the ships and was in contact with Confederate agents. The French government blocked the sale under pressure from the United States, but L'Arman was able to sell the ships illegally to Denmark and Prussia, which were then fighting on opposite sides of the Second Schleswig War. The *Cheops* was sold to Prussia as the *Prinz Adalbert*, while the *Sphynx* was sold to Denmark under the name *Stærkodder*.

Manned by a Danish crew, the ship left Bordeaux for its shakedown cruise on June 21, 1864. The crew tested the vessel while final negotiations were conducted between the Danish Naval Ministry and L'Arman. Intense haggling over the final price and a disagreement over compensation from L'Arman for late delivery led to his calling off the deal on October 30. The Danish government refused to relinquish the vessel, claiming confusion in regards to the negotiations.

American career as CSS *Stonewall*

View of bow

Profile view

Closeup

On January 6, 1865 the vessel took on a Confederate crew at Copenhagen under the command of Captain T. J. Page, CSN and was recommissioned the CSS *Stonewall* while still at sea.

The arrival of the "formidable" *Stonewall* in America was dreaded by the Union, and several ships tried to intercept her, among them the USS *Kearsarge* and the USS *Sacramento*. The *Stonewall* sprung a leak, however, after leaving Quiberon, Brittany and Captain Page steamed her in to Spain for repairs. In February and March, the USS *Niagara* and the *Sacramento* kept watch from a distance as the *Sumter* lay anchored off Corunna during February 1865. On March 24, the *Stonewall* steamed out to sea, while Captain Page challenged the U.S. Navy vessels, which turned and fled, fearful to engage in the attack. Finding that the enemy had run, Captain Page steamed for Lisbon, with the intent to cross the Atlantic Ocean from there and attack at Port Royal, the base of Major General Sherman's attack on South Carolina.

The *Stonewall* reached Nassau on May 6, and then sailed on to Havana, Cuba, where Captain Page learned of the war's end. There he decided to turn her over to the Spanish Captain General of Cuba for the sum of $16,000. The vessel was then turned over to United States authorities in return for reimbursement of the same amount. She was temporarily de-commissioned, stationed at a U.S. Navy dock, until she was offered for sale to the Japanese government of the Tokugawa shogunate.

Japanese career

Kōtetsu was supposed to be delivered to the Tokugawa shogunate in 1868, in order to reinforce the ongoing modernization of its army and navy. US$30,000 had already been paid, and the remaining US$10,000 were to be paid on delivery. When the Boshin War between the shogunate and pro-Imperial forces broke out however, Western powers took a neutral stance, retrieved any military advisors they had in Japan, and stopped the delivery of military material, including the delivery of *Kōtetsu* to the shogunate. The ship actually arrived under Japanese flag, but US Resident-Minister Van Valkenburgh ordered her put back under American flag on arrival in Japan under a caretaker crew of the US naval squadron then stationed there.

Kōtetsu was finally delivered to the new Meiji government in February 1869. She was immediately put to use and dispatched with seven other steam warships to the northern island of Hokkaidō, to fight the remnant of the Shogun's forces, who were trying to form an independent Ezo Republic there, with the help of French ex-military advisors.

On March 25, 1869, in the Naval Battle of Miyako Bay, *Kōtetsu* successfully repulsed a surprise night attempt at boarding by the rebel *Kaiten* (spearheaded by survivors from the Shinsengumi), essentially thanks to the presence of a Gatling gun onboard.

The *Kōtetsu* leading the line of battle, at the Naval Battle of Hakodate.

She then participated in the invasion of Hokkaidō and various naval engagements in the Naval Battle of Hakodate Bay.

Kōtetsu was renamed *Azuma* in 1871 and remained in military service until 1888, when she was turned to non-combat harbor service.

Kōtetsu was well-armed with casemated rotating turret guns, and considered a "formidable" and "unsinkable" ship in her time. She could sustain direct hits without her armour being pierced, and prevail against any wooden warship.

In effect, Japan was thus equipped with advanced ironclad warships only ten years after the launch of the first ocean-going ironclad warship in history, the French Navy's *La Gloire* ("Glory", launched in 1859).

Source (edited): "http://en.wikipedia.org/wiki/Japanese_ironclad_K%C5%8Dtetsu"

Laurent Millaudon (1856)

Laurent Millaudon was a wooden sidewheel river steamboat launched at Cincinnati, Ohio, in 1856 operating in the New Orleans, Louisiana area, and captained by W.S. Whann. At the beginning of the American Civil War she was taken into service by the Confederate Navy as **CSS *General Sterling Price***. On 6 June 1862, she was sunk at the Battle of Memphis. She was raised and repaired by the Union army, and on 16 June 1862 was moved into Union service as **USS *General Price*** and served until the end of the war. (Dictionary of American Naval Fighting Ships 1968 p525)

CSS General Sterling Price

CSS *General Sterling Price*, often referred to as *General Price* or *Price*, was built as *Laurent Millaudon*, (or *L. Millandon* or *Milledon*) at Cincinnati, Ohio, in 1856. She was acquired for Confederate service and fitted out at New Orleans, Louisiana, for the River Defense Fleet (See DANFS appendix II) and was renamed after the confederate general Sterling Price. On 25 January 1862, Captain Montgomery began to convert her into a cottonclad ram by placing a 4-inch oak sheath with a 1-inch iron covering on her bow, and by installing double pine bulkheads filled with compressed cotton bales. (This evidently increased her displacement from the 483 tons specified for the Laurent Millaudon to the 633 tons specified for the *General Price*.) On 25 March, *General Price* commanded by Capt. J. H. Townsend, sailed from New Orleans to Memphis, Tennessee, where she stayed until 10 April having her ironwork completed. She was then sent to Fort Pillow, Tennessee, where she operated in defense of the river approaches to Memphis.

On 10 May 1862, off Fort Pillow, *General Price* under First Officer J. E. Henthorne (or Harthorne), in company with seven other vessels under Captain Montgomery attacked the ironclad gunboats of the Union Mississippi River Squadron. In the action of Plum Point Bend, which followed, the Confederate ram USS *General Bragg* struck USS *Cincinnati* halting her retreat. This allowed *General Price* to violently ram the Federal gunboat, taking away her rudder, stern post, and a large piece of her stern, decisively disabling her. At the same time *General Price's* well directed fire silenced Federal Mortar boat No. 16, which was being guarded by *Cincinnati*. *General Price* was heavily hit in this action. Her upper works were severely damaged, and she was struck by a 128-pound shell which cut off her supply pipes and caused a dangerous leak.

Destruction of the Confederate force at the Battle of Memphis. The CSS *General Sterling Price* is the ship directly behind the bow of the closest ship (?)

The Confederates quickly repaired *General Price* and later she participated with Montgomery's force in holding off Federal vessels until Fort Pillow was successfully evacuated on 1 June. The Confederate vessels then fell back on Memphis to take coal.

Following the Federal capture of Fort Pillow, Flag Officer Charles H. Davis USN, commanding the Mississippi River Squadron, pressed on without delay and appeared off Memphis with a superior force on 6 June. Montgomery, unable to retreat to Vicksburg, Mississippi because of his shortage of fuel, and unwilling to destroy his boats, determined to fight against heavy odds. In the ensuing Battle of Memphis, *General Price* charged the Federal ram USS *Monarch* but instead collided with the Confederate ram CSS *General Beauregard*, also attacking *Monarch*. *General Price* lost her wheel and was disabled. While the two Confederate vessels were entangled, Federal rams attacked them mercilessly. *General Price* collided with the Federal ram USS *Queen of the West* under Col. Charles Ellet, Jr., USA, commander of the two rams of the Davis Flotilla. As *Queen of the West* captured her crew, *General Price* sank slowly onto a sand bar. She was later raised by the Union army and taken into Federal service.

USS General Price

USS *General Price* was a cottonclad river ram and gunboat in the United States Navy during the American Civil War. She was formerly a Confederate ram named **CSS *General Sterling Price*** that was sunk and captured during the battle of Memphis on 6 June 1862 by Union naval forces under Flag Officer Charles H. Davis. After the Union victory, she was raised by the Union army and taken to Cairo, Illinois for repairs. She was moved into the Union service under Lt. LeRoy Fitch on 16 June 1862 and was moved to Cairo for repairs. The ram was formally transferred to the Navy by Quartermaster H. A. Wise at Cairo on 30 September 1862. Although at that time she was renamed **USS *General Price***, she continued to be referred to as *General Sterling Price* in Union dispatches.

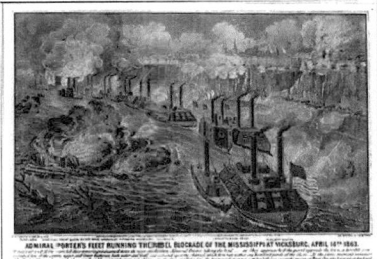

Lithograph of the Mississippi River Squadron running the Confederate blockade at Vicksburg on 16 April 1863. The lead ship is the flagship USS *Benton* with a coal tender, followed by USS *Lafayette* with *General Price* lashed to her starboard (right) side.

Completing repairs and conversion at Cairo on 11 March 1863, *General Price* departed for duty with the Mississippi River Squadron, arriving at Black Bayou a few days later, to join in the Union's Vicksburg campaign. The commander of the squadron, Rear Admiral David Dixon Porter was at that time attempting to move up the shallow and overgrown Steele's Bayou on the Mississippi river in a move to cut off Vicksburg Mississippi from the rear, and *General Price* joined the expedition. After several days of slow and difficult progress, harassed by Confederate troops, the gunboats were forced to withdraw on 22 March 1863. General Ulysses S. Grant and Admiral Porter then conceived a plan to attack Vicksburg from the south. This would require the Mississippi squadron to slip past the Confederate blockade of the river at Vicksburg in order to defend and transport Grant's army across the Mississippi south of the city. As a member of Admiral Porter's flotilla, *General Price* ran the Confederate blockade at Vicksburg on 16 April 1863. Lashed to the starboard side of the ironclad USS *Lafayette* during the run, she suffered little damage, and arrived safely at New Carthage, Louisiana early the next day with the rest of the fleet. Porter was then in a position to assault Grand Gulf, Mississippi, and, during the heavy engagement with the batteries there on 29 April and 3 May 1863, *General Price*, under the command of Commander Selim E. Woodworth, carried troops across the river and conveyed transports under fire. The Confederacy was forced to evacuate this vital point on the river, and the fate of Vicksburg was sealed.

General Price departed Grand Gulf for the Red River on 3 May and took part in the capture of Alexandria, Louisiana, and assisted in the partial destruction of Fort De Russy, Louisiana between 3 May and 17 May. During this period, *General Price* acted briefly as Admiral Porter's flagship, and on 10 May she was sent on a reconnaissance up the Black River, where she engaged strong Confederate batteries at Harrisonburg, Louisiana. On 22 June 1863 the Sterling price received 8 replacements to augment the 12 aboard that were fit for duty, the remainder of the crew being ill.

As Union pressure against Vicksburg mounted, *General Price* played a major part in the continuing bombardment of the city and in gunfire support of the Union troops until the Confederacy's river stronghold finally surrendered on 4 July. She was at Bayou Sara, Louisiana below Vicksburg on 7 July 1863 and was in Memphis on 16 July and left there for Cairo and much-needed repairs, which were not completed until about 19 November.

General Price rejoined the squadron at Memphis on 2 December 1863 and soon became part of Rear Admiral Porter's planned expedition up the Red River. Before joining Porter, she accidentally rammed the USS *Conestoga* on 8 March 1864 after a confusion in whistle signals, causing the latter ship to sink quickly as a total loss. Accompanying the Red River expedition as far as Alexandria, Louisiana, *General Price* returned to the mouth of the river on 6 April convoying transports.

She then took up regular cruising station on the lower Mississippi River, protecting transports, landing reconnaissance parties, and keeping the river free from Confederate guerrillas. While on this duty, she engaged a Confederate battery off Tunic Bend, Louisiana on 19 May forced it to withdraw, and landed a shore party which burned the Confed-

List of ships of the Confederate States Navy

Confederate States Navy (CSN) Department Seal

This is a list of ships of the Confederate States Navy (CSN), used by the Confederate States of America during the American Civil War between 1861 and 1865. Included are some types of civilian vessels, such as blockade runners, steamboats, and privateers which contributed to the war efforts by the CSN. Also included are special types of floating batteries and harbor defense craft.

CSN Warships

The Secretary of the CS Navy, Stephen Mallory, was very aggressive on a limited budget in a land-focused war, and developed a two-pronged warship strategy of building ironclad warships for coastal and national defense, and commerce raiding cruisers, supplemented with exploratory use of special weapons such as torpedo boats and torpedoes.

Batteries

Based upon the successful employment of ironclad warships, particularly batteries, at the Battle of Kinburn, Britain and France decided to focus on armor plated warships, starting with coastal battery designs. Initial ocean-going ironclad cruisers, such as the French battleship *La Gloire* and the British battleship HMS *Warrior* were only just emerging in 1859 and 1860, and were beyond the budget and timeline necessary for rapid force deployment that the CS Navy needed for immediate coastal defenses in 1861.

Therefore, the Confederate Congress voted $2 million in May 1861 to buy ironclads from overseas, and in July and August started work on construction and converting wooden ships locally. On 12 October 1861, the CSS *Manassas* became the first ironclad to enter battle when she fought Union warships on the Mississippi. In February 1862, the even larger CSS *Virginia* joined the Confederate Navy, having been built at Norfolk. The Confederacy built a number of ships designed as versions of the CSS *Virginia*, of which several saw action. In the failed attack on Charleston on April 7, 1863 two small ironclads, CSS *Palmetto State* and CSS *Chicora* participated in the successful defense of the harbor. For the later attack at Mobile Bay, the Union faced the CSS *Tennessee*, the Confederacy's most powerful ironclad.

Ironclad steam-powered batteries

The CS Navy ironclad steamer batteries were all designed for national coastal defense.

- CSS *Albemarle* twin-screw steamer, ironclad, sunk: Oct 28, 1864
- CSS *Arkansas* twin-screw steamer, ironclad ram, destroyed: Aug 5, 1862
- CSS *Atlanta* triple-screw steamer, ironclad, captured: Jun 17, 1863
- CSS *Baltic* surrendered: May 10, 1865
- CSS *Charleston* steamer, ironclad, destroyed: Feb 18, 1865
- CSS *Chicora* steamer, ironclad ram, destroyed: Feb 18, 1865
- CSS *Columbia* single screw steamer, ironclad ram, captured: Apr 26, 1865
- CSS *Eastport* incomplete, captured: Feb 8, 1862
- CSS *Fredericksburg* twin-screw steamer, ironclad ram, destroyed: Apr 4, 1865
- CSS *Georgia* ironclad steam battery, scuttled: Dec 21, 1864
- CSS *Huntsville* ironclad steam battery, scuttled: Apr 12, 1865
- CSS *Louisiana* twin screw and double center-wheel steamer, ironclad, destroyed: Apr 28, 1862
- CSS *Manassas* screw steamer, ironclad ram, sunk: Apr 24, 1862
- CSS *Milledgeville* steamer ironclad, burned/sunk: Dec 21, 1864
- CSS *Mississippi I* 3-screw steamer, ironclad, burned: Apr 25, 1862
- CSS *Missouri* steam sloop, ironclad, surrendered: Jun 3, 1865
- CSS *Mobile* screw steamer, burned before launching: May 21, 1863
- CSS *Muscogee* twin-screw with center-wheel steamer, ironclad, burned: Apr 17, 1865
- CSS *Nashville* side-wheel steamer, ironclad, surrendered: May 10, 1865
- CSS *Neuse* twin-screw steamer, ironclad, destroyed: Mar 14, 1865
- CSS *New Orleans* floating steam battery, sunk
- CSS *North Carolina II* steamer, ironclad, accidentally sank: Sep 27, 1864
- CSS *Palmetto State* sloop, ironclad, destroyed: 18 Feb 1865
- CSS *Raleigh* sloop, ironclad, wrecked: May 7, 1864
- CSS *Richmond* screw steamer, ironclad, scuttled: Apr 3, 1865
- CSS *Savannah* steam sloop ironclad, burned: Dec 21, 1864
- CSS *Tennessee I* ironclad ram, destroyed before launching: Jun 5, 1862
- CSS *Tennessee II* single screw steamer, ironclad, captured: Aug 5, 1864
- CSS *Texas* twin-screw steamer, ironclad ram, never completed, captured Apr 4, 1865

- CSS *Tuscaloosa* ironclad steam battery, scuttled: Apr 12, 1865
- CSS *Virginia* screw steamer, ironclad ram, destroyed: May 11, 1862
- CSS *Virginia II* ironclad, destroyed: Apr 4, 1865
- CSS *Wilmington* twin-screw steamer, ironclad, destroyed before completion: Jan 1865

Ironclad floating batteries

CS Navy ironclad floating batteries lacked steam engines for propulsion and were towed into firing positions.
- CSS *Arctic* ironclad floating battery, burned: 1865
- CSS *Phoenix* ironclad floating battery, destroyed: 1865

Wooden floating batteries

CS Navy wooden floating batteries were towed into firing positions, and as in the case at Charleston Harbor, used for makeshift defense.
- Floating Battery of Charleston Harbor
- CSS *Memphis* floating battery

Cruisers

CS Navy cruisers were ocean-going ships designed primarily for the Confederate Navy's strategy of *guerre de course*. Confederate States Navy cruisers were typically lightly armed, with a couple of large guns or a pivot gun, and often very fast. The Navy planned to add ironclad cruisers to their fleet, successfully procuring one, but too late to be of benefit for the war.

Wooden cruisers

- CSS *Alabama* screw steamer, sloop-of-war, built in Birkenhead, England by John Laird Sons and Company, sunk: Jun 19, 1864
- CSS *Alexandra* - screw steamer, bark-rigged, built in Liverpool, England, seized before delivery: April 5, 1863
- *America* racing yacht, scuttled: 1862
- CSS *Archer* schooner, captured: Jun 28, 1863
- CSS *Caleb Cushing* revenue cutter, burned: Jun 28, 1863

- CSS *Chickamauga* screw steamer, burned
- CSS *Clarence* brig, burned: Jun 12, 1863
- CSS *Florida* screw steamer, sloop, captured: Oct 7, 1864
- CSS *Georgia* screw steamer, iron, sold: Jun 1, 1864
- CSS *Georgiana* steamer, destroyed: after Mar 20, 1863
- CSS *Lapwing* bark, burned: Jun 20, 1863
- CSS *Nashville* side-wheel steamer, brig rigged, sold: 1862
- CSS *Rappahannock* screw steamer, sloop-of-war, turned over at war's end
- CSS *Shenandoah* screw steamer, full rigged, iron-framed, turned over to British Government
- CSS *Sumter* screw steamer, sloop, sold: Dec 19, 1862
- CSS *Tacony* bark, burned: Jun 25, 1863
- CSS *Tallahassee* twin-screw steamer, sloop, seized: Apr 9, 1865 by British Government
- CSS *Tuscaloosa* bark, seized: Dec 29, 1863
- CSS *United States* frigate, sail, harbor defense use only, scuttled

Ironclad cruisers

But the CS Navy attempts to procure ironclad cruisers from overseas were frustrated as European nations confiscated ships being built for the Confederacy. Only the CSS *Stonewall* was completed and successfully delivered, and she arrived in American waters just in time for the end of the war.
- CSS *North Carolina I* - seized Oct 1863 and commissioned as HMS *Scorpion*
- CSS *Mississippi II* - seized Oct 1863 and commissioned as HMS *Wivern*
- CSS *Stonewall* twin-screw steamer, brig rigged, ironclad, sold to Japan after capture by Union and renamed Kōtetsu
- *Cheops* - sister to CSS *Stonewall*, built in France and sold to Prussia Oct 29, 1865 and named SMS *Prinz Adalbert*
- Ironclad Frigate No. 61, arranged by Captain James H. North, CSN, sold to Denmark, commissioned as HDMS *Danmark*

Gunboats
- CSS *Appomattox* tugboat, burned: Feb 10, 1862
- CSS *Bartwo* schooner
- CSS *Bayou City*
- CSS *Beaufort* screw steamer, burned: Apr 4, 1865
- CSS *Bienville* side-wheel steamer, destroyed: 1862
- CSS *Black Warrior* schooner, burned Feb 10, 1862
- CSS *Bombshell* steamer, captured: May 5, 1864
- CSS *Calhoun* side-wheel gunboat, captured: Jan 23, 1862
- CSS *Carondelet* side-wheel steamer, destroyed: 1862
- CSS *Chattahoochee* twin-screw steamer, scuttled: Dec, 1864
- CSS *Clifton* side-wheel gunboat, Texas Marine Department, scuttled March 1864
- CSS *Curlew* side-wheel river steamer, sunk: Feb 7, 1862
- CSS *De Soto* side-wheel steamer, captured: Sep 30, 1862
- CSS *Defiance* river steamer, destroyed: Apr 28, 1862
- CSS *Diana* steamer, burned: Apr 12, 1863
- CSS *Drewry* steamer, tender, destroyed: Jan 24, 1865
- CSS *Ellis* steamer, tugboat, captured: Feb 10, 1862
- CSS *Equator* steamer, burned: 1865
- CSS *Fanny* screw steamer, iron hull, burned: Feb 10, 1862
- CSS *Fashion* schooner
- CSS *Forrest* steamer, tugboat, burned: Feb 10, 1862
- CSS *Fulton*
- CSS *Gaines* side-wheel steamer
- CSS *General Quitman* steamer, destroyed: Apr 24, 1862
- CSS *General Polk* steamer, destroyed: Jun 26, 1862
- CSS *George Page* side-wheel river steamer, burned
- CSS *Germantown* sloop-of-war, burned
- CSS *Governor Moore* side-wheel steamer, schooner rigged, destroyed

- Apr 23, 1862
- CSS *Hampton* screw steamer, burned: Apr 4, 1865
- CSS *Harmony* steamer, tug
- CSS *Henry Dodge* cutter, schooner rigged
- CSS *Huntress* side-wheel steamer
- CSS *Isondiga* steamer, burned: Dec 21, 1864
- CSS *Ivy* side-wheel river steamer, burned: 1863
- CSS *J. A. Cotton* side-wheel river steamer, burned: Jan 1863
- CSS *Jackson* side-wheel river steamer, tug, sunk
- CSS *Jamestown* side-wheel steamer, sunk: May, 1862
- CSS *Junaluska* steamer, tug, dismantled: 1862
- CSS *Kate Bruce* schooner, scuttled
- CSS *Lady Davis*, steamer tug, iron, machinery mounted in CSS *Palmetto*
- CSS "Launch No. 3 steamer, captured: Apr, 1862
- CSS "Launch No. 6 steamer, destroyed: Apr 24, 1862
- CSS *Livingston* side-wheel steamer, destroyed: Jun 26, 1862
- CSS *Macon* steamer
- CSS *Matilda* bark
- CSS *Maurepas* side-wheel steamer, sunk: June, 1862
- CSS *McRae* screw steamer, sloop rigged, sunk: Apr 28, 1862
- CSS *Morgan* side-wheel steamer, surrender: 1865
- CSS *Morgan* cutter
- CSS *Morning Light* sail, burned: Jan 23, 1863
- CSS *Nansemond* twin-screw gunboat, burned: Apr 3, 1865
- CSS *Neptune* steamer, sunk: Jan 1, 1863
- CSS *Nina* steamer
- CSS *Oregon* steamer, scuttled: Apr, 1862
- CSS *Pamlico* side-wheel river steamer, burned: 1862
- CSS *Patrick Henry* side-wheel steamer, CSNA school ship, burned: Apr 4, 1865
- CSS *Pedee* screw steamer, sunk: 1865
- CSS *Pickens* cutter, schooner rigged

- CSS *Plymouth* sloop-of-war, burned: 1862
- CSS *Polk* side-wheel river steamer, burned
- CSS *Pontchartrain* side-wheel steamer, burned: 1863
- CSS *Raleigh* steamer
- CSS *Rappahannock* side-wheel steamer, burned: Apr, 1862
- CSS *Rattlesnake* steamer, destroyed: Feb 28, 1863
- CSS *Rescue* cutter, schooner rigged
- CSS *Resolute* burned: Apr 24, 1862
- CSS *Roanoke* screw steamer, destroyed: Apr 4, 1865
- CSS *Queen of the West*
- CSS *Sampson* side-wheel river steamer
- CSS *Savannah* steamer, foundered: Aug 18, 1863
- CSS *Sea Bird* side-wheel river steamer, sunk: Feb 10, 1862
- CSS *Selma* side-wheel steamer, captured: Aug 5, 1864
- CSS *Spray* steam tug, sunk
- CSS *St. Mary* side-wheel river steamer, burned
- CSS *Stono* burned: 1865
- CSS *Talomico* side-wheel steamer, sunk: 1863
- CSS *Teaser* tug, captured: 1862
- CSS '"Tiger
- CSS *Torpedo* screw steamer, tug/tender, iron, burned: Apr 4, 1865
- CSS *Tropic*
- CSS *Tuscarora* side-wheel steamer, burned
- CSS *Velocity*
- CSS *Washington* schooner
- CSS *Water Witch* side-wheel steamer, burned: Dec 19, 1864
- CSS *Winslow* side-wheel river steamer, wrecked
- CSS *Yadkin* steamer, burned: 1865

Torpedo boats

- CSS *David*
- CSS *David II* - larger version of David, captured incomplete: Feb, 1865
- CSS *Midge* steam torpedo boat, captured: Feb, 1865
- CSS *Saint Patrick* semi-submersible torpedo boat
- CSS *Squire*
- CSS *Squib* spar torpedo boat

- CSS *Hornet* spar torpedo boat
- CSS *Scorpion* spar torpedo boat
- CSS *Wasp* spar torpedo boat

CSN Support ships

Government blockade runners

- CSS *Advance* side-wheel steamer, captured: September 10, 1864
- CSS *Florida* screw steamer
- CSS *Harriet Lane* side-wheel steamer
- CSS *Kate Dale*
- CSS *Lady Stirling* side-wheel steamer, captured: Oct 28, 1864
- CSS *Owl*
- CSS *Rob Roy*
- CSS *Robert E. Lee*
- CSS *William G. Hewes* (later SS *Ella and Annie*), captured: Nov 9, 1863

Government steamers

- CSS *Admiral* side-wheel river steamer, captured: April 7, 1862
- CSS *Atlanta*
- CSS *Appomattox* screw steamer, burned: Feb 10, 1862
- CSS *Beaufort*
- CSS *Beauregard* side-wheel coastal steamer, captured: Dec, 1864
- CSS *Capitol* side-wheel river steamer burned: Jun 28, 1862
- CSS *Champion* side-wheel river steamer, captured: April 7, 1862
- CSS *Curlew*
- CSS *Ellis*
- CSS *Fanny*
- CSS *George Page*
- CSS *Governor Moore*
- CSS *Grampus* stern-wheel river steamer, scuttled: Apr 7, 1862
- CSS *Grand Duke*
- CSS *Ida* side-wheel coastal steamer, captured/burned: Dec 10, 1864
- CSS *Jamestown*
- CSS *Nashville* - 1861
- CSS *Ohio Belle* side-wheel river steamer, captured: April 7, 1862
- CSS *Patrick Henry*
- CSS *Prince* side-wheel river steamer, sunk: April 7, 1862
- CSS *Raleigh* - 1861
- CSS *Red Rover* side-wheel river steamer, captured: April 7, 1862
- CSS *Sea Bird*
- CSS *Selman*

- CSS *Tennessee* side-wheel steamer, captured: January, 1862
- CSS *Winchester* side-wheel river steamer, captured: April 7, 1862

Government transports
- CSS *Bombshell*
- CSS *City of Vicksburg* - side-wheel steamer transport, damaged then destroyed: Feb/Mar 1863
- CSS *Cotton Plant*
- CSS *Darlington*
- CSS *Mars* side-wheel river steamer, captured: April 7, 1862
- CSS *The Planter* side-wheel steamer, captured by its slave pilot, 13 May 1862
- CSS *Sumter*
- CSS *Yazoo* side-wheel river steamer, sunk: April 7, 1862

Cutters
- CSS *Duane* revenue cutter, schooner rigged
- CSS *Lewis Cass* revenue cutter, schooner rigged
- CSS *Manassas* revenue cutter, schooner rigged, dismantled
- CSS *Robert McClelland* revenue cutter, schooner rigged

Hospital ships
- CSS *Kanawha Valley* stern-wheel river steamer, burned: April 7, 1862

Tenders and tugs
- CSS *Alert* lighthouse tender, schooner rigged
- CSS *Beaufort* tugboat
- CSS *Caswell* side-wheel steamer tender, burned
- CSS *Firefly* side-wheel steamer tender, burned: Dec 21, 1864
- CSS *Indian Chief* receiving ship, burned
- CSS *Resolute* side-wheel steamer, tugboat, captured: Dec 12, 1864
- CSS *Retribution* steam tugboat, sold: Mar 8, 1863
- CSS *Satellite* tugboat, destroyed: August, 1863
- CSS *Shrapnel* tender, burned: Apr 4, 1865
- CSS *St. Philip* receiving ship, sunk
- CSS *Uncle Ben* steam tugboat, machinery mounted into CSS *North Carolina II*

Civilian auxiliary
Privateers
- *A.C. Gunnison* privateer steam tug
- *Beauregard* privateer cutter, schooner rigged, sunk: Jul 28, 1861
- *Calhoun* privateer side-wheel steamer, burned: 1862
- *Dixie* privateer schooner, captured: Apr 15, 1862
- *Gibralter* privateer schooner
- *Governor A. Mouton* privateer steamer, captured: May 11, 1862
- *Isabella* privateer screw steamer
- *J. M. Chapman* privateer schooner, captured: March 15, 1863
- *J. O. Nixon* privateer schooner
- *Jefferson Davis* privateer brig, ran aground: mid-August, 1861
- *Judah* privateer schooner, destroyed: Sep 14, 1861
- *Lorton* privateer schooner
- *Mariner* privateer screw steamer
- *Music* privateer steamer
- *Sallie* privateer schooner
- *Savannah* privateer schooner, captured: Jun 3, 1861
- *Sealine* privateer brig
- *Theodora* privateer side-wheel steamer
- *V. H. Ivy* privateer steamer
- *York* privateer pilot boat, schooner rigged, burned: Aug 9, 1861

Privateer submersible torpedo boats
- Bayou St. John Confederate Submarine
- *H. L. Hunley* hand-cranked, sunk: Feb 17, 1864
- *Pioneer*

Civilian steamers
- SS *Dick Keys* captured: May 7, 1861
- SS *Lewis* captured: May 7, 1861
- SS *Swan* of Savannah

Civilian transports
- Berwick Bay
- *Era No. 5* - shallow-draft steamer, captured: Feb 14, 1863

Civilian blockade runners
- *Caroline* (a.k.a. USS *Arizona*)
- SS *Bat* side-wheel steamship, captured: Oct 10, 1864
- SW *Colonel Lamb* side-wheel steamer
- SW *Constance Decimer* (a.k.a. *Constance*)
- SW *Flamingo*
- PS *Lelia*
- SW *Mary Bowers*
- *Memphis* (later USS *Memphis*)
- *Monticello*, Cuban blockade runner
- SS *Norseman*
- SW *Ruby*
- *San Quintin*, Cuban blockade runner
- SW *Stonewall Jackson* (ex-SW *Leopard*)

Foreign blockade runners
- *Denbigh* (ship) side-wheel steamer, schooner rigged

CS Army
CSA cotton-clads
Used for river defense, CS Army cottonclads were typically more lightly armored and reinforced than a regular ironclad, such as the CSS *General Sterling Price*, which was converted by placing a 4-inch oak sheath with a 1-inch iron covering on her bow, and by installing double pine bulkheads filled with compressed cotton bales. Many of the cottonclads were outfitted with rams.

River Defense Fleet cotton-clads:
- CSS *Colonel Lovell* side-wheel steamer, cotton-clad ram, sunk: Jun 6, 1862
- CSS *General Beauregard* steamer, cotton-clad ram, sunk: Jun 6, 1862
- CSS *General Bragg* steamer, cotton-clad ram, captured: Jun 6, 1862
- CSS *Breckinridge* stern-wheel steamer, cotton-clad ram, burned: Apr, 1862
- CSS *Defiance* side-wheel steamer, cotton-clad ram, burned: 1862
- CSS *General Earl Van Dorn* steamer, cotton-clad ram, burned
- CSS *General M. Jeff Thompson* steamer, cotton-clad ram, sunk: June 6, 1862
- CSS *General Sterling Price* steamer, cotton-clad ram, sunk: Jun 6, 1862
- CSS *General Sumter* steamer, cotton-clad ram, captured: Jun 6 1862

- CSS *Governor Moore* steamer, schooner rigged, cotton-clad ram, destroyed: Apr 24, 1862
- CSS *Little Rebel* steamer, cotton-clad ram, captured: Jun 6, 1862
- CSS *Resolute* side-wheel steamer, cotton-clad ram
- CSS *Stonewall Jackson* side-wheel steamer, cotton-clad ram, burned: Apr 24, 1862
- CSS *Warrior* side-wheel steamer, cotton-clad ram, destroyed: Apr, 1862

Other CS Army cotton-clads:
- CSS *Grand Duke* steamer, cotton-clad, burned: 1863
- CSS *Josiah A. Bell* steamer, cotton-clad, operated by Texas Marine Department
- CSS *Queen of the West* river steamer, cotton-clad and ironclad ram, exploded: Apr 14, 1863
- CSS *Uncle Ben* steamer, cotton-clad, operated by Texas Marine Department
- CSS *Webb* river steamer, cotton-clad ram, transferred to CS Navy early 1865, burned: Apr, 1865

Other CSA boats
- CSA *Bayou City* - CS Army gunboat, side-wheel steamer
- CSA *General Lee* - CS Army transport
- CSA *John Simonds* - CS Army support ship, side-wheel steamer, sunk: Apr 7, 1862
- CSA *Louisville* - CS Army cargo steamer, captured: Jul 13, 1863
- CSA *Planter* - CS Army transport, side-wheel steamer, surrendered: May 13, 1862
- CSA *Neptune* - CS Army tugboat, sank: Jan 1, 1863

Other

Prizes
- *Alvarado* - prize bark, captured: by privateer *Jefferson Davis*, July 21, 1861
- *Enchantress* - prize schooner, captured: by privateer *Jefferson Davis* July 6, 1861

Undetermined
- CSS *Segar*
- CSS *Smith*
- CSS *St. Nicholas*
- CSS *W. R. Miles*

Source (edited): "http://en.wikipedia.org/wiki/List_of_ships_of_the_Confederate_States_Navy"

Monticello (privateer)

The **Monticello** was a Confederate blockade runner during the American Civil War. She was a two-masted schooner out of Havana, Cuba and of unknown nationality. She ran ashore about 6 to 8 miles east of Fort Morgan and the main inlet to Mobile Bay in Alabama on June 26, 1862, after sailing from Havana, and was then set on fire by the crew to prevent her capture. A landing party from the USS *Kanawha* attempted to board the vessel, but were driven off by Confederate soldiers firing from nearby on the shore. Her length was 136 feet. She was likely cruising just off shore along the Swash Channel when she ran aground.

Some experts believe that a wreck uncovered by Hurricane Ike on Fort Morgan Road in Fort Morgan, Alabama may be the *Monticello*.

Source (edited): "http://en.wikipedia.org/wiki/Monticello_(privateer)"

PS *Alfred* (1863)

PS *Alfred* was a passenger vessel operated under the name **P.S. *Prince Arthur*** by the London and North Western Railway and the Lancashire and Yorkshire Railway from 1871 to 1877.

History

Ordered by the Bristol General Steam Navigation Company, but before she was put into service she was purchased in May 1864 by George Campbell and Henry Collis, acting for the Virginia Importing and Exporting Company. She was renamed *Old Dominion* and used as a Blockade runner.

She arrived at Wilmington, North Carolina on 28 June 1864 from Bermuda, sailed back on 15 July 1864. A second voyage from Bermuda saw her arrive on 10 August 1864 again in Wilmington, North Carolina. She was used in the blockade running until February 1865. She made six successful runs through the blockade.

On her return to the UK, she was reregistered as **P.S. *Sheffield*** for the Liverpool and Dublin Steam Navigation Company.

In 1867 she was bought by Lancashire and Yorkshire Railway and London and North-Western Railway and renamed **P.S. *Prince Arthur*** for their Fleetwood to Belfast and Londonderry service.

She was sold by the Lancashire and Yorkshire Railway in 1877 to T. Seed in Liverpool.

Source (edited): "http://en.wikipedia.org/wiki/PS_Alfred_(1863)"

SS Rob Roy

The **CSS Rob Roy** was a Confederate blockade runner which, commanded by Captain William Watson, ran to and from Bermuda, the Bahamas and Cuba from 1862 to 1864, during the American Civil War.

Watson, who had immigrated from Great Britain several years before, had originally enlisted in the Confederate Army as a sergeant before being wounded at the Battle of Corinth, and discharged due to his injuries. Hiring out a schooner, commissioned as the *Rob Roy*, Williams would bring in desperately needed supplies into blockaded southern ports, specifically Galveston, Texas before selling the ship after financial disagreements with business associates. Williams would later write about his wartime naval career in an autobiography *The Civil War Adventures of a Blockade Runner* in 1892.

Source (edited): "http://en.wikipedia.org/wiki/SS_Rob_Roy"

SS *Scotia* (1847)

PS *Scotia* was a paddle steamer passenger vessel operated by the Chester and Holyhead Railway from 1847 to 1858, and the London and North Western Railway from 1859 to 1861.

History

She was built in Blackwall Yard, London by Money and Wigrams in 1847 for the Chester & Holyhead Railway Company for a passenger service between Holyhead and Kingstown (Dun Laoghaire) and Howth.

From 1858 to 1859 she was loaned to the Scilly Isles Steam Navigation Company until their new ship the SS Little Western was ready.

She was transferred in 1859 to the London & North Western Railway Company. At Liverpool in December 1861, she was sold as a Blockade runner and she made four runs and on the fifth attempting to reach Charleston she was captured by the Federals on 24 October 1862 at Bull's Bay, South Carolina.

By 23 January 1863, she had been sold and was registered at New York as the PS *General Banks*. By then end of 1863 she had again been sold a number of times and ended up registered at Nassau as the PS *Fanny and Jenny*.

She made two more runs against the Blockade but was driven ashore by the USS Florida on Wrightsville Beach, Masonboro Inlet, North Carolina on 10 February 1864.

Source (edited): "http://en.wikipedia.org/wiki/SS_Scotia_(1847)"

Spanish cruiser Tornado

The **Tornado**, was a 2100-ton and maneuverable at 13 knots bark-rigged screw steam cruiser of the Spanish Navy, first launched at Clydebank, Scotland in 1863, as the Confederate raider *CSS Texas*. She is most famous for having captured the North American filibustering ship *Virginius*, which led to the Virginius Affair and to the Spanish-American Crisis of 1873.

Design and construction

She was built as the Confederate raider *CSS Texas* but was seized by the British Government in 1863 and acquired in 1865. She was purchased by the Chilean government for 75,000 Pounds, through Isaac Campbell & Co, in February 1866. Being *officially* known as both the *Texas* and the *Canton*, she was later given the name *Pampero* in an attempt to conceal her true identity.

Body plan of CSS Alabama.

In early 1862, Lt. George T. Sinclair was sent to England, with orders to build a *clipper propellor for cruising purposes*, and to take command of her when she was ready for sea. His instructions were to confer with Commander Bulloch in Liverpool, as to the design of the vessel, and the building, fitting out and arming of her. Bulloch received orders to help Sinclair with funds and advice. He showed Sinclair the drawings and specifications for the CSS Alabama, also the contract with Lairds, and they both decided to use these as a basis for the new cruiser.

What Sinclair did was to arrange, with the help of the Southern diplomat James M. Mason, for an issue of bonds, each equal to twenty-five bales of cotton, weight 12,500 pounds. Seven individuals took up these bonds, and were effectively the owners of this new vessel. The new cruiser was contracted by James and George Thomson of Glasgow, in October of 1862. The same firm that was contracted to build an ironclad ram for Lt. North. The *Pampero* was modelled on the Alabama, even though she was somewhat larger.

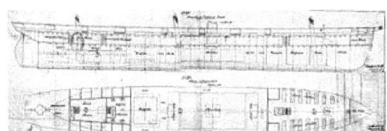

A plan showing body plan, upper deck, hold and platforms of the CSS Alabama, sister ship of the Tornado.

The *Pampero* was to be 231 feet in length, 33 feet in breadth, powered by both sail and steam. Bark rigged, she was equipped for cruising under canvas or steam, with telescopic funnels, and a raiseable screw. Similar, but larger engines to the Alabama were placed below the waterline for protection. Her frame was iron, with a mixture of iron and wood for the planking. Her armament was to be three 8-inch pivot guns, and a broadside battery of four or more guns. The original contract called for the Pampero to be ready fo sea by July of 1863, but the schedule could not be maintained. Guns and gun carriages were ordered, and Sinclair received £10,000 ($40,000) from Bulloch, and perhaps more. For his crew, Sinclair made arrangements for some men to come out from Baltimore. By the spring of 1863 Sinclair was becoming very concerned about the *Pampero*, and feared that the British Government would not permit the departure of any vessel suspected to be Confederate.

He visited Paris to duscuss with John Slidell the possibility of transferring the vessel to France. Slidell suggested Hamburg in Germany would be a better alernative. However, Sinclair investigated this, but did not proceed with it. Meanwhile the completion of the *Pampero* was further delayed by labour troubles, and the seizure of the *Alexandria*, another Confederate vessel in production at Lairds, by the British Government. The Alexandria trial was indecisive, and Mason put off the launching of the Pampero *until a final verdict was reached*.

The *Pampero* herself first came to the attention of Thomas H. Dudley, United States Consul in Liverpool, in the spring of 1863, when he made an investigative tour of Northern England andd Scotland, looking for any warships being built for the Confederates. He learned that Thomsons were building a screw steamer "of about 1500 tons," designed for great speed. He was told that she was to have an angle-iron frame and teak planking, and he found that among the workmen it was geneally believed that she was for the South.

On his next trip to Scotland in August 1863, his suspicions increased as new details on the vessel came to light. The builders insisted that the boat was for the Turkish Government, but Dudley`s informants in the yard insisted the boat was for the South, being supervised by the same men as those who supervised the building of the ironclad ram. Dudley left behind a spy in Thomsons yard, who soon reported that the vessel was rigged in the same manner as the Alabama, the drawings of which, he was told, were in Glasgow.

The Pampero by a Mrs. Galbraith, the vessel finally slid down the slipway on October 29th 1863. On November 10th, the American consul in Glasgow, W. L. Underwood formally requested that the Pampero be detained. Although the British Government did not make any immediate legal moves, in late November a British warship was moored abreast of the Pampero, and she was placed under a 24 hour scrutiny by customs officers. Court proceedings against the Pampero commenced on march 18th 1864, and were never satisfactorily concluded.

Capture

Spanish frigate *Gerona* chasing the British-built Chilean steamer Tornado

During the Chincha Islands War, the South American allies sent agents to European shipyards in search of unsold warships originally laid down for the Confederate states; Peru purchased two screw corvettes in France, and Chile, purchased one in Britain, the Tornado. She set sail from Leith with a British register, British flag, with a British crew, after having been duly examined by the Custom-house authorities, on the 19th of August 1866. Bound for a neutral destination, she had no chilean men on board.

She should had been in rendez vous with the British filibustering ship steamer *Greathem Hall*, aiming to interfere against the Spanish trade. But the later was captured by HMS Caledonia and taken into Portland. The *Pampero* (also known as Tornado) waited patiently in the rendez vous point, until the crew were ordered to re-coal and head for the desolate islands of Fernando de Noronha, an old pirate haunt off the Brazilian coast, in order to collect unpaid wages and bonuses offered by the delivery of the vessel.

The Spanish frigate, brought strict orders from the Spanish government to capture these ships. However, the Peruvian vessels made it to Latin American waters but the Chilean *Pampero* was about to be captured. The *Gerona* sailed from Cadiz in the early morning of the 20th instant, arriving at Madeira, Portugal on the 22nd instant. At 6'15 in the evening; before arriving at the anchoring ground, she discovered a suspicious steamer weighing anchor and apparently getting ready to put to sea, for which reason the Commander of the *Gerona* Don Benito Escalera, thought fit to proceed towards her to see if he could obtains news, and to be at the same time in readiness to follow in her track, should she turn out to be ither of the vessels indicated to him by the Spanish government.

At 8 o'clock at night the frigate, thinking that she perceived that the *Tornado* was putting herself in motion, and having been confirmed in that opinion by the showing of the signal agreed upon on board the Spanish schooner, commenced to move in pursuit. The course which the *Tornado* took was in every way suspicious, for she kept as close into the north-west shore of this island as she could, coasting along it at a very short distance as far as Cape Tristão, where she put to sea steering towards the north.

Notwithstanding that the *Tornado* was some distance off at 10-30 at night, and at a distance of more than four miles from the coast, the Captain of the *Gerona*, a slower ship, resolved to call her attention by discharging at her a cannon loaded with blank cartridge, but seeing that she kept on her course, he fired another shotted cannon at her, and this he repeated three times, the Tornado then stopped.

He sent on board of her tow boats manned and tow officers to examine her, which was done in due form, although it could not be affirmed positively whether she carried munitions of war or not on account of th egreat quantity of coal with which she was stowed. The Commander made the captain come on board the *Gerona*, and this latter answered the questions that were put to him with insolent and insulting words so that he was obliged to be called to order. He then ordered the said captain to return to the "Tornado" which was navigated to Cadiz, by the 1st Lieutenant Don Manuel del Bustillo, 2nd Lieutenant, four marines (guardia marinas), one engineer, and fifty-one men armed, and the crew of the *Tornado* composed of fifty-five men, amonst whom were five Portuguese taken on board at Funchal, were transferred to the *Gerona*.

Captain John MacPherson and the crew of the Tornado were treated with great severity, both on their way to Cádiz and after their arrival in that city. The case led to negotiations between the British and Spanish governments expressed the opinion that the Spanish Government ha dno right to treat the crew as prisoners of war, much less to chain them up.

Spanish Service

U.S steamer *Virginius* surrenders to the Spanish corvette *Tornado*. Oil on Canvas 1873.

She was brought into spanish service as *Tornado,* and rated as screw corvette. During the Ten Years' War, she saw service in Cuban Waters and had a notorious incident with the American filibustering steamer *Virginius*, that had been bought for the purpose of being used for landing military expeditions on Cuba in aid of the insurgents, and she had been engaged in this work for months, being even called by one of the Havana newspapers as *the famous filibuster steamer Virginius*.

On October 31, 1873 she was bound from Kingston, Jamaica to some point in Cuba, flying the American flag, and carrying a cargo of war material. Having a crew of 52 (chiefly Americans and Britons) and 103 passengers (mostly Cubans), the *Virginius* was sighted by the *Tornado*, and she immediately fled in a northerly direction toward Jamaica, but was chased by her, captured and taken into Santiago de Cuba. Fifty-three of the crew and passengers were condemned to death by court-martial, and between November 4 and 8 were shot; among them were eight American citizens.

Joseph Fry, captain of the *Virginius*.

Relations between Spain and the United States became strained, and war seemed imminent, but on December 8, the Spanish government agreed to surrender the Virginius to the U.S. on December 16, to deliver the survivors of the crew and passengers to an American warship at Santiago, and to salute the American flag at Santiago on December 25 if it was not proved before that date that the Virginius was not entitled to sail under American colors. The Virginius foundered off Cape Hatteras as she was being towed to the United States, by the Ossipee. George Henry Williams, the Attorney General of the United States decided before December 25 that the Virginius was the property of General Quesada and other Cubans, and had had no right to carry the American flag.

Under an agreement of the February 27 1875, the Spanish government paid to the United States an indemnity of $80,000 for the execution of the Americans, and another indemnity to the British government.

Resumed service

She was converted to a torpedo-training vessel in 1886. From 1898 until its destruction by the Nationalist aviation in 1938, she served as a hospice for poor children of sailors and fishermen killed or drowned by maritime accidents, in the port of Barcelona. She was finally broken up in 1939.

The Tornado, serving as powder hulk, before being sunk by Nationalist Air Raid.

Source (edited): "http://en.wikipedia.org/wiki/Spanish_cruiser_Tornado"

Star of the West

Steamship *Star of the West* approaching Fort Sumter. Illustration from Frank Leslie's Weekly

The ***Star of the West*** was a civilian steamship hired by the United States government to transport military supplies and reinforcements to the garrison of Fort Sumter in the run-up to the American Civil War. The ship was a substitute for the USS *Brooklyn*, an armed screw sloop which continued to escort the *Star of the West* on its journey.

Background

The Star of the West was a 1172 ton steamship built by Jeremiah Simonson, of New York for Cornelius Vanderbilt, and launched June 17, 1852. Its length was 228.3ft and its beam 32.7ft, with wooden hullside paddle wheels and two masts. She started service between New York and San Juan de Nicaragua on October 20, 1852 and continued this service for Charles Morgan from July 1853 to March 1856. In June 1857, she started the New York to Aspinwall service for the United States Mail Steamship Company until September 1859 when it went onto the New York, Havana, New Orleans service. In January 1861, she was chartered to the War Department.

Civil War

On January 9, 1861, before the Confederacy was formed, the *Star of the West* was fired upon by cadets from The Citadel stationed at the Morris Island battery as the ship entered Charleston Harbor. This prevented the *Star of the West* from resupplying Major Robert Anderson's garrison at Fort Sumter. The *Star of the West* was given a warning shot across the bow and turned about to leave the harbor mouth. She was hit three times by what were effectively the first shots of the American Civil War. The mission was abandoned and the *Star of the West* headed for her home port of New York Harbor.

The ship was then hired out of New York as a troop transport for $1,000 a day under its master, Elisha Howes. The *Star of the West* sailed for Texas to pick up seven companies of United States troops assembled at Indianola. On April 18, 1861, while anchored off Pass Caballo bar leading into Matagorda Bay, the ship was captured by Colonel Earl Van Dorn and members of two Galveston militia units, the Wigfall Guards and the Island City Rifles. Two days later the ship was taken to New Orleans, where Louisiana's Governor Moore changed its name to the CSS *St. Philip*. The old name persisted, however, and the *Star of the West* served as a naval station and hospital ship until Admiral David Farragut captured New Orleans.

Still under Confederate control, the *Star of the West* escaped recapture by transporting millions in gold, silver, and paper currency to Vicksburg and continued to Yazoo City, Mississippi. When federal Lieutenant Commander Watson Smith tried to lead two ironclads and five smaller vessels through the Yazoo Pass into the Tallahatchie River to attack Vicksburg from the rear, Confederate defenders hurriedly constructed Fort Pemberton, and Major General William W. Loring had the *Star of the West* sunk broadside in the Tallahatchie near Greenwood to block the passage of the Union flotilla. In a skirmish on April 12, 1863, the Union forces suffered heavy casualties and were forced to withdraw.

Following the war, the owners of the *Star of the West* collected $175,000 in damages from the United States government for their loss.

Popular culture

The incident looms large in a novel by John Updike, *Memories of the Ford Administration* (1992). Although Updike's protagonist is trying (in the early 1990s) to write about the mid-1970s, he spent those years seeking to write a book about President Buchanan, and his mind keeps reverting to the 19th century and, among other incidents, the mission of this sloop to Sumter.

The Star of the West Medal is awarded annually to the "best drilled cadet" at The Citadel, The Military College of South Carolina. Each medal awarded has a small piece of wood salvaged from the original Star of the West ship.
Source (edited): "http://en.wikipedia.org/wiki/Star_of_the_West"

USS *Atlanta* (1861)

The first ***Atlanta*** was a casemate southern ironclad, converted from a Scottish-built blockade runner serving in the Confederate Navy. She was later captured in battle and then served in the Union Navy for the duration of the Civil War.

Atlanta was built in Glasgow, Scotland by James and George Thompson at the Clyde Bank Iron Shipyard and was completed as the *Fingal* early in 1861. She briefly operated between Glasgow and other ports in Scotland for Hutcheson's West Highland Service.

As *Fingal*

Just as the *Fingal* was beginning her career as a merchantman, on the other side of the Atlantic, the United States was sinking deeper and deeper into the secession crisis. Soon after the Southern attack upon Fort Sumter plunged the nation into war in mid-April 1861, the Confederate Secretary of the Navy, Stephen Mallory, sent James Dunwoody Bulloch to England to buy the warships, ordnance, and widely varied supplies needed by the South's fledgling navy. After reaching Liverpool on 4 June, Bulloch—a former naval officer who had resigned his commission as a lieutenant in the United States Navy on 5 October 1854—quickly arranged for the construction of two fast and powerful cruisers to prey upon Union shipping. He also purchased a large quantity of naval supplies. Next—realizing that he must arrange for a steady flow of new funds before he could go much farther with his purchasing program and also prompted by the fact that the materiel of war that he had already acquired would be useless to the Confederate cause as long as it remained in England—decided to buy a steamship, to fill it with the ordnance that he and an agent of the Southern War Department had accumulated, and to sail in her to America.

To carry out this plan, the enterprising Southern naval agent chartered *Fingal* with an option to buy her upon a moment's notice if circumstances should arise which made such a move seem to be advisable. Under this arrangement, the ship would appear to be a British vessel under the command of a certified English master while she would actually be completely under Bulloch's control. Thus, *Fingal* would enjoy the protection of neutral English colors; yet, in the event she encountered an overinquisitive but none too powerful Union blockader, the English commanding officer might exercise his power of attorney as the agent of the steamer's owner and sign her over to the Confederate Government. In this way, *Fingal*, under Bulloch's command, could fight for her freedom without compromising British neutrality.

In an attempt to avoid suspicious eyes, the Southern arms were carried by rail and by the coastal steamer Colletis from the vicinity of London to Greenock, Scotland, where *Fingal* was moored. When the prospective blockade runner was fully loaded, she got underway on the morning of 10 October; moved down the Firth of Clyde; transited the North Channel; and proceeded south through the Irish Sea to Holyhead, Wales, where Bulloch and other Confederate officials and passengers awaited. On the night of the 14th, as she was slowly rounding the breakwater shielding that port, *Fingal* suddenly came upon unlighted brig *Siccardi*, slowly swinging at anchor. Although *Fingal* barely had steerage way and despite the fact that she quickly reversed her engines, she collided with the dark sailing ship. The steamer's sharp bow pierced *Siccardi*'s starboard quarter, and the brig went down before a boat could be lowered.

While *Fingal*'s boats were carrying out rescue operations, Bulloch and the passengers embarked in the steamer. Bulloch sent a letter ashore to request that Messrs. Fraser, Trenholm and Co.—Confederate financial agents in England—settle damages with the brig's owners. Then, lest *Fingal* be held up by an investigation of the accident which might well bring his whole project to naught, Bulloch ordered the steamer to get underway immediately. She headed for the Azores and replenished her water supply at Praia on the island of Terceira. When the ship reached Bermuda on 2 November, she found CSS *Nashville* in port; and that Confederate side-wheel cruiser supplied her with coal and a pilot familiar with ". . . Savannah and the inlets to the southward . . . ." While *Fingal* was at Bermuda preparing for a dash to the Confederate coast, the United States consul, suspicious of her purpose, attempted in vain to persuade her crew to leave the ship.

On the afternoon of the 7th, *Fingal*, cleared for Nassau in the Bahamas, got underway again. Soon after she left port, Bulloch informed the crew that the steamer's real destination was Savannah, Georgia; but he offered to take anyone who objected to the plan to Nassau. However, all agreed to join in the effort to run the Union blockade; and the ship headed for the Georgia coast. Her two 4½-inch rifled guns were then mounted in her forward gangway ports, and her two breech loading 2½-inch boat guns were put in place on her quarterdeck. The weather was clear as she approached the entrance to Wassaw Sound on the night of 11 and 12 November; but, in the wee hours of the morning, a heavy fog settled over the coastal waters and screened the ship from Union eyes, enabling her to slip safely into the Savannah estuary.

The cargo which she brought to the munitions-hungry South consisted of 14,000 Enfield rifles, 1,000,000 cartridges, 2,000,000 percussion caps, 3,000 cavalry sabers, 1,000 short rifles with cutlass bayonets, 1,000 rounds per rifle, her own ordnance, 400 barrels of coarse cannon powder, medical supplies, much military clothing, and a large quantity of cloth for sewing still more uniforms. Recalling the voyage after the war, Bulloch proudly stated that "No single ship ever took into the Confederacy a cargo so entirely composed of military and naval supplies ..." and every bit of it was desperately needed by Southern forces.

While *Fingal* was discharging her most welcome cargo, Bulloch went to Richmond to confer with Secretary of the Navy Mallory and other Confederate leaders seeking approval of what he had done and what he intended to do. His plans called for him next to return to his ship, to fill her with cotton and naval stores, then to escape through the blockade to sea, and finally to steam on to England.

Bulloch returned to Savannah on 23 November heartened by Mallory's approval of his past performance and of his projected course of action, and he promptly went to work to obtain a cargo of cotton and rosin for *Fingal's* outward voyage. However, the very next day, the first of a series of events occurred that would keep *Fingal* in port and ultimately would make her useless to the South.

Optimistic because of his great victory at Port Royal, South Carolina, earlier in the month, Flag Officer Samuel F. Du Pont—the commanding officer of the newly established South Atlantic Blockading Squadron—ordered a Union naval force to waters off Savannah. On the 24th, in response to Du Font's instructions, Comdr. John Rodgers led a party of Union sailors and marines ashore on Tybee Island, which controlled the mouth of the Savannah River, closing to Fingal that avenue of escape. The next day, Bulloch wrote Mallory reporting this development, explaining that "the only egress left for Fingal is through Warsaw [sic] Inlet . . ."and warning that". . . it can scarcely be supposed that the enemy will permit it to remain open many days . . . ."

Yet, despite the urgency of loading the steamer and preparing her for sea, other pressing demands upon Southern railroads delayed the arrival of her coal and cargo. Thus, she was not ready to sail until 20 December; and, by that time, Union blockaders had sealed off Wassaw Sound, ending the steamer's last chance to reach the Atlantic.

Slow to abandon hope that changed conditions might yet enable him to slip out to sea, Bulloch remained on board the steamer until mid-January 1862. Then, yielding to the inevitable and prodded by pressing business abroad, he turned her over to Lt. George T. Sinclair, CSN, so that he might proceed to England independently and resume his duties there.

Under Sinclair, *Fingal* for a time continued to seek an opportunity to dash out to sea; but this hope was abandoned before spring; and the ship was taken into the Confederate Navy. She was stripped to her deck; covered with a slanted, armored roof, flat at the center; and fitted with a sharp reinforced-steel bow which could be used to pierce the hulls of wooden enemy vessels. The contract for converting her into an ironclad ram was awarded to the Tift brothers, Nelson and Asa F.; and her metamorphosis— financed largely by contributions from the ladies of Savannah— was completed during the summer. The new warship was renamed **Atlanta**.

As *Atlanta*

CSS *Atlanta*

However, in her new configuration as a fighting ship, *Atlanta* suffered from several serious shortcomings. Her new armor and ordnance increased her draft to almost 16 feet, making it difficult for her to operate in the inland waters approaching Savannah. Moreover, her modifications made her extremely slow to respond to her helm and reduced her speed from 13 to 10 knots. She also leaked significantly, and her armored roof all but eliminated circulation of air, turning her into a humid oven during hot weather.

On 31 July, *Atlanta*—under the command of Lt. Charles H. McBlair, CSN—steamed down the Savannah River toward Fort Pulaski to a point where she could be seen from Union blockaders, but she soon retired above the obstructions. Efforts were then made to correct her defects but with poor results.

USS Weehawken captures the Confederate ram Atlanta, 17 June 1863

In January 1863, Flag Officer Josiah Tattnall—who then commanded the naval defenses of Georgia and, although residing ashore, flew his flag in Atlanta—felt pressure from Mallory to engage Northern naval forces. The Confederate Secretary of the Navy and other officials in Richmond were highly impressed by the performance of *Virginia*—the former screw frigate Merrimack rebuilt as an ironclad ram—in Hampton Roads the previous March and hoped that *Atlanta* could boost Southern morale by repeating *Virginia's*, victory over wooden-hulled Union warships. Accordingly, Tattnall made plans to have *Atlanta* descend the Savannah. However, obstructions blocking the channel leading to sea prevented Tattnall from launching the operation. In March, the disappointed and frustrated Mallory reacted by relieving Tattnall from the command afloat and later placed Lieutenant William A. Webb, CSN, in command of *Atlanta*, leaving no doubt that he expected great accomplishments from the ironclad ram in the near future.

On 10 June 1863, Rear Admiral Du Pont—sensing that *Atlanta* was about to descend the Wilmington River for a foray into Wassaw Sound and remembering that *Monitor* had ended *Virginia's* destructive rampage—ordered monitors USS *Weehawken* and USS *Nahant* to enter Wassaw Sound to stop the Southern ironclad ram's attack, should she make one, and to prevent her escape. Captain John Rodgers in *Weehawken* had overall command of this Union force.

Five days later, in the early evening of the 15th, *Atlanta* got underway and passed over the lower obstructions in the Wilmington River to get into position for a strike at the Union forces in Wassaw Sound. Webb dropped anchor at 8:00 p.m. and spent the remainder of the night coaling. The next evening ". . . about dark . . .," Webb later reported, he ". . . proceeded down the river to a point of land which would place me in 6 or 7 miles of the monitors, at the same time concealing the ship from their view, ready to move on them at early dawn the next morning."

Atlanta, accompanied by wooden steamers CSS Isondiga and CSS Resolute, got underway before daylight on the 17th. A percussion torpedo was fitted to a long spar projecting forward from the ram's bow, "which," Webb wrote, "I knew should do its work to my entire satisfaction, should I but be able to touch the *Weehawken* . . . ." *Atlanta* grounded coming into the channel, was gotten off, but repeatedly failed to obey her helm and ran hard aground again. *Weehawken* poured five shots from her heavy guns into the Confederate ram, and *Nahant* moved into attacking position. With two of his gun crews out of action with two of three pilots severely injured, and with his ship stranded and helpless, Webb was compelled to surrender to prevent further futile loss of life. His two wooden escorts had returned upriver without engaging.

Captain Rodgers reported, "The *Atlanta* was found to have mounted two 6-inch and two 7-inch rifles, the 6-inch broadside, the 7-inch working on a pivot either as broadside or bow and stern guns. There is a large supply of ammunition for these guns and other stores, said to be of great value by some of the officers of the vessel." At the time of capture, 21 officers and 124 men, including marines were on board.

In the United States Navy

After completion of temporary repairs at Port Royal, Du Pont placed the prize in temporary commission on 26 September and sent her to Philadelphia where she was condemned by a prize court, repaired in the Federal navy yard, and commissioned again on 2 February 1864. Still bearing her Confederate Navy name while in the Federal Navy, *Atlanta* was assigned to the North Atlantic Blockading Squadron.

During most of her career under Union colors, *Atlanta* was stationed up the James River helping other Northern warships support General Grant's operations against Richmond. Under the command of Acting Lieutenant Thomas J. Woodward, her main service was to guard against a foray from the Confederate capital of the small fleet of Southern warships. On 21 May 1864, she and the schooner-rigged screw steamer *Dawn* shelled Confederate cavalry which was attacking Fort Powhatan on the James. Their gunfire broke up the assault and dispersed the Southern troopers.

After the collapse of the Confederacy, *Atlanta* steamed north to Philadelphia where she was decommissioned on 21 June 1865. She was sold at auction at the Philadelphia Navy Yard to Sam Ward on 4 May 1869. Haiti purchased *Atlanta* for $160,000 in gold, but while sailing to the country in December 1869, she sank off Cape Hatteras.
Source (edited): "http://en.wikipedia.org/wiki/USS_Atlanta_(1861)"

USS *Cornubia* (1858)

The **SS *Cornubia*** was built in Hayle, Cornwall, by Harvey & Co. in 1858 as a packet ship and ferry for the Hayle Steam Packet Company. Sleek and painted white, with two funnels mounted close together amidships and with a high bridge over her paddle wheels, she plied the Hayle/St Ives to Bristol route in the days when the Great Western Railway had not penetrated as far as West Cornwall.

She was given the name *Cornubia* from the Latinised name for Cornwall and was a fast iron paddle steamer, long and narrow at 210 ft (64 m) long and with a 24 ft 6 in (7.47 m) beam. Her Harveys-built twin oscillating sidewheel engines with four boilers and 9 ft (2.7 m) stroke produced 230 hp (170 kW) and was capable of propelling the vessel at over 18 kn (21 mph; 33 km/h). Her shallow, 9 ft (2.7 m) draft was initially designed to cope with the shallow harbours in Cornwall, but proved to be very useful in her later life.

Confederate Navy Service

During the American Civil War, agents for the Confederacy purchased *Cornubia* and took her over the Atlantic where she was officially renamed *Lady Davis* though by all accounts her old name *Cornubia* was also commonly used.

She proved to be a very good investment. Her speed, manoeuvrability and shallow draft making her an excellent blockade runner. She successfully avoided and outran Union forces on 22 occasions bringing vital supplies to the confederate army at Wilmington.

On her 23rd run on 8 November 1863, however luck ran out for *Cornubia*. She was pursued by *Niphon* and was forced to run up onto the beach at New Inlet. The ship's captain, Richard Gayle, the ship's carpenter and one seaman remained onboard and helped other crew and passengers to escape to shore.

Later that same day, *James Adger* arrived on the scene and on the rising tide towed the still-intact *Cornubia* free. She was then sent to Boston as a Prize together with the bags of waterlogged mail. The abandoned mail proved to be a vital aid to the Union, gaining an insight into the Confederacy plans and in particularly the role that British seamen were taking in blockade running.

Union Navy Service

Cornubia was purchased from the Boston Prize court and then commissioned in the Union Navy on 17 March 1864 and assigned to the role of blockading the waters around Mobile and Pensacola, before later being reassigned to the coast of Texas. The blockade runner had now become a blockader.

On 21 April 1865, *Cornubia* captured

the blockade-running schooner *Chaos*. On 24 May, *Cornubia* captured the guard boat *Le Compt* where a cache of arms was found. Later the same day, *Cornubia* assisted *Princess Royal* in the pursuit and sinking of the Confederate steamer *Denbigh*.

Following the evacuation of Galveston on 22 May, *Cornubia* was put on duty removing the harbour obstructions.

On 3 August, *Cornubia* was officially decommissioned from the Union Navy and was sold on 25 October.

Source (edited): "http://en.wikipedia.org/wiki/USS_Cornubia_(1858)"

USS *Planter* (1862)

USS *Planter* (1860) was a steamer taken over by Robert Smalls, a Southern slave and ship's pilot who steered the ship past Confederate defenses and surrendered it to Union Navy forces on 13 May 1862 during the American Civil War.

For a short period, *Planter* served as a gunboat for the Union Navy. As the ship burned wood, which was scarce where the Navy was operating, the Navy turned the ship over to the Union Army for use at Fort Pulaski on the Georgia coast. In 1863 Smalls was appointed captain of *Planter*, the first black man to command a United States ship, and served in that position to 1866.

Service under the Confederacy

Planter was a sidewheel steamer built at Charleston, South Carolina in 1860 that was used by the Confederacy as an armed dispatch boat and transport attached to the engineer department at Charleston, under Brigadier General Ripley, CSA.

Robert Smalls, pilot

At 04:00 on 13 May 1862, while her captain, C. J. Relyea, was absent on shore, Robert Smalls, a slave who was *Planter*'s pilot, quietly took the ship from the wharf, and with a Confederate flag flying, steamed past the successive Confederate forts. He saluted the installation as usual by blowing the steam whistle. As soon as the steamer was out of range of the last Confederate gun, Smalls hauled down the Confederate flag and hoisted a white one. Then he turned *Planter* over to the *Onward* of the Union blockading force.

Besides Smalls, *Planter* carried 15 other slaves to freedom behind Union lines: seven crewmen, five women, and three children. In addition to the cargo of artillery and explosives, Smalls brought Flag officer Samuel Francis Du Pont valuable intelligence, including word that the Confederates had abandoned defensive positions on the Stono River.

Smalls pilots *Planter* to Samuel DuPont in South Carolina

The next day, *Planter* was sent to Flag Officer Du Pont at Port Royal Harbor, South Carolina, who later assigned Robert Smalls as *Planter*'s pilot. At the time she was taken over by the Union, *Planter* was carrying four guns as cargo beside her usual armament.

Smalls and his crew are awarded half the value of *Planter*

The United States Senate and House of Representatives passed a private bill on 30 May 1862, granting Robert Smalls and his African-American crew one half of the value of *Planter* and her cargo as prize money. At the very time of the seizure she had on board the armament for Fort Ripley. The Planter was taken by the Government at a valuation of $9,000, one-half of which was paid to the captain and crew, the captain receiving one-third of one-half, or $1,500. Upon what principle the Government claimed one-half of this capture can not be divined, nor yet how this disposition could have been made of her without any judicial proceeding. That $9,000 was an absurdly low valuation for the Planter is abundantly shown by facts stated in the affidavits of Charles H. Campbell and E. M. Baldwin, which are appended. In addition thereto their sworn average valuation of the Planter was $67,500. The report of Montgomery Sicard, commander and inspector of ordinance, to Commodore Patterson, navy-yard commandant, shows that the cargo of the Planter, as raw material, was worth $3,043.05; that at antebellum prices it was worth $7,163.35, and at war prices $10,290.60. For this cargo the Government has never paid one dollar. It is a severe comment on the justice as well as the boasted generosity of the Government that, while it had received $60,000 to $70,000 worth of property at the hands of Captain Smalls, it has paid him the trifling amount of $1,500, and for twenty years his gallant, daring, and distinguished and valuable services which he has rendered to the country have been wholly unrecognized.

Service in the Union Navy

Du Pont took *Planter* into the Union Navy and placed her under command of Acting Master Philemon Dickenson. On 30 May he ordered the side-wheeler to North Edisto, where Acting Master Lloyd Phoenix relieved Dickenson. *Planter* served the South Atlantic Blockading Squadron through the summer of 1862. On a joint expedition under Lieutenant Rhind, the *Crusader* and *Planter* carried troops to Simmons Bluff, Wadmelaw River, South Carolina, where they destroyed a Confederate encampment.

Planter transferred to the Union Army

The Southern steamer had been designed to use only wood as fuel, a scarce commodity for the Union blockaders off Charleston, South Carolina. In the fall of 1862, Du Pont ordered her transferred to the Union Army for service near Fort Pulaski on the coast of Georgia. .

Planter under fire

After his escape, Smalls served as a pilot for Union ships in the Charleston area. He was eventually assigned to serve aboard *Planter* again. On December 1, 1863, *Planter* was caught in a crossfire between Union and Confederate forces. The ship's commander, a Captain Nickerson, ordered her surrendered. Smalls refused, saying he feared her black crewmen would not be treated as prisoners of war and might be killed by the Confederates.

Smalls took command and piloted the ship out of range of the Confederate guns. As a reward for his bravery, he was appointed captain of the *Planter*, becoming the first black man to command a United States ship. Smalls served as captain until the Army sold *Planter* in 1866 after the end of the war. Source (edited): "http://en.wikipedia.org/wiki/USS_Planter_(1862)"

USS *Red Rover* (1859)

USS *Red Rover* (1861) was a 650-ton Confederate States of America steamer that the United States Navy captured. After refitting the vessel, the Union used it as a hospital ship during the American Civil War.

Red Rover became the U.S. Navy's first hospital ship, serving the Mississippi Squadron until the end of the American Civil War. Her medical complement included nurses from the Catholic order Sisters of the Holy Cross, the first female nurses to serve on board a Navy ship. In addition to caring for and transporting sick and wounded men, she provided medical supplies to Navy ships along the Western Rivers.

Service under the Confederacy

Red Rover was a side-wheel steamer built in 1859 at Cape Girardeau, Missouri. The Confederacy purchased her on 7 November 1861, and initially put her to use as a barracks ship for the floating battery at New Orleans, Louisiana. Serving from 15 March 1862, at Island No. 10, near New Madrid, Missouri, she was holed by Union fire during a bombardment of that island sometime before 25 March, leading the Confederates to abandon her as a barracks ship.

Captured by the Union Army

When the island fell to Union forces on 7 April, the Union gunboat *Mound City* captured *Red Rover*. The Union forces repaired her, fitting her out as a summer hospital ship for the Army's Western Flotilla. Her role was to augment the limited Union medical facilities, to minimize the hazards to sick and wounded in fighting ships, and to facilitate delivery of medical supplies to and evacuation of personnel from forward areas.

Civil War care of the sick and wounded

Hospital ward on *Red Rover*

At the time of *Red Rover*'s commissioning as a hospital ship, the Union was already using steamers such as the *City of Memphis* as medical transports to carry casualties upriver. However, these transports lacked necessary sanitary accommodations and medical staff, and thus were unable to prevent the spread of disease. Barges, housed over or covered with canvas, were ordered for the care of contagious diseases, primarily smallpox, and were moored in shady spots along the river.

Rapid mobilization at the start of the Civil War had vitiated efforts to prevent the outbreak and epidemic communication of disease on both sides of the conflict. Vaccination was slow; sanitation and hygiene were generally poor. Overworked military medical personnel were assisted by voluntary societies coordinated by the U.S. Sanitary Commission founded in June 1861. But by 1865, typhoid fever, typhus, dysentery, diarrhea, cholera, smallpox, measles, and malaria would claim more lives than gunshot.

Conversion to hospital ship

Red Rover, serving first with the Union Army, then with the Union Navy, drew on both military and voluntary medical personnel. Her conversion to a hospital boat, begun at St. Louis, Missouri, and completed at Cairo, Illinois, was accomplished with both sanitation and comfort in mind. A separate operating room was installed and equipped. A galley was put below, providing separate kitchen facilities for the patients. The cabin aft was opened for better air circulation. A steam boiler was added for laundry purposes. An elevator, numerous bathrooms, nine water closets, and gauze window blinds "... to keep cinders and smoke from annoying the sick" were also included in the work.

Civil War service

Mound City hospital service

On 10 June 1862, *Red Rover* was ready for service. Her commanding officer was Captain McDaniel of the Army's Gunboat Service. Assistant Surgeon George H. Bixby became Surgeon in Charge.

On 11 June, *Red Rover* received her first patient, a cholera victim. By the 14th, she had 55 patients. On the 17th, *Mound City* exploded during an engagement with Confederate batteries at St. Charles, Arkansas. Casualties amounted to 135 out of a complement of 175. *Red Rover*, dispatched to assist in the emergency, took on board extreme burn and wound cases at Memphis, Tennessee, and transported them to less crowded hospitals in Illinois.

Vicksburg, Mississippi, hospital service

From Mound City, Illinois, the hospital ship moved down-stream again and joined the Western Flotilla above Vicksburg, Mississippi. Through the summer, she treated the flotilla's sick and wounded while the Ram Fleet engaged at Vicksburg and along the Mississippi River to Helena, Arkansas. While off Helena, *Red Rover* caught fire, but — with assistance from the gunboat *Benton* — she extinguished the blaze and continued her work.

Transferred to the Union Navy's Mississippi operating area

In September 1862, *Red Rover* — still legally under the jurisdiction of an Illinois prize court — was sent to Cairo, Illinois, to be winterized. The Navy purchased her on the 30th. The next day, the Union transferred the vessels of the Western Flotilla, with their officers and men, to the Navy Department to serve as the Mississippi Squadron under acting Rear Adm. David Dixon Porter. The Navy Medical Department of Western Waters was organized at the same time under Fleet Surg. Edward Gilchrist.

In December *Red Rover*, used during the fall to alleviate crowded medical facilities ashore, was ready for service on the river. On the 26th, she was commissioned under the command of Acting Master William R. Wells, USN. Her complement was 47, while her medical department, remaining under Assistant Surgeon Bixby, was initially about 30. Of that number, three were Sisters of the Order of the Holy Cross, later joined by a fourth member of their order and assisted by lay nurses' aides. These women were the forerunners of the U.S. Navy Nurse Corps. The Western Sanitation Commission, which also donated over $3,000 worth of equipment to the ship, coordinated the work of these and other volunteers.

In December 1862, Fleet Surg. Ninian A. Pinckney relieved Fleet Surg. Gilchrist. Pinckney imposed such strict standards on the department's day-to-day activities and ran them so well run from his headquarters in Red Rover that by 1865, he was able to claim "there is less ... sickness in the Fleet than in the healthiest portion of the globe."

Supporting the White River expedition

On the 29th, *Red Rover* headed downstream. During January 1863, she served with the expedition up the White River. While the expedition took the Port of Arkansas (Fort Hindman), she remained at the mouth of the river to receive the wounded. On her departure, she was fired on and two shots penetrated into the hospital area, but caused no casualties.

From February to the fall of Vicksburg early in July, she cared for the sick and wounded of that campaign and supplemented her medical support of Union forces by provisioning other ships of the Mississippi Squadron with ice and fresh meat. She also provided burial details and sent medical personnel ashore when and where needed.

Red Rover continued her service along the river, taking on sick and wounded and delivering medicine and supplies until the fall of 1864. In October of that year, she began her last supply run. After delivering medical stores to ships at Helena and on the White, Red, and Yazoo Rivers, she transferred patients to Hospital Pinckney at Memphis, Tennessee and headed north.

Post-war decommissioning

Arriving at Mound City, Illinois on 11 December, she remained there, caring for Navy patients, until she was decommissioned on 17 November 1865. Having admitted over 2,400 patients during her career, she transferred her last 11 to *Grampus* on that date. On 29 November, she was sold at public auction to A. M. Carpenter.

Source (edited): "http://en.wikipedia.org/wiki/USS_Red_Rover_(1859)"

USS *United States* (1797)

USS *United States* was a wooden-hulled, three-masted heavy frigate of the United States Navy and the first of the six original frigates authorized for construction by the Naval Act of 1794. Joshua Humphreys designed the frigates to be the young Navy's capital ships, and so *United States* and her sisters were larger and more heavily armed and built than standard frigates of the period. She was built at Humphrey's shipyard in Philadelphia, Pennsylvania and launched on 10 May 1797 and immediately began duties with the newly formed United States Navy protecting American merchant shipping during the Quasi-War with France.

In 1861 the *United States* was in port at Norfolk and was seized and subsequently commissioned into the Confederate States Navy as **CSS *United States***, but was later scuttled by Confederate forces. Union forces raised the scuttled ship, and retained control of the ship until it was broken up in 1865.

Design & construction

During the 1790s American merchant vessels began to fall prey to Barbary Pirates in the Mediterranean, most notably from Algiers. Congress's response was the Naval Act of 1794. The Act provided funds for the construction of six frigates; however, it included a clause stating that construction of the ships would cease if the United States agreed to peace terms with Algiers.

Joshua Humphreys' design was long on keel and narrow of beam (width) for mounting very heavy guns. The design incorporated a diagonal scantling (rib) scheme to limit hogging while giving the ships extremely heavy planking. This gave the hull greater strength than those of more lightly built frigates. Humphreys developed his design after realizing that the fledgling United States could not match the navy sizes of the European states. He therefore designed his frigates to be able to overpower other frigates, but with the speed to escape from a ship of the line.

Originally designated as "Frigate A" and subsequently named *United States* by President George Washington, her keel was laid down in 1795 at Humphreys' shipyard in Philadelphia

Pennsylvania. Humphreys was assigned as her constructor and US Navy Captain John Barry as superintendent. As Philadelphia was at the time America's capital, many visitors walked through observing her construction as it progressed. Humphreys personally led President Washington and First Lady Martha on a tour. The President expressed his admiration of the great size of the ship. A less desirable visitor, Benjamin Franklin Bache (grandson of Benjamin Franklin) was physically assaulted by Clement Humphreys (Joshua's son) allegedly over Bache's opposition to the Federalist Party and his opposition newspaper, the *Philadelphia Aurora*.

Fearing sabotage, Humphreys was concerned about the open nature of his ship yard which allowed anyone to wander in. He requested from the War Department a number of guards which were posted to keep out visitors but to little effect.

Construction slowly continued until a peace treaty was announced between the United States and Algiers in March 1796. In accordance with the clause in the Naval Act, construction of *United States* was discontinued. President Washington requested instructions from Congress on how to proceed. Several proposals circulated before a final decision was reached allowing Washington to complete the three frigates nearest to completion; *United States*, *Constellation* and *Constitution* were chosen.

She was the first American warship to be launched under the Naval Act of 1794, and the first ship of the United States Navy. She was fitted out at Philadelphia during the spring of 1798 and, on 3 July ordered to proceed to sea. Relations with the French government had deteriorated, starting the Quasi-War.

Armament

United States's nominal rating was that of a 44-gun ship. However, she usually carried over 50 guns. *United States* was originally armed with a battery of 55 guns: thirty-two 24-pounder (10.9 kg) cannon; twenty-two 42-pounder (19 kg) carronades; and one 18-pounder (8 kg) long gun.

Unlike modern Navy vessels, ships of this era had no permanent battery of guns. Guns were portable and often exchanged between ships as situations warranted. Each commanding officer modified his vessel's armaments to his liking, taking into consideration factors such as the overall tonnage of cargo, complement of personnel aboard, and planned routes to be sailed. Consequently, a vessel's armament would change often during its career; records of the changes were not generally kept.

Quasi-War

United States sailed with *Delaware* to Boston where they were to meet with *Herald* and *Pickering* to form a patrol squadron. Shortly afterward Barry sighted a frigate showing French colors. Raising his own French flag, Barry maneuvered closer and when reaching it, hoisted the American colors. As Barry was about to open fire on the frigate, she changed to the English flag and identified herself as HMS *Thetis*, narrowly avoiding being fired upon. When reaching Boston, Barry learned that *Herald* and *Pickering* were not ready to sail and he decided to continue without them. *United States* and *Delaware* departed for the West Indies on 26 July

Portrait of John Barry c. 1801

In the ensuing two months two French privateers, *Sans Pareil* and *Jalouse* were captured and brought into New Castle, Delaware on 20 September. *United States* put to sea again on 17 October with orders to cruise along the New England coast and eastward. However, a severe gale arose the following day and *United States* was disabled with a sprung bowsprit and slackened rigging. Emergency repairs had to be made. After the storm passed, she made her way back to Delaware, arriving on 9 November. Barry received orders in December which returned *United States* to the West Indies, taking command of the American squadron there. This squadron, in addition to *United States*, would by early 1799 include: *Constitution*, *George Washington*, *Merrimack*, *Portsmouth*, *Herald* and the revenue cutters *Pickering*, *Eagle*, *Scammel*, and *Diligence*.

On 3 February 1799, *United States* sighted a French ship and began a five hour pursuit of the schooner *L'Amour de la Patrie*. After coming in close to the vessel, *United States* opened fire; the third shot went completely through *L'Amour de la Patrie*, sinking her rapidly. Barry sent out his boats to collect survivors of the schooner and they were taken prisoner. *United States* then set a course for Guadaloupe to arrange a prisoner exchange with the French but Barry's flag of truce was ignored when shore batteries opened fire on the boat carrying Barry's envoy. Barry returned to *United States* and ordered his gun crews to bombard the batteries in return. On 26 February, *United States* pursued the French privateer *Democrat* which had recently taken prize of the English ship *Cicero*. *Cicero* was recaptured but the pursuit of *Democrat* ended when she escaped into shallow water. Returning to Guadaloupe, Barry made another attempt at a prisoner exchange. However, Governor Desfourneax told Barry he held no prisoners because there was no war with the United States. Though skeptical, Barry released his prisoners.

On 26 March, *United States* took the French privateer *La Tartueffe* and its prize, the American ship *Vermont* southeast of Antigua. Also recorded is the capture of *Le Bonaparte* sometime in 1799. In April, Barry turned over command of the squadron to Thomas Truxtun. *United States* sailed for home and arrived at New Castle, Delaware on 9 May. Barry recruited new crew members to replace the ones whose enlistments had expired while *United States* underwent refitting and repairs. She sailed again 1 July with orders to patrol the southern Atlantic coast of the United States. Encountering a storm on the 6th which sprung her bowsprit, she continued on to deliver an artillery company to Fort Moultrie and then put into the Gosport Navy Yard for repairs on the 22nd. Returning to patrols on 13 August, *United States* experienced an uneventful period and at times sailed in company with *George Washington* and *Insurgent*.

United States returned to Newport, Rhode Island in September and Barry waited for further orders. In October those orders were to deliver Oliver Ellsworth and William Davie as envoys to France to negotiate a settlement of the Quasi War. *United States* departed on 3 November and returned in April 1800. She remained in port for needed repairs until December when Barry was ordered to return to the West Indies. The treaty of peace with France was ratified on 3 February 1801 and *United States* returned home in April. An act of Congress passed on 3 March 1801 and signed by President John Adams, retained thirteen frigates. Seven of those frigates, including *United States*, were to be placed in a reserve fleet. Ordered to the Washington Navy Yard, *United States* was decommissioned there along with *Congress* and *New York*.

War of 1812

United States remained in the Washington Navy Yard throughout the First Barbary War of 1801–1805 and up until 1809 when orders were given to ready her for active service. On 10 June 1810, now under the command of Stephen Decatur, she sailed to Norfolk, Virginia for refitting.

While she was at Norfolk, Captain John S. Carden of the Royal Navy, commander of the new British frigate HMS *Macedonian*, wagered Captain Decatur a beaver hat that his vessel would take *United States* if the two should ever meet in battle. Ichabod B. Crane, whose name was appropriated for the main character in The Legend of Sleepy Hollow, served under Decatur as a lieutenant in the Marine detachment aboard ship.

The United States declared war against Britain on 18 June 1812. Three days later Decatur and *United States* sailed from New York City within a squadron under the command of Commodore John Rodgers in *President*. Other ships of the squadron were *Congress*, *Hornet*, and *Argus*; departed on a seventy-day North Atlantic cruise. A passing American merchant ship informed Rodgers about a fleet of British merchantmen en route to Britain from Jamaica. Rodgers and his squadron sailed in pursuit, and on 23 June encountered what was later learned to be HMS *Belvidera*.

United States and the squadron returned to pursuing the Jamaican fleet and on 1 July began to follow the trail of coconut shells and orange peels the Jamaicans had left behind them. *United States* sailed to within one day's journey of the English Channel but never sighted the convoy. Rodgers called off the pursuit on 13 July. During their return trip to Boston, the squadron captured seven merchant ships and recaptured one American vessel.

After some refitting, *United States*, still under Decatur's command, sailed again 8 October with Rodgers but on the 12th parted from the squadron for her own patrol.

Three days later, after capturing *Mandarin*, *United States* parted company and continued to cruise eastward. At dawn, on the 25th, five hundred miles south of the Azores, lookouts on board *United States* reported seeing a sail 12 miles (19 km) to windward. As the ship rose over the horizon, Captain Decatur made out the familiar lines of HMS *Macedonian*.

United States vs Macedonian

Both ships were immediately cleared for action and commenced maneuvers at 0900. Captain Carden elected not to risk crossing the bows of *United States* to rake her, but chose instead to haul closer to the wind on a parallel course with the American vessel. For his part, Decatur intended to engage *Macedonian* from fairly long range, where his 24 pounders (11 kg) would have the advantage over the 18 pounders (8 kg) of the British.

Naval Battle Between the United States & The Macedonian on Oct. 30, 1812 by Thomas Birch, 1813

The actual battle developed according to Decatur's plan. *United States* began the action at 0920 by firing an inaccurate broadside at *Macedonian*. This was answered immediately by the British vessel, bringing down a small spar of *United States*. Decatur's next broadside destroyed *Macedonian*'s mizzen top mast, letting her driver gaff fall and so giving the advantage in maneuver to the American frigate. *United States* next took up position off *Macedonian*'s quarter and proceeded to riddle her with shot. By noon, *Macedonian* was a dismasted hulk and was forced to surrender. She had suffered 104 casualties against 12 in *United States*, which emerged from the battle relatively unscathed.

The two ships lay alongside each other for over two weeks while *Macedonian* was repaired sufficiently to sail. *United States* and her prize entered New York Harbor on 4 December amid jubilation over the victory. Captain Decatur and his crew were received with praise from both Congress and President James Madison.

Aftermath

Macedonian was subsequently purchased by the United States Navy, repaired, and placed in service. After repairs, *United States* — accompanied by USS *Macedonian* and the sloop *Hornet*—sailed from New York on 24 May 1813. On 1 June, the three vessels were driven into New London, Connecticut, by a powerful British squadron, and *United States* and *Macedonian* were kept blocked there until the end of the war. *Hornet* managed to slip through the blockade on 14 November 1814 and escape to sea.

Decatur was transferred to the frigate *President* in the spring of 1814, and he took the officers and crew of *United States* with him to his new command.

Second Barbary War

Soon after the United States declared war against Britain in 1812, Algiers took advantage of the United States' preoccupation with Britain and began intercepting American merchant ships in the Mediterranean. On 2 March 1815, at the request of President James Madison, Congress declared war on Algiers. Work preparing two American squadrons promptly began—one at Boston under Commodore William Bainbridge, and one at New York under Commodore Steven Decatur. *United States* was assigned under Bainbridge but required repairs and refitting from her period in port for the latter part of the War of 1812. She was not ready for sea when Bainbridge departed Boston on 3 July.

United States finally departed for the Mediterranean two months later under the command of Captain John Shaw; arriving at Gibraltar on 25 September. Soon after, Shaw learned that Commodore Decatur had already secured a peace treaty with Algiers. Now part of a large gathering of U.S. Navy ships, *United States* was chosen to remain behind with *Constellation*, *Erie*, and *Ontario*. They were later joined by *John Adams*, *Alert* and *Hornet*.

The senior American naval officer in the region, Captain Shaw became commodore and commanded the squadron consisting of *Constellation*, *Java*, *Erie* and *Ontario* until Commodore Isaac Chauncey arrived 1 July 1816 and took overall command. Nevertheless, *United States*, despite losing her position as flagship, continued to serve in the Mediterranean until she sailed for home in the spring of 1819 and reached Hampton Roads on 18 May. The frigate was decommissioned on 9 June 1819 and laid up at Norfolk.

Squadron duty

United States returned to duty in November 1823 under the command of Commodore Isaac Hull. After repairs and preparation she sailed on 5 January 1824, to relieve Commodore Charles Stewart in the Pacific. Accompanying Hull was his wife and sister-in-law Jeanette Hart.

United States made a stop enroute to the Pacific at Rio de Janeiro and reached Valparaiso, Chile by 7 March. Commodore Hull found that Chile was now independent and had been acknowledged by Spain, though hostilities still continued with Peru; Callao was held by the Spaniards and blockaded by the Peruvian fleet. The United States' position was one of strict neutrality in the war and Hull's orders contained the main objective of overseeing and protecting American commerce. *United States* sailed for Callao, arriving on 4 April. Commodore Stewart, in command of *Franklin* was relieved by Hull and sailed for home. Under Hull's command, a squadron of US Navy ships consisted of *Vincennes*, *Peacock*, and *Dolphin*.

United States remained in the vicinity of Peru and her duty there was mostly uneventful. In the autumn of 1825, Hull placed Lieutenant John Percival in command of *Dolphin* and tasked him with searching for mutineers from the American whaling ship *Globe*. Percival found only two of the mutineers but discovered an uncharted island which he named "Hull's Island"; now known as Îles Maria. Percival continued on to Hawaii and reportedly caused discontent with the tribal chiefs and missionaries. Hull placed Thomas ap Catesby Jones in command of *Peacock* and dispatched him to Hawaii to ascertain the behavior of Percival. However, upon Jones' arrival, Percival had already departed. With Hull's tour of duty now expired, *United States* departed from Callao on 16 December 1826 and arrived at the New York Navy Yard on 24 April 1827.

She put into the Philadelphia Navy Yard in 1828 for extensive repairs and remained there until 1830 when she was placed in reserve at the New York Navy Yard. The frigate remained at New York through 1832 and was thoroughly modernized. On 3 July 1832, she sailed under Capt. J. B. Nicholson to join Commodore Patterson's squadron in the Mediterranean, returning to New York 11 December 1834. From 1836 to 1838, under Capt. J. Wilkinson, the United States was again in the Mediterranean, and from 1839 to 1840 she was in the Home Squadron under Captain Lawrence Kearney.

Capture of Monterey

United States was repaired at Norfolk in 1841 and was designated the new flagship of the Pacific Squadron of Thomas ap Catesby Jones, now a Commodore. On 9 January 1842 she sailed from Norfolk via Cape Horn under Captain James Armstrong. On the night of 6 September 1842, while lying in Callao, the British frigate HMS *Dublin*, flagship of Rear Admiral Richard Darton Thomas, appeared off the port, and, seeing the American fleet, at once put to sea. The suspicions of Commodore Jones were immediately aroused, and, having heard that war was about to be declared between the United States and Mexico, the Commodore suspected *Dublin* intended to run up the coast and take possession of California, a country that England had long had her eye upon. *United States* got under way, and in company with *Cyane* Jones hastened north. They captured Monterey on 16 October when Jones demanded a surrender. The next day he realized that the United States and Mexico were still at peace, so tried to make amends for his action.

While waiting for further orders, Jones heard British Captain Lord George Paulet had claimed the Hawaiian

Islands. He sailed there, arriving on 22 July. Admiral Thomas arrived a few days later, and restored the government of the Kingdom of Hawaii.

Herman Melville

Melville ca. 1860

Herman Melville, the future author of *Moby-Dick*, enlisted as an ordinary seaman on board *United States* at Honolulu, Hawaii, on 17 August 1843. His novel *White-Jacket*, published in 1850 is a fictionalized account of his experiences on board, highly critical of the captain of the *United States* and of naval customs in general. Melville observed that Armstrong often appeared on deck intoxicated. From Hawaii, *United States* proceeded to the Marquesas Islands and lost a man overboard en route. From the Marquesas she visited Valparaiso, Chile; Lima and Callao Peru.

United States remained at Callao for 10 weeks and the crew was denied shore leave while Commodore Jones was in port with his flagship *Constellation*. Jones inspected every ship under his command during the 10 weeks expecting formal ceremonies at each inspection. The only break in the crew's boredom came when *United States* challenged *Constellation* and the British ship HMS *Vindictive* to a race out of the harbor. *United States* handily defeated both of them.

Setting a course back home in mid 1844, *United States* arrived at Rio de Janeiro, Brazil for resupply. Departing 24 August for Boston she challenged and won a race with the French sloop *Coquette*. *United States* arrived in Boston on 2 October and decommissioned there on the 14th.

She was recommissioned there on 18 May 1846 and detailed to the African Squadron to suppress the illicit slave trade under command of Captain J. Smoot as the flagship of Commodore George C. Read. *United States* joined the Mediterranean Squadron in 1847 and served in European waters until ordered home late in 1848. She returned to Norfolk on 17 February 1849, was decommissioned on 24 February and placed again in ordinary.

Civil War

Norfolk Navy Yard burns

United States rotted away at Norfolk until April 20, 1861 when the navy yard was captured by Confederate troops. Before leaving the yard, Union fire crews failed to burn the vessel along with other abandoned ships, thinking it unnecessary to destroy the decayed relic. The Confederates, pressed for vessels in any condition, thought otherwise. They pumped her out and commissioned the frigate CSS *United States* (though they often called her *Confederate States*) on April 29. On June 15, she was fitted out as a receiving ship with a deck battery of 19 guns for harbor defense.

In this role, she served her new owners well but was ordered sunk in the Elizabeth River, Virginia, to form an obstruction to Union vessels when the Confederates abandoned the navy yard in May 1862. The ancient timbers of the frigate were so strong and well-preserved they ruined one whole box of axes when attempts were made to scuttle her, and it was necessary to bore through the hull from inside before she settled to the muddy bottom of the river.

Shortly after the destruction of ironclad ram *Virginia* on May 11, 1862 and the surrender of the Norfolk Navy Yard to Union troops, *United States* was raised and towed to the yard by federal authorities. She remained there until March 1864, when the Bureau of Construction and Repair decided to break her up and sell the wood. This was delayed until the Bureau ordered on December 18 that the gallant old frigate be docked at Norfolk and finally broken up.

Source (edited): "http://en.wikipedia.org/wiki/USS_United_States_(1797)"

Arkansas toothpick

The **Arkansas Toothpick** is a heavy dagger with a 12–20-inch (30–51 cm) pointed, straight blade. The "toothpick" is balanced and weighted for throwing and can be used for thrusting and slashing. James Black, known as the inventor of the Bowie knife, is credited with inventing the *Arkansas Toothpick*.

Some sources use Arkansas Toothpick as a synonym for the Bowie Knife as opposed to the image of a large dagger. Its versatility had such an impact that two of Arkansas's nicknames became "The Bowie State" and "The Toothpick State".

Legal status

Although many jurisdictions worldwide have knife legislation regulating the length of a blade or the dagger-like profile of the Arkansas Toothpick that one

Beaumont-Adams Revolver

The **Beaumont-Adams Revolver** was a muzzle-loading percussion revolver. Originally adopted by the British Army in .442 calibre (54-bore, 11.2mm) in 1856, many were later converted to use centrefire cartridges. It was replaced in British service in 1880 by the .476 calibre (actually 11.6mm) Enfield Mk I revolver.

History

On 20 February 1856, Lieutenant Frederick E.B. Beaumont of the Royal Engineers was granted a British patent for improvements to the Adams revolver which allowed them to be cocked and fired either cocking the hammer as in Colt single-action revolvers, or by just pulling the trigger. It was the first true double-action system. The Adams revolvers had previously been double-action only, which had led to doubts regarding their accuracy. Beaumont was granted a US Patent (no. 15,032) on 3 June of the same year.

In partnership with George and John Deane, the company of Deane, Adams & Deane produced the new revolver in a variety of calibres and sizes, from pocket pistols to large military versions. The United Kingdom officially adopted the 54-bore (.442 calibre) Beaumont-Adams in 1856, Holland and Russia following soon after. To meet the growing demand for its weapons, Deane, Adams & Deane contracted companies in Birmingham and Liége to manufacture their weapons under licence. The new revolver enabled Robert Adams to regain public confidence and forced Samuel Colt to shut his London factory due to a drop in sales.

In the US, the Massachusetts Arms Company was licensed to manufacture about 19,000 specimens of the gun in .36 calibre, of which about 1,750 were purchased by the Union Army at the beginning of the American Civil War.

The Beaumont-Adams was favoured by British officers in the Crimean War and colonial conflicts due to the stopping power of its large bullet, which was considered superior to Colt revolvers of the period. In close-quarters, the speed of its action was preferred over long-range accuracy.

Source (edited): "http://en.wikipedia.org/wiki/Beaumont-Adams_Revolver"

Blakely rifle

A **Blakely rifle** was a type of muzzle-loading rifled cannon that the Confederate States used during the U.S. Civil War and that owed its design to a British army officer, Captain Theophilus Alexander Blakely. Blakely tried to interest the British government in his designs, but without success. His designs involved a cast-iron core with wrought-iron or steel banding to reinforce the breech, a design similar to that of the Armstrong guns of Sir William George Armstrong. Blakely believed that Armstrong had infringed upon his patents so when Armstrong became superintendent of the Royal Arsenal at Woolwich, Blakely stopped offering his designs to the British Army.

He turned, instead, to selling cannons of his design to the Confederacy. He did not actually manufacture the guns, but rather contracted out the manufacturing to such companies as Fawcett, Preston, & Company of Liverpool, Vavasseur of London, George Forrester and Company of Liverpool, Low Moor Iron Company, and the Blakely Ordnance Company of London, in which he may have had an interest. In all, the cannon foundries produced some 400 guns to Blakely's design, most being made of iron. Blakely also sold some guns to Russia, and apparently Massachusetts bought eight 9" and four 11" models.

Because Blakely continued to experiment with designs, there are at least five and possibly ten different designs, many of which came in several variants. There were at least nine varieties of 3.5" 12-pounder rifles. The two primary rifling types appear to have involved flat-sided bores or bores with grooves cut in them into which flanges on the shells would fit.

The foundries manufactured Blakely rifles in 2.5" (6-pounder), 2.9", 3. 5" (12-pounder), 3.75" (16-pounder), 4" (18-pounder), 4.5" (20-pounder), 6.4" (100-pounder), 7" (120-pounder), 7.5" (150-pounder), 8" (200-pounder), 9" (250-pounder), 11" and 12.75" (450 pounder shells or 650-pound solid shot) bores.

One famous Blakely rifle was "The Widow Blakely", a 7.5" rifle that the Confederates used during their defense of Vicksburg, Mississippi, in 1863. On May 22, 1863, a shell exploded while in the gun's barrel while The Widow was firing at a Union gunboat. The explosion only took part of the end of the muzzle off. The Confederates cut what had been a 124 inch long barrel back to 100 inches and continued to use the rifle as a mortar until Vicksburg fell.

Source (edited): "http://en.wikipedia.org/wiki/Blakely_rifle"

Bowie knife

A **Bowie knife** (pronounced /ˈboʊ.iː/ *boh-ee* or /ˈbuː.iː/ *boo-ee*) is a style of fixed-blade knife first popularized by Colonel James "Jim" Bowie in the early 19th Century. It was first made by James Black, although its common use refers to any large sheath knife with a clip point.

The "Jim Bowie knife" first became famous due to Bowie's use of a large knife at a duel known as the Sandbar Fight. The knife pattern is still popular with collectors; in addition to various knife manufacturing companies there are hundreds of custom knife makers producing Bowies and variations.

Description

An early Bowie of the type made for Rezin Bowie and commissioned by the Bowies to Searles and Constable. This is a copy of the Fowler Bowie currently displayed at the Alamo.

The historical Bowie knife was not a single design, but was a series of knives improved several times by Jim Bowie over the years. The earliest such knife, made by Jesse Clifft at Rezin Bowie's request resembled the Spanish hunting knives of the time and differed little from a common butcher knife. The blade, as later described by Rezin Bowie, was 9.5 inches (24 cm) long, 0.25 inches (0.64 cm) thick and 1.5 inches (3.8 cm) wide. It was straight-backed having no clip point nor any hand guard with simple riveted wood scale handle. Rezin presented the knife to his brother because of a recent violent encounter with one Norris Wright. This is the knife that became famous after the sandbar duel of 1827. Bowie and Wright were attendants on opposite sides of the duel. When the principals quit the field, a fight broke out among the attendees and Bowie, though seriously injured by a rifle shot, killed the 3 men, by almost decapitating one, splitting the skull of another, and disembowelling the third. Bowie and his knife, described by witnesses as "a large butcher knife," quickly attained celebrity and the Bowie brothers received many requests for knives of the same design. They commissioned more ornate custom blades from various knife makers including Daniel Searles and John Constable. George William Featherstonhaugh described them as: *These formidable instruments...are the pride of an Arkansas blood, and got their name of Bowie knives from a conspicuous person of this fiery climate.*

The version most commonly known as the historical Bowie knife would have a blade of at least 6 inches (15 cm) in length, some reaching 12 inches (30 cm) or more, with a relatively broad blade that was an inch and a half to two inches wide (4 to 5 cm) and made of steel usually between ∕ to ∕ in (4.763 to 6.350 mm) thick. The back of the blade sometimes had a strip of soft metal (normally brass or copper) inlaid which some believe was intended to catch an opponent's blade while others hold it was intended to provide support and absorb shock to help prevent breaking of poor quality steel or poorly heat treated blades. Bowie knives often had an upper guard that bent forward at an angle (an S-guard) intended to catch an opponent's blade or provide protection to the owner's hand during parries and corps-a-corps.

Some Bowie knives had a notch on the bottom of the blade near the hilt known as a "Spanish Notch." The Spanish Notch is often cited as a mechanism for catching an opponent's blade; however, some Bowie researchers hold that the Spanish Notch is ill-suited to this function and frequently fails to achieve the desired results. These researchers, instead, hold that the Spanish Notch has the much more mundane function as a tool for stripping sinew and repairing rope and nets, as a guide to assist in sharpening the blade (assuring that the sharpening process starts at a specific point and not further up the edge), or as a point to relieve stress on the blade during use.

One characteristic of Bowie knives is the "Clip point" at the top of the blade, which brings the tip of the blade lower than the spine for better control. As the goal is to produce a sharp, stabbing point, most Bowie knives have a bevel ground along the clip, typically 1/4 of the way, but sometimes much further running the entire top-edge. This is referred to as a "false edge" or a "swedge" as from a distance it looks sharpened, although it may or may not be. Regardless of whether or not the false edge is sharp, it serves to take metal away from the point, streamlining the tip and thus enhancing the penetration capability of the blade during a stab. The version attributed to blacksmith James Black had this "false edge" fully sharpened in order to allow someone trained in European techniques of saber fencing to execute the maneuver called the "back cut" or "back slash". A brass quillon, usually cast in a mold, was attached to protect the hand.

Noted knife expert Bernard Levine has reported that the first known Bowie knife showed a strong Mediterranean influence insofar as general lines were concerned. This would have involved the single, principal cutting edge, regardless of the false edge's existence or not. It is noted that in the Old West many "Bowie knives" were made that in fact did not show Mediterranean influence, but were just large knives, often with two full edges.

The curved portion of the edge, toward the point, is for removing the skin from a carcass, and the straight portion of the edge, toward the guard, is for chores involving cutting slices, similar in concept to the traditional Finnish hunting knife, the "puukko" (though the typical early 19th-century Bowie knife was far larger and heavier than the typical puukko). Arkansas culturalist and researcher Russell T. Johnson describes the James Black knife in the following manner and at the same time captures the quintessence of the Bowie Knife: "It must be long enough to use as a sword, sharp enough to use as a razor, wide enough to use as a paddle, and heavy enough to use as a hatchet." Most such knives intended for hunting are only sharpened on one edge, to reduce the danger of cutting oneself while butchering and skinning the carcass.

History

The Sandbar Fight

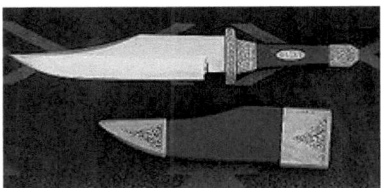

A coffin handled Bowie Knife.

The first knife, with which Bowie became famous, allegedly was designed by Jim Bowie's brother Rezin in Avoyelles Parish, Louisiana and smithed by blacksmith Jesse Cleft out of an old file. Period court documents indicate that Rezin Bowie and Cleft were well acquainted with one another. Rezin's granddaughter claimed in an 1885 letter to Louisiana State University that she personally witnessed Cleft make the knife for her grandfather.

This knife became famous as the knife used by Bowie at the Sandbar Fight, which was the famous 1827 duel between Bowie and several men including a Major Norris Wright of Alexandria, Louisiana. The fight took place on a sandbar in the Mississippi River across from Natchez, Mississippi. In this battle Bowie was stabbed, shot, and beaten half to death but managed to win the fight using the large knife.

Jim Bowie's older brother John claimed that the knife at the Sandbar Fight was not Cleft's knife, but a knife specifically made for Bowie by a blacksmith named Snowden.

James Black's Bowie Knife

The most famous version of the Bowie knife was designed by Jim Bowie and presented to Arkansas blacksmith James Black in the form of a carved wooden model in December 1830. Black produced the knife ordered by Bowie, and at the same time created another based on Bowie's original design but with a sharpened edge on the curved top edge of the blade. Black offered Bowie his choice and Bowie chose the modified version. Knives such as this, with a blade shaped like that of the Bowie knife, but with a pronounced false edge, are today called "Sheffield Bowie" knives, because this blade shape became so popular that cutlery factories in Sheffield, England were mass-producing such knives for export to the U.S. by 1850, usually with a handle made from either hardwood, deer antler, or bone, and sometimes with a guard and other fittings of sterling silver.

Bowie returned, with the Black-made knife, to Texas and was involved in a knife fight with three men who had been hired to kill him. Bowie killed the three would-be assassins with his new knife and the fame of the knife grew. Legend holds that one man was almost decapitated, the second was disemboweled, and the third had his skull split open. Bowie died at the Battle of the Alamo five years later and both he and his knife became more famous. The fate of the original Bowie knife is unknown; however, a knife bearing the engraving "Bowie No. 1" has been acquired by the Historic Arkansas Museum from a Texas collector and has been attributed to Black through scientific analysis.

Black soon had a booming business making and selling these knives out of his shop in Washington, Arkansas. Black continued to refine his technique and improve the quality of the knife as he went. In 1839, shortly after his wife's death, Black was nearly blinded when, while he was in bed with illness, his father-in-law and former partner broke into his home and attacked him with a club, having objected to his daughter having married Black years earlier. Black was no longer able to continue in his trade.

Black's knives were known to be exceedingly tough, yet flexible, and his technique has not been duplicated. Black kept his technique secret and did all of his work behind a leather curtain. Many claim that Black rediscovered the secret of producing true Damascus steel.

In 1870, at the age of 70, Black attempted to pass on his secret to the son of the family that had cared for him in his old age, Daniel Webster Jones. However, Black had been retired for many years and found that he himself had forgotten the secret. Jones would later become Governor of Arkansas.

The birthplace of the Bowie knife is now part of the Old Washington Historic State Park which has over 40 restored historical buildings and other facilities including Black's shop. The park is known as "The Colonial Williamsburg of Arkansas". The American Bladesmith Society established the William F. Moran School of Bladesmithing at this site to instruct new apprentices as well as journeyman, and mastersmiths in the art of bladesmithing.

Variations and collecting

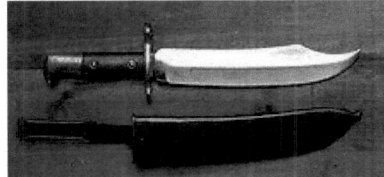

Krag Bolo bayonet US stamped, on the reverse date 1900

Over the years many knives have been called Bowie knives and the term has almost become a generic term for any large sheath knife. During the early days of the American Civil War Confederate soldiers carried immense knives called D-Guard Bowie knives. Many of these knives could have qualified as short swords and were often made from old saw or scythe blades.

The Bowie knife is sometimes confused with the "Arkansas toothpick," possibly due to the interchangeable use of the names "Arkansas toothpick", "Bowie knife", and "Arkansas knife" in the antebellum period. The Arkansas toothpick is essentially a heavy dagger with a straight 15-25-inch blade. While balanced and weighted for throwing, the toothpick can be used for thrusting and slashing. James Black is credited with inventing the "Arkansas Toothpick" but no firm evidence exists for this claim.

Knives made in Sheffield, England, were quick to enter the market with "Bowie Knives" of a distinctive pattern that most modern users identify with the true form Bowie. The Sheffield pattern blade is thinner than the Black/Musso knives while the false edge is often longer with a less pronounced clip.

The shape and style of blade was such that the Bowie knife could serve usefully as a camp and hunting tool as well as a weapon, and is still popular as such with hunters and sportsmen even in the present day. However, some camping authorities dissent as to its usefulness as a camping knife on the grounds that it is far too large.

Since the 1960s, Bowie knives with sawteeth machined into the back side of the blade appeared inspired by the United States Air Force survival knife (NSN 7340-00-098-4327). The sawteeth were intended to cut through the acrylic glass canopy of a downed aircraft. During the Vietnam War the United States Army issued them to helicopter crews for the same purpose.

The Bowie remains popular with collectors. In addition to various knife manufacturing companies there are hundreds of custom knife makers and bladesmiths producing Bowies and variations. The Bowie knife dominates the work produced by members of the American Bladesmith Society. Collecting antique Bowie knives is one of the higher-end forms of knife collecting with rare models selling as high as $200,000. Even mass-produced Sheffield Bowies from the 19th century can sell in the range of $5,000US to $15,000US.

The USMC Ka-Bar of World War II fame is based on the Bowie design. Custom knife maker, Ernest Emerson originally used a Bowie knife in his logo and manufactures a folding Bowie known in his line-up as the CQC13.

A Bowie knife appears on the shoulder sleeve insignia of the 39th Infantry Brigade Combat Team, headquartered in Little Rock, Arkansas. Jim Bowie was posthumously inducted into the Blade Magazine Cutlery Hall of Fame at the 1988 Blade Show in Atlanta, Georgia in recognition for the impact that his design made upon generations of knife makers and cutlery companies. Rock star David Bowie (born David Robert Jones) took the name Bowie after the Bowie knife because, in his words "it cuts both ways".

Legal status

Sheffield pattern blades are not quite as wide as the Black design but most variations carry a false-edged clip point.

Although many jurisdictions worldwide have knife legislation regulating the length of a blade one may own or carry, certain locales in the United States have legislation mentioning "Bowie knives" in particular. These laws were passed in the late 1830s, in several southern states as an attempt to curtail the manufacture and sale of these knives.

In 1837, the Alabama legislature imposed a $100 transfer tax on Bowie knives and stipulated that any killing with a Bowie knife was murder regardless of the circumstances.

In Texas, the state where Jim Bowie died, it is a criminal offense (generally a Class A misdemeanor) to carry a Bowie knife, as a Bowie knife is classified in Texas as an "illegal knife". This law does not apply if you are traveling in a private vehicle because it is legal to carry a handgun, knife, or club while en route to or from the vehicle or engaged in a sporting activity involving the use of such equipment.

Source (edited): "http://en.wikipedia.org/wiki/Bowie_knife"

Brooke rifle

An 8-inch (203 mm) double-banded Brooke rifle

The **Brooke rifle** was a type of rifled, muzzle-loading naval and coast defense gun designed by John Mercer Brooke, an officer in the Confederate States Navy. They were produced by plants in Richmond, Virginia and Selma, Alabama between 1861 and 1865 during the American Civil War. They served afloat on Confederate ships and ashore in coast defense batteries manned by the Confederate States Army.

Design and production

Brookes can be best identified by the presence of at least one band of wrought iron at the breech and a rough-finished, tapering barrel. The barrels were made of cast iron for ease of manufacture, but one or more wrought iron bands was welded around the chamber to reinforce it against the high chamber pressure exerted when the gun fired. Because no southern foundries had the capacity to wrap the rifles in a single band like the Parrott design, a series of smaller bands were used, each usually 2 inches (51 mm) thick and 6 inches (152 mm) wide. All of Brooke's rifles used the same seven-groove rifling with a right-hand twist. Most of Brooke's guns had a Gomer-style powder chamber, shaped like a truncated cone with a hemispherical tip, but the 6.4-inch rifles had a simple hemispherical powder chamber.

These weapons were manufactured at the Tredegar Iron Works (sometimes referred to as J.R. Anderson & Co, after owner Joseph Reid Anderson) in Richmond, Virginia and at Selma Naval Ordnance Works in Selma, Alabama.

Markings

Guns manufactured at Selma bear the foundry imprint "S", those from Tredegar "TF". "R.N.O.W" may be found on some guns as they were bored and rifled by the Richmond Naval Ordnance Works in Richmond, Virginia after a fire in May 1863 temporarily crippled Tredegar's boring shop.

Types

6.4-inch Rifle

Brooke reported fourteen single-banded 6.4 in (163 mm) rifles were completed by 8 January 1863, although Tredegar records only list eleven as some were double-banded before being shipped. Three were cast in 1861 with the remainder in 1862. Two of the earliest were mounted on the broadside of the CSS *Virginia*. Two others were mounted on the broadside of CSS *Atlanta* and survive today in Willard Park of the Washington Navy Yard.

Double-banded rifles were produced from 28 October 1862 by direction of Stephen Mallory, Confederate Secretary of the Navy. Twenty-four were cast by Tredegar between 1862 and 1864 while Selma cast twenty-seven, but only fifteen were shipped due to casting problems. Five of the damaged gun blocks were rebored as 8-inch (203 mm) double-banded smoothbores. Nine survivors exist, including four from CSS *Tennessee II* and one from CSS *Albemarle*.

7-inch Rifle

drawing of a single-banded Brooke for the CSS *Texas*

The first seven single-banded 7-inch (178 mm) were bored and rifled from 11-inch (279 mm) Dahlgren gun blocks between July and December 1861. Two of these were the front and rear pivot guns of the CSS *Virginia*. Tredegar made another nineteen to the Brooke pattern between 1862 and 1863 of which three survive. Two of these are found at the Washington Navy Yard as trophies from CSS *Atlanta*.

Selma cast fifty-four double-banded rifles in 1863 and 1864, but only shipped thirty-nine due to casting flaws. Tredegar cast thirty-six between 1863 and 1865. Eight survive, two as trophies from CSS *Tennessee II*, one in the Washington Navy Yard and the other in Selma.

Three triple-banded rifles were cast by Tredegar in 1862. These were 15 inches (380 mm) longer than the other 7-inch rifles and were unique among Brooke guns in that they lacked cast trunnions. Instead a separate trunnion strap was fitted around the breech. One was mounted on the CSS *Richmond* and another was sent to the harbor defenses of Charleston, South Carolina where it remains as a trophy in Ft. Moultrie.

8-inch Rifle

Tredegar cast four double-banded 8 in (203 mm) rifles in April and May 1864. One was mounted in CSS *Virginia II* while another was sent to the batteries defending the James River. It was present, but lacked shells during the fighting at Dutch Gap Canal on 13 August and 22 October 1864. Shells were delivered on 27 October and 2 November 1864. No known survivors.

Brooke smoothbores

Brooke designed a series of smoothbores that were produced in small numbers by the Selma and Tredegar foundries. Selma re-bored five flawed 6.4-inch blanks as 8-inch double-banded guns, one of which survives in Selma Alabama. Brooke's 1863 report to Secretary Mallory shows a plate of an unbanded 8-inch smoothbore, but nothing further is known of it. Similar attempts to bore out flawed 7-inch gun blocks to 9-inch (229 mm) smoothbores were unsuccessful. Seven 10-inch (254 mm) double-banded guns were cast by Selma and four by Tredegar in 1864. Two survive, one of which is a trophy from CSS *Columbia* in the Washington Navy Yard. Selma cast twelve 11-inch double-banded smoothbores in 1864, although only eight were shipped. One survives in Columbus, Georgia. In 1863 and 1864 two 11-inch triple-banded guns were cast by Tredegar, but none are known to survive.

Ammunition

Brooke's rifles fired both armor-piercing and explosive shells of his own design. The former were solid cylindrical projectiles with a blunt or flat nose to reduce the chance of a ricochet, and were often referred in contemporary accounts as "bolts". The latter were hollow cylinders with rounded or pointed noses. They were filled with black powder with a fuse set to detonate a variable amount of time after being fired. His smoothbores used spherical solid shot for armored targets and hollow spherical explosive shells against unarmored targets.

- Note: Data for 8-inch smoothbore is approximate

Source (edited): "http://en.wikipedia.org/wiki/Brooke_rifle"

Burnside carbine

The **Burnside carbine** was a breech-loading carbine that saw widespread use during the American Civil War.

Design

The carbine was designed and patented by Ambrose Burnside, who resigned his commission in the U.S. Army to devote himself full time to working on the weapon. The carbine used a special brass cartridge, also invented by Burnside. Pressing the weapon's two trigger guards opened the breech block and allowed the user to insert a cartridge. When the trigger was pulled, the hammer struck a percussion cap and caused a spark; a hole in the base of the cartridge exposed the black powder to this spark. The unique, cone-shaped cartridge sealed the joint between the barrel and the breech. Most other breech-loading weapons of the day tended to leak hot gas when fired, but Burnside's design eliminated this problem.

Service history

In 1857, the Burnside carbine won a competition at West Point against 17 other carbine designs. In spite of this, few of the carbines were immediately ordered by the government, but this changed with the outbreak of the Civil War, when over 55,000 were ordered for use by Union cavalrymen. This made it the third most popular carbine of the Civil War; only the Sharps carbine and the Spencer carbine were more widely used. They saw action in all theatres of the war. There were so many in service that many were captured and used by Confederates. A common complaint by users was that the unusually shaped cartridge sometimes became stuck in the breech after firing.

By using ordnance returns and ammunition requisitions, it has been estimated that 43 Union cavalry regiments were using the Burnside carbine during the 1863-1864 period. Additionally, 7 Confederate cavalry units were at least partially armed with the weapon during this same period.

Five different models were produced. Toward the end of the Civil War, production was discontinued when the Burnside Rifle Company was given a contract to make Spencer carbines instead.

Effect of the carbine on Burnside's career

Though he was actually a poor military officer, Ambrose Burnside rose through the ranks partly because his carbine was so well known. He was pressured by President Lincoln several times to take command of the Union Army of the Potomac. He repeatedly declined, saying "I was not competent to command such a large army as this." When he eventually did accept command, he led the Army of the Potomac to defeat at the Battle of Fredericksburg. The battle and the subsequent retreat left Burnside's "officers complaining loudly to the White House and the War Department about his incompetence." He also performed poorly at the Battle of Spotsylvania Court House, and a court of inquiry blamed him for the Union failure at the Battle of the Crater.

Source (edited): "http://en.wikipedia.org/wiki/Burnside_carbine"

Colt 1851 Navy Revolver

The **Colt Revolving Belt Pistol of Naval Caliber** (i.e., .36 cal), later known as the **Colt 1851 Navy** or **Navy Revolver**, is a cap and ball revolver. It was designed by Samuel Colt between 1847 and 1850. It remained in production until 1873, when revolvers using fixed metallic cartridges came into widespread use. Total production numbers were exceeded only by the Colt Pocket models in concurrent development, and numbered some 250,000 domestic units and about 22,000 produced in the Colt London Armory. (Wilson, 1985)

The designation "Colt 1851 Navy" was applied by collectors, though the popular name "Navy Revolver" is of early origin, as the gun was frequently called the "Colt Revolving Belt Pistol of Naval Caliber." (ibid, Wilson) The cylinder was engraved with a scene of the victory of the Second Texas Navy at the Battle of Campeche on May 16, 1843. The Texas Navy had purchased the earlier Colt Paterson Revolver, but this was Colt's first major success in the gun trade; the naval theme of the engraved cylinder of the Colt 1851 Navy revolver was Colt's gesture of appreciation. Despite the "Navy" designation, the revolver was chiefly purchased by civilians and military land forces(ibid Wilson 1985).

Famous "Navy" users included Wild Bill Hickok, John Henry "Doc" Holliday, Richard Francis Burton, Ned Kelly, and Robert E. Lee. Usage continued long after more modern cartridge revolvers were introduced in 1873.

Characteristics

The .36 caliber Navy revolver was much lighter than the contemporary Third Model Dragoon revolvers developed from the .44 Walker Colt revolvers of 1847, which, given their size and weight, were generally carried in saddle holsters. It is an enlarged version of the .31 caliber pocket revolvers that evolved from the earlier Baby Dragoon, and, like them, is a mechanically improved and simplified descendant of the 1836 Paterson revolver. As the factory designation implied, the Navy revolver was suitably sized for carrying in a belt holster. It became very popular in North America at the time of Western expansion. Colt's aggressive promotions distributed the Navy and his other revolvers across Europe, Asia, and Africa.

As with many other Colt revolvers, it has a six round cylinder.

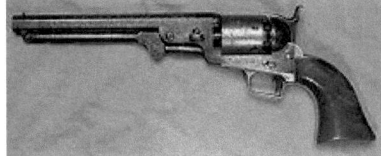

Early Colt Navy Mod 1851, Second Model squareback trigger guard

The .36 caliber (.375-.380-inch) round lead ball weighs 86 grains and, at a velocity of 1,000 feet per second, is comparable to the modern .380 pistol cartridge in power. Loads consist of loose powder and ball or bullet, metallic foil cartridges (early), and combustible paper cartridges (Civil War era), all combinations being ignited by a fulminate percussion cap applied to the nipples at the rear of the chamber.

combustible paper cartridges. Six to a box

Sighting consists of a bead front sight with a notch in the top of the hammer, as with most Colt percussion revolvers. In spite of the relative crudity of the sighting arrangement, these revolvers and their modern replicas generally are quite accurate.

Loading and Handling Sequence Common to Percussion Revolvers

The loading sequence and basic operation of the Colt revolvers remained constant throughout the percussion period, and mirrors the operation of most other percussion revolvers. A shooter familiar with the basic operation of the Colt would find the function of a Remington, LeMat, Adams, or Cooper double action essentially identical.

Percussion revolvers are carried with the hammer down between chambers, with a groove or protuberance in the hammer engaging either a safety peg or notch in the rear of the cylinder. This method prevents inadvertent rotation of the cylinder, and prevents the hammer from touching the percussion caps and firing the weapon unintentionally. Patersons and a few later revolvers such as the Rogers and Spencer lacked these safety detents, requiring that they be carried with the hammer down on an empty chamber.

To load:

1. Draw the hammer back to the first detent, placing it on "half cock" and allowing the cylinder to rotate for loading;
2. Fill the chambers with powder, leaving enough room to seat a bullet or ball, and place a ball on the chamber mouth with the sprue (mark or projection left from filling the mould) facing exactly forward;
3 Rotate the chamber under the rammer and use the loading lever (if present) to seat the projectile firmly on top of the powder column and at or below the chamber mouth;

The cylinder arbor serves as a bullet seater on models without loading levers

4. Place percussion caps on each of the nipples at the rear of the chambers;
5. Rotate the cylinder as necessary and return the hammer to down position (pull it back slightly, squeeze trigger and let hammer down carefully) engaging the safety detents; or
6. Draw the hammer back to full cock for immediate firing.

A single-action revolver is thumbcocked before firing, which rotates the cylinder and puts a loaded chamber under the hammer; the trigger then is pulled to fire. With double-action revolvers, a single long pull on the trigger cocks the hammer, rotates the cylinder and fires the arm.

Variations:

A. In the case of foil or combustible-paper cartridges containing bullet and powder, place the cartridge in the chamber and use the loading lever to fully seat the projectile. In the case of foil cartridges, insert a nipple pick through the cone openings to pierce the rear of the cartridge envelopes, then cap the nipples.

B. After #3 above, it was (and still is) common practice to put heavy grease over and around the seated bullet, to lubricate the ball, reduce fouling and prevent multiple (chain) fires; or

C. After #2 above, some early shooters (and modern shooters, too) placed a rigid, greased felt wad over the powder column before seating the bullet, as a hedge against chain fires which may occur with undersized or poorly-shaped bullets or chambers (Bates, Cumpston 2005). It also effectively minimizes fouling buildup in the bore and allows for accurate extended shooting (Keith 1956). It also is common to run a bristle brush or patch dampened with black-powder solvent through the bore before reloading.

D. Most modern target shooters use less than full charges, filling the remaining space over the powder with an inert filler (often Cream of Wheat) so the ball is at the front of the cylinder when loaded. This procedure improves accuracy by reducing the "jump" of the ball before it enters the barrel.

Safety peg between cylinder chambers

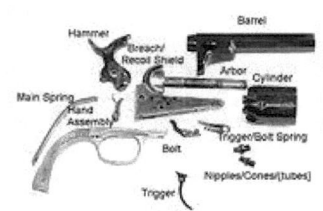

Post 1850 Colt Revolvers

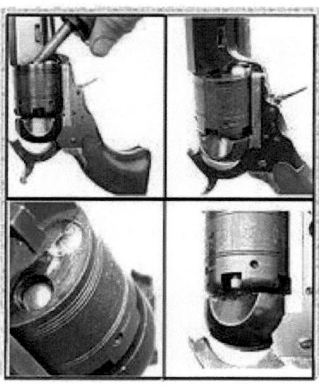

Loading sequence for percussion revolvers

Source (edited): "http://en.wikipedia.org/wiki/Colt_1851_Navy_Revolver"

Colt M1861 Navy

The **Colt Model 1861 Navy** cap & ball .36-caliber revolver was a six-shot, single-action percussion weapon produced by Colt's Manufacturing Company from 1861 until 1873. It incorporated the "creeping" or ratchet loading lever and round barrel of the .44-caliber Army Model of 1860 but had a barrel one half inch shorter, at 7.5 inches. Total production was 38,000 revolvers.

Like its forerunner, the Colt 1851 Navy Revolver, it saw widespread use in the American Civil War and on the American Western frontier, though far fewer were produced. It has the same general specification as the earlier model, but with a rounded barrel and somewhat different rammer. While similar in design to the Colt Army Model 1860, the lighter recoil of the 1861 Navy's .36 caliber was preferred by some cavalry soldiers.

There were few variations of the Model 1861 Navy Colt. Approximately 100 of the first guns made had fluted cylinders with no cylinder scene. Another 100, made between the serial ranges of 11,000 and 14,000 were cut for a shoulder stock — the lower portion of the recoil shield was milled away and a fourth screw for the stock was added to the frame. With the exception of the first fifty or so of this model, all guns had a capping groove. A brass trigger guard and back strap, silver plated, were standard.

During the Civil War its main competitor in England was the Adams self-cocking revolver. The Adams fired a .49 caliber bullet and did not require the shooter to pull the hammer back. Colt's revolver was more popular because Colt mass-produced his weapons while Adams' products were handmade by skilled artisans. In the United States, Colt's main rival was the Remington Model 1858 revolver.

The Colt 1861 Navy typically was used with paper cartridges, that is, with a cartridge consisting of nitrated paper, a pre-measured black powder charge, and a bullet that was either a lead round ball or a lead conical bullet. The nitrated paper of the cartridge was completely consumed upon use, and the use of paper cartridges enabled faster re-loading. Alternatively, it was always possible to load with measured powder charges and lead round balls.

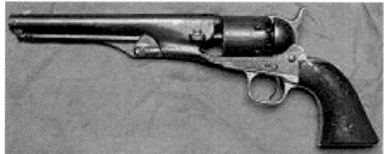

Colt Navy Mod 1861, shipped 1863

Source (edited): "http://en.wikipedia.org/wiki/Colt_M1861_Navy"

E. C. Singer

E. C. Singer was an American engineer (and the nephew of Isaac Singer, inventor of the sewing machine) who worked on secret projects for the benefit of the Confederate States of America during the Civil War and who invented the spar torpedo. Singer's torpedo was a large explosive device mounted on the tip of a long spar. It was detonated by means of a trigger mechanism adapted from a rifle lock (see flintlock mechanism for a similar device). The spring-loaded trigger was detonated by means of a long cord attached to the attacking vessel. The attacking vessel rammed its target, embedding the barbed torpedo in its hull, then backed off. When the attacker reached the limit of the trigger cord, the torpedo was detonated.

Source (edited): "http://en.wikipedia.org/wiki/E._C._Singer"

Fayetteville rifle

The **Fayetteville Rifle** was a 2 banded rifled musket of rifle length produced at the Confederate States Arsenal in Fayetteville, North Carolina. The machinery which produced these weapons was primarily that captured at the United States Arsenal at Harpers Ferry, Virginia, which was previously used to produce the US Model 1855 Rifle.

The weapon was produced in .58 caliber from early in 1862 until the capture and destruction of the arsenal by Union forces under General W.T. Sherman on March 11, 1865.

In February, 1862, the Fayetteville Observer, in describing the beginning of arms' manufacturing at the arsenal, reported:

A few days ago we were shown one of a number of rifles furnished at the C. S. Armory here. It is much the same in general appearance, as the U.S. rifle for some years made at Harper's Ferry and at Springfield, Mass.; but for certain improvements, in the matter of sword bayonet, Maynard primer, and perfection of finish in all parts, it must be pronounced very superior. The back sights are set for 800 and 500 yards.

Altogether, we think it the handsomest specimen of small arms, rifle or musket, we have ever seen-reflecting the greatest credit upon all concerned with its manufacture."

The first examples were manufactured using assorted M1855 lock blanks and are mounted in iron with high and medium high lockplate humps. Later examples are mounted in brass with a graceful "S" shaped hammer. Only the very early examples are known to have a patchbox.

The rifle was made both with and without a special bayonet lug which allowed the use of a sword bayonet.

The weapons are highly collectible and pristine examples will command prices in excess of $25,000.

Source (edited): "http://en.wikipedia.org/wiki/Fayetteville_rifle"

Gorgas machine gun

The **Gorgas machine gun** was a manually operated weapon used by the confederate states. It was fed from a horizontal rotating cylinder and was made from a cast iron receiver.

Source (edited): "http://en.wikipedia.org/wiki/Gorgas_machine_gun"

Hawken rifle

The **Hawken rifle** was a brand of black powder long rifle used on the prairies and in the Rocky Mountains of the United States during the early frontier days. It has become synonymous with the "plains rifle", the buffalo gun, and the fur trapper's gun. Born in the 1820s, it was eventually displaced by breechloaders (such as the Sharps rifle) and lever-action rifles which flourished after the Civil War.

The Hawken "plains rifle" was made by Jacob and Samuel Hawken, or by their St Louis, Missouri shop, which they ran from 1815 to 1858. Their shop continued to operate and sell rifles bearing the "Hawken" name under later owners William S. Hawken, William L. Watt, and J. P. Gemmer, until Gemmer closed down the business and retired in 1915.

Samuel and Jacob were trained by their father as rifle smiths on the east coast. They moved west and opened a business in St. Louis at the beginning of the Rocky Mountain fur trade. The brothers' claim to fame is the "plains rifles" produced by their shop. They produced what their customers needed in the west, a quality gun, light enough to carry all the time, capable of knocking down big targets at long range. They called their guns "Rocky Mountain Rifles," reflecting their customers: fur trappers, traders and explorers.

History

The earliest known record of a Hawken rifle dates to 1823 when one was made for William Henry Ashley. The Hawkens did not mass-produce their rifles but rather made each one by hand, one at a time. A number of famous men were said to have owned Hawken rifles, including: Daniel Boone, Jim Bridger, Kit Carson, Orrin Porter Rockwell, Joseph Meek and Theodore Roosevelt.

Hawken rifles had a reputation for both accuracy and long range.

The Hawken rifle company was sold in 1862, and the last rifle actually made by a Hawken was built in 1884. Although popular with mountain men and hunters of the fur trade era, up through the mid part of the 19th century, muzzleloaders were generally replaced by mass-produced, breech-loading weapons such as the Sharps Rifle and the Winchester Rifle.

Design

The rifles are generally shorter and of a larger caliber than earlier "Kentucky rifles" from which they descend. The style of the rifles is the same as the Harpers Ferry Model 1803, a half stock rifle (although they also made some with full stock), with the same lines as the Kentucky Rifle. The "plains rifle" style would become the "sporter" for much of the United States during the 1840s.

Their "Rocky Mountain" guns were typically .50 caliber or .53 caliber, but ranged as high as .68 caliber. They averaged 10 and 1/2 pounds, although there are examples of 15 pound guns. Barrels were of varying lengths (33 and 36 inch examples are described), and are octagonal on the outside. The walnut or maple stocks have a curved cheek piece, often looking like a beaver's tail and called that. They tend to have double triggers; the rear trigger is a "set" trigger. When the rear trigger is pulled, the hammer does not fall but rather the action "sets" the front trigger, the front trigger becoming a "hair trigger," tripped with a light touch. When the front trigger is used without using the rear "set" trigger, it requires a firm pull. The front site was a blade sight. Unlike many modern reproductions, the butt plate and other trim was not made of bronze, but of iron.

The 1972 film *Jeremiah Johnson* starring Robert Redford as a mountain man who used such a rifle, and contributed to general interest in replicas and a resurgence in the popularity of muzzleloaders among modern hunters.

Source (edited): "http://en.wikipedia.org/wiki/Hawken_rifle"

Hughes Breech-loading cannon

The **Hughes breech-loading cannon** 38.1mm gun was designed in 1861 by the Confederate States of America and produced by the manufacturer *Street & Hungerford Company*. It was a breech-loading cannon; the breech of the cannon is uniquely like a bolt-action but has no firing pin in its bolt.

Source (edited): "http://en.wikipedia.org/wiki/Hughes_Breech-loading_cannon"

Kerr's Patent Revolver

Kerr's Patent Revolver was an unusual 5-shot single-action revolver manufactured from 1859 to 1866 by the London Armoury Company. It was used by Confederate cavalrymen during the U. S. Civil War. It is easily recognized by its side-mounted hammer.

History

James Kerr had been the foreman for the Deane, Adams and Deane gun factory. Robert Adams, one of the partners and inventor of the Adams revolver, was Kerr's cousin. Kerr developed an improvement to the Adams revolver, British Patent No. 1722 of July 28, 1855, and when Adams left the Deane brothers to found the London Armoury Company on February 9, 1856, Kerr went with him.

The London Armoury Company manufactured military rifles and revolvers. Kerr designed rifles for the company based on the 1853 pattern Enfield rifled musket. When the company directors decided to focus on rifle production in 1859 Adams left, taking his revolver patents with him.

Kerr designed a new revolver in .36 caliber and .44 caliber (54 bore in British measurement). Production began in April 1859. The British government did not initially purchase the weapon and civilian sales were modest.

However, the U.S. Civil War began in 1860 and the governments of both the United States and the Confederacy began purchasing arms in Britain. In November of 1861 1600 revolvers were purchased for the Union army, at $18.00 apiece. However Confederate arms buyers Maj. Caleb Huse and Cpt. James D. Bulloch contracted for all the rifles and revolvers the Armoury could produce (and the Confederate government could pay for.) As a result, the London Armoury Company become a major arms supplier to the Confederacy, selling the most of the 11,000 Kerr revolvers produced to Huse. The Kerr revolvers sold to the Confederacy were said by William Edwards in his book *Civil War Guns* to be those between serial number 3,000 and 10,000, but earlier serial numbers are thought by collectors to have also been shipped to the South, and there are no good records to show the exact number sold to the Confederate buyers.

As with all Confederate imports from England (and Europe), these weapons had to pass through the Union blockade and the number that actually reached the Confederate army is unknown. Modern writers often state that the confederates acclaimed the London Armoury Company's guns (which would include the first-class model 1853 rifle-muskets on the Enfield pattern) as the best weapons delivered to the Confederacy. The London Armoury Company supplied more revolvers to the Confederacy than the total produced by all the efforts of southern manufacturers to make revolver.

As the Civil War progressed, the London Armoury Company was almost completely dependent on sales to the

Confederacy and survived for only a year after the end of the war, dissolving in the Spring of 1866.

Operation

The Kerr Revolver featured a side-mounted hammer on a back-action lockplate. Unlike other revolvers of the day, the lock mechanism of the Kerr revolver was identical to that of back-action rifle and single shot pistol percussion locks of the time. The simple action was designed to be easily repairable in the field without requiring model-specific spare parts. The Kerr had a top strap over the cylinder, which is held in place by a pin that runs into the back of the frame below the hammer. The pistol is 12.25 inches overall with a barrel length of about 5 inches. Nearly all were made in .44, or "54 bore," caliber; a few in the smaller .36 caliber.

The Kerr is often described as a double action revolver. That is true as to only the earliest Kerrs produced, but all the later production were of the simpler single action mechanism. With this simpler single action type, the hammer must be manually pulled back until it locks in the full cock position. This cocking action causes the cylinder to revolve, thus bringing a fresh chamber into line with the barrel. Once the hammer has been cocked and locked back, the user must pull the trigger to cause the hammer to fall, striking the percussion cap over the chamber and firing the weapon. If the hammer is left down, and the trigger is pulled back, the cylinder will revolve, but the hammer will not be cocked back, as would be the case with true double action revolver. The term "single action" means that the pulling of the trigger has only one effect - it releases the cocked hammer. In a "double action" revolver, the pulling of the trigger has two effects - it caused the hammer to cock back, and then as the trigger pull is continued, it releases the hammer. The double action mechanism in the early Kerrs was more complicated to manufacture and to keep in good adjustment and repair, and was early on dropped in favor of the simpler single action mechanism.

The London Armoury Company manufactured Kerrs have engraved on the side of the frame "KERRS PATENT No. xxxx" with the xxxx representing a number. This is the serial number of the gun, and not the patent number. This serial number is also on the side of the cylinder. Mistaking this serial number for a patent number is an error often repeated from Edwards, *Civil War Guns*, by many writers. This same serial numbering convention used on the Kerr was used on the Adams Revolver (made by the London Armoury Company, among others), and also is seen on Samuel Colt's percussion revolvers of all models, where the serial number of each revolver (stamped on various places on the Colt revolver) was stamped on the cylinder following the words "COLTS PATENT No. " On the Kerr Revolvers, as with the Adams and Colts, these numbers are sequential and are serial numbers and not the patent number.
Source (edited): "http://en.wikipedia.org/wiki/Kerr%27s_Patent_Revolver"

LeMat Revolver

The **LeMat revolver** was a .42 or .36 caliber cap & ball black powder revolver invented by Dr. Jean Alexandre LeMat of New Orleans, which featured a rather unusual secondary 16 gauge smoothbore barrel capable of firing buckshot, and saw service with the armed forces of the Confederate States of America during the American Civil War of 1861–1865.

History and design

The mid-19th century was a time in American history that gave birth to a number of innovative firearm designs, and this unique sidearm was also known as the "Grape Shot Revolver." It was developed in New Orleans in 1856 by Dr. Jean LeMat and backed by Pierre G.T. Beauregard, who was to become a general with the Confederacy. Roughly 2,900 were produced.

The distinguishing characteristic of LeMat's revolver is that its 9-shot cylinder revolves around a separate central barrel of larger caliber than the chambers in the cylinder proper. The central barrel is smoothbore and can function as a short-barrelled shotgun (hence the name "Grape Shot Revolver") with the shooter selecting whether to fire from the cylinder or the smoothbore barrel by flipping a lever on the end of the hammer. Flipping the lever down caused the moveable striker to fall upon the primer set directly under the hammer, discharging the lower barrel, while leaving it in the standard position would fire the chambers in the cylinder, much like any other revolver.

LeMat originally chambered his pistol for .40 (or 42) caliber revolver bullets, with a .60 (16 gauge) smoothbore barrel, and had a jointed ramrod (mounted on the right-hand side of the frame), which was used to load both barrels. Later, during the American Civil War, a lighter .35-caliber pistol with a .50 caliber (28-gauge) smoothbore barrel was produced, but as these were non-standard ammunition sizes (.36 or .44 caliber were most common for contemporary revolvers) LeMat owners had to cast their own bullets (as opposed to being issued them from general military stores.) The final models of the LeMat were produced in .36 or .44 caliber in response to these criticisms, but too few of them managed to get past the Union blockade of the South during the Civil War to be of any real use.

Civil War use

LeMat hoped to market his adaptable revolver as a primary sidearm for dragoons and other mounted troops. He entered into a partnership with then-Major P.G.T. Beauregard in April 1859 to market his handgun to the U.S. Army. Beauregard — besides being LeMat's cousin — was one of the first U.S. officers to join the Confederacy.

When war broke out LeMat received Confederate contracts for the production of five thousand revolvers, and plans were laid to manufacture the gun abroad and then import them into the Confederacy, which lacked the necessary facilities to produce the weapon locally. Confederate gun runners were able to slip shipments of the gun through the Union naval blockade and it is estimated that about 2,500 made it into Confederate service.

In addition to General Beauregard and Colonel LeMat, LeMat's revolver was used by such famous Confederate officers as Major Generals Braxton Bragg, J.E.B. Stuart and Richard H. Anderson, and Major Henry Wirz.

The LeMat revolver was manufactured from 1856 to 1865, with approximately 2900 being produced. The first models were manufactured by John Krider of Philadelphia, with the second model (the first overseas model), being produced by Charles Frederic Girard and Son of Paris. Quality concerns prompted LeMat to consider production at the Birmingham Small Arms Company in Birmingham, England, but production was never mounted there. LeMat revolvers from France were shipped to the Confederate forces via the United Kingdom, and all firearms landed in the UK were (and still are) required to be proofed. The LeMats which found their way through the Union blockade were stamped with British proof marks from the Birmingham Proof House, leading to the misapprehension that the pistols were actually manufactured in the UK. A handful are known to have been made illegitimately in the UK by an unknown manufacturer, believed to be the London Armoury Company, but only two examples survive to the present day and it is doubtful any of the English-made LeMats ever saw service during the U.S. Civil War.

The original revolver, constructed of blued steel with grips of polished walnut, was not considered to be a very accurate weapon although it was deadly at close range. Civil War cavalrymen, particularly in the South, preferred to carry several pistols anyway as it was faster to draw another loaded weapon than it was to try and reload a cap and ball revolver in combat.

After the introduction of cartridge-firing firearms, the LeMat system appeared in pinfire, but this version is exceedingly rare. A centerfire version in 12mm Perrin or 11mm Chamelot-Delvigne, with a 24 gauge shot barrel was made in later years in Belgium. While having better sales than its pinfire relative, the centerfire LeMat also had no real commercial success due to the invention of the double-action system. With both weapons, loading was accomplished via a loading gate located at the 4 o' clock position for the cylinder, and by swinging the breech of the shot barrel up and left.

Variants
Muzzle Loader
The first variant of the LeMat.
Pinfire Cartridge

A close-up of the hammer on a LeMat Pinfire Revolver, showing the pivoting striker that could be used to fire either the pinfire cartridges in the revolving chambers or the secondary smoothbore barrel.

Second variant, can be recognised by cylinder.

Centrefire
The centrefire variant came with a distinctive grip.

Carbine
A rare variant with extended barrels and a rifle type stock.

Modern reproductions

Modern reproduction of a LeMat Revolver.

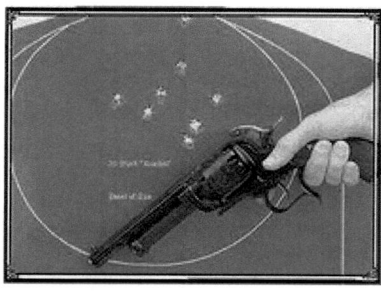

The Pietta company of Brescia, Italy has manufactured modern reproductions of the LeMat revolver since 1985. United States distributors include Navy Arms Company, Dixie Gunworks and Cabela's. Canadian Distributors include Marstar Canada, among others.

- General Beauregard's personal, engraved LeMat, which he carried throughout the war, is preserved at the Museum of the Confederacy in Richmond, Virginia.
- Elmer Keith, *Sixguns* 1955, noted that early 20th century percussion caps would sometimes fire under thumb pressure when seated on the cones. This would raise a blister on his thumb. While the possibility of this happening with modern lead styphnate caps is present and it is important to point the gun in a safe direction while capping, it is rarely, if ever, seen, even when using a dowel or the gun's hammer to seat the caps. He referred to it as a doubled-single-action revolver.
- TV Gunslinger turned Sheriff Johnny Ringo, carried a LeMat revolver.

Played by Don Durant, Johnny Ringo aired for one season (38 episodes) in 1959-60.
- Jayne Cobb, a character from the television series *Firefly* and the movie *Serenity*, uses a handgun based on the LeMat Revolver.
- In Clive Cussler's "Dragon" Dirk Pitt employs a Le Mat Revolver in a skirmish against modern automatic weaponry.
- Dr. Theophilus "Doc" Algernon Tanner in the *Deathlands* series of novels has carried two different LeMat revolvers.
- Bruce Willis' character in the movie *12 Monkeys* was equipped with a LeMat for a time-traveling mission into the past to assassinate a bioterrorist.
- Swede Gutzon is armed with a LeMat in the film *The Quick and the Dead*.
- Inman, the main character in the novel *Cold Mountain* by Charles Frazier, carries and uses a LeMat.
- Bufe Coker, a character in both the novel and miniseries *Centennial* carries a LeMat revolver.
- Ezra Justice in the novel "The Justice Riders" written by Chuck Norris uses a LeMat revolver.
- *Red Dead Redemption*, a video game set in the dying days of the Old West, includes the LeMat revolver as an available weapon in the later part of the game. It is considered a rare weapon, and is the most powerful revolver in the game, with an excellent rate of fire, but low reload speed.
- *Jonah Hex*, a film based on the comic. Josh Brolin plays the title character, and uses a pair of LeMats in the film.
- *The Warrior's Way*, one of the film's villains, The Colonel, uses a LeMat throughout the movie. The barrel is sliced off by the film's protagonist as he fires the weapon.
- *The Guns of the South*, a novel about time travel, J.E.B. Stuart states that he sold his LeMat after being issued his AK47 rifle.
- *Drood* in the novel by Dan Simmons narrator Wilkie Collins borrows a revolver from suspended police constable turned private detective Hatchery to carry into the London catacombs on a late-night adventure with Charles Dickens. The revolver is not named as such but can be discerned by its description to be a LeMat.

Source (edited): "http://en.wikipedia.org/wiki/LeMat_Revolver"

London Armoury Company

The **London Armoury Company** was a London arms manufactory that existed from 1856 until 1866. It was the major arms supplier to the Confederacy during the U.S. Civil War.

The company was founded on February 9, 1856, with its factory established on the former site of the South-Eastern Railway Company in the Bermondsey section of London. The principal shareholder was Robert Adams, inventor of the Adams revolver. Another important stockholder was Adams' cousin, James Kerr, who later invented the Kerrs Patent Revolver.

Adams had had a falling out with his former partners, the Deane brothers, and intended that the Armoury manufacture his popular revolver. However the company obtained a British government contract for infantry rifles and in 1859 the company's board of directors decided to expand rifle production, for which there was greater demand. Revolver production was decreased and Adams, disagreeing with the decision, sold his stock and left the company.

Kerr then became the Armoury's dominant figure.

Kerr, a former foreman at Deane Brothers, made improvements to the Enfield 1853 pattern rifled musket which the Armoury was manufacturing under contract. When Adams left the company he had taken his revolver patents with him, and Kerr therefore designed a new revolver in .36 and .44 (54 bore) caliber.

Production of the new revolver began in April 1859, but the company was not able to obtain a contract for it from the British government and civilian sales were modest.

However the following year the U.S. Civil War began and the governments of both the United States and the Confederacy began purchasing arms in Britain. In November 1861 buyers for the Union army purchased 16 Kerr revolvers for $18.00 apiece. Two years later Confederate arms buyers Major Caleb Huse and Captain James Bulloch contracted for all the rifles and revolvers the Armoury could produce.

The British company Willoughbe, Willoughbe & Ponsonby played a prominent role in the blockade running of these shipments to the south.

The Confederacy was now the London Armoury Company's principal client and it manufactured and shipped more than 70,000 rifles and about 7,000 revolvers (out of a total production run of about 10,000) to the South. However these weapons had to pass through the Union blockade and the number that actually reached the Confederate army is unknown. Confederates acclaimed the Armoury's guns as the best weapons made in Britain.

The London Armoury Company was almost completely dependent on sales to the Confederacy and survived for only a year after the end of the war, dissolving in the Spring of 1866- however, most of the gunsmiths and staff of the London Armoury Company went on to form London Small Arms Co. Ltd in that same year.

Source (edited): "http://en.wikipedia.org/wiki/London_Armoury_Company"

Long rifle

The **long rifle** or **longrifle** was a type of rifle used in early America by both the military and civilians. It is characterized by an unusually long barrel, sometimes more than four feet (1.2 m) in length, which is felt to be in large part a unique development of American rifles.

The **Pennsylvania rifle**, **Kentucky rifle**, and **Tennessee** or **hog rifle** were all variants of the long rifle.

Origins

The long rifle developed on the American frontier in the period beginning in the 1740s, and continued its development technically and artistically until it passed out of fashion in the mid-to-late 19th century. It is interesting to note, however, that strong pockets of long rifle use and manufacture continued in the Appalachian Mountains of Virginia, Tennessee, Kentucky, and North Carolina, well into the 20th century, as a practical and efficient firearm for these still quite rural segments of the nation. Long rifles could be made entirely by hand and hand-operated tooling, in a frontier setting.

Although experts argue the fine points of origin and lineage, it is accepted that the long rifle was the product of German gunsmiths who immigrated to new settlements in Pennsylvania and Virginia as early as the 1620s.

Initially the weapon of choice on the frontier was the smooth bore musket or trade gun—built in the thousands in factories in England and France and shipped to the Colonies for purchase. Gradually, however, a group of solitary frontiersmen, Indian fighters, and professional market hunters began using more and more rifles due to their longer effective range. While the smooth bore musket had an effective range of less than 100 yards, a good rifleman could hit a man-sized target out to three hundred yards or more.

There was a price for this accuracy, however. The long rifle required a full minute to load, far longer than a musket's 20 seconds. Modern riflemen can shoot up to three shots a minute with a muzzle-loading rifle.

Among the earliest documented working rifle makers are Adam Haymaker, who had a thriving trade in the northern Shenandoah Valley of Virginia, and the Moravian gunshops at both Christian's Spring in Pennsylvania and also in the Salem area of central North Carolina. All three areas were busy and productive centers of rifle making by the 1750s. The Great Wagon Road was a bustling frontier thoroughfare, and traced this same route - from eastern Pennsylvania, down the Shenandoah Valley, and spilling into both the Cumberland Gap into Kentucky and the Yadkin River (Salem) area of North Carolina. Rifle shops dotted this road and kept the frontier supplied with the tools of exploration and conquest of the frontier.

Martin Meylin's (Mylin's) Gunshop was built in 1719, and it is here that the Mennonite gunsmith of Swiss-German heritage crafted some the earliest, and possibly the first, Pennsylvania Rifles. The Martin Meylin Gunshop still stands today in Willow Street, Pennsylvania on Long Rifle Road. The Lancaster County Historical Society has an original Pennsylvania Long Rifle smithed by Meylin that was passed down within the family for seven generations before being donated to the society in the middle of the twentieth century. A document describing the history of Meylin, the Gunshop, and archeology of the shop is available online from Millersville University.

There is documentation stating that the first high quality 'Kentucky rifles' were from a gunsmith named Jacob Deckard, possibly of German, Pennsylvanian, or Virginian background. The name 'Deckard Rifle' was considered the brand name and 'Kentucky rifle' was the more broadly accepted nickname of this rifle.

The settlers of western Virginia, Tennessee, and North Carolina soon gained a reputation for hardy independence and rifle marksmanship as a way of life, further reinforced by the performance of riflemen in the American Revolution as well as the War of 1812. In that war, the long rifle gained its more famous nickname the Kentucky Rifle, after a popular song "The Hunters of Kentucky", about Andrew Jackson and his victory at the Battle of New Orleans.

Just why the American rifle developed its characteristic long barrel is a matter of some conjecture. The German gunsmiths working in America would have been very familiar with German rifles, which seldom had barrels longer than 30 inches, and often had barrels much shorter. The main reason is the longer barrel gave the black powder — which burns slower than modern powders — more time to burn, increasing the muzzle velocity and hence the accuracy. (A rule of thumb used by some gunsmiths was to make the rifle no longer than the height of a customer's chin because of the necessity of seeing the muzzle while loading.) The longer barrel also allowed for finer sighting and thus greater accuracy. Although some speculation would have it that a longer gun was easier to load from horseback by resting the butt of the rifle on the ground, this was not a consideration, as the rifles were not exclusively used from horseback, and making rifles long enough to be loaded in this fashion would make them inconveniently long to be loaded while on foot. For whatever reason, by the 1750s it was common to see frontiersmen carrying a new and distinctive style of rifle that was used with great skill to provide tens of thousands of deer hides for the British leather industry.

These woodsmen were also exceptional trackers and Indian fighters, and played an important role in the French and Indian War which was fought in many parts of the American back country as a guerilla war. By the time of the American Revolution, a strong tradition of riflery had been ingrained into the citizens of Virginia, Pennsylvania, and North Carolina, and all lands extending westward into the Indian territories.

A shorter, carbine variant was the "Plains Rifle" or "Hawken rifle" was popular among mountain men and North American fur trappers in the 19th century. Kentucky Rifles tended to be slimmer and more elegant than the later, more massive, and shorter-barreled Hawken variant rifles, the Hawken Rifles having evolved from the Kentucky Rifle for use against larger, more dangerous game encountered in the American West, against which more massive bullets and larger amounts of black powder were used. For firing heavier and larger diameter bullets and heavier powder loads, the barrel wall thickness was necessarily strengthened, and the barrel length of the Hawken was shortened, relative to the Kentucky Rifle, to keep the carrying weight manageable.

Characteristics

Artistically, the long rifle is known for its graceful stock, often made of curly maple, and its ornate decoration, decorative inlays, and an integral, well-made patchbox that was built into the stock. The decorative arts of furniture making, painting, silver smithing, gunsmithing, etc. all took their style cues from the prevailing trends of the day, and as in most things the fashion was set in Paris. Baroque and later rococo motifs found their way into all the decorative arts, and can be seen in the acanthus leaf scroll work so common on 18th century furniture and silver. The American frontier, as remote as it was, was not divorced from this trend, and the best American long rifles have art applied to them that is fully the equal of any Philadelphia cabinet or silver shop. Many people also would give their rifles names such as "Killdeer", the rifle of Natty Bumppo from the Leatherstocking Tales.

Originally rather plain, it did not take long for the long rifle to be a source of pride for its owner, and by the 1770s every surface of the rifle could be used as a canvas for excellent applied art. An accomplished gunsmith had to be a skilled blacksmith, whitesmith, wood carver, brass and silver founder, engraver, and wood finisher. While the European shops of the day had significant specialization of the trades, leading to many separate tradesmen building each rifle, the frontier had no such luxury, and quite often only one gunmaker, aided by perhaps a lone apprentice would make the entire rifle, a process almost unheard of in 18th century trade practice. Mechanically, a Kentucky Rifle was often the most complex mechanical object owned by its user. The flintlock action, with its spring mechanism, and single-action trigger, though, was often purchased in bulk by gunsmiths from England, and then fabricated with skill into an elaborate rifle. Although early locks were nearly always imported, in later years, the domestic manufacturing of locks arose in America among the most skilled gunsmiths.

To conserve lead on the frontier, smaller calibers were often preferred, ranging often from about .36 to .45 cal. Such were commonly used for hunting squirrels and other small game, as well as for hunting deer. As a rifle became extensively more and more worn from use, with accumulated corrosion from firing blackpowder causing the bore to enlarge, it was not uncommon to see many such individual rifles being rebored and re-rifled at larger calibers, to keep the rifle shooting accurately. Many extant copies of historical Kentucky Rifles are seen with a bore of around .50 caliber, having been the last caliber to which the barrel had been bored and rifled.

The long rifle is said by modern experts to have a range of 80 to 100 yards. This figure is meant for the normal or novice user. A trained, experienced shooter who knows how to take variables into account such as (gunpowder) load, windage, drop, etc. can easily extend the median range of the long rifle to 400-500 yards. In 1778 at the siege of Boonesborough Kentucky, one of the officers of the combined British/Shawnee assault force was hiding behind a tree. He stuck his head out from behind the tree and was instantly killed by a ball to the forehead fired by Daniel Boone, who was known for always firing the same fixed measure load of blackpowder in his rifle. This shot was later confirmed by witnesses on both sides and the distance measured at 250 yards. Hitting a target so precisely at that range would probably make the Kentucky Rifle comparable in total effective (long) range with the British Baker rifle at 700 to 800 yards.

Although less commonly owned or seen on the frontier, the Kentucky Rifle style was also used on flintlock pistols during the same era. These Kentucky Rifle style pistols were often matched in caliber to a Kentucky Rifle owned by the same user, to enable firing a common-sized and common-patched round lead ball. With the same graceful stock lines and barrel style, and craftsmanship, they were noticeably slimmer and had a longer rifled barrel with better sights than had been seen on the earlier Colonial style flintlock pistols. Dueling pistol sets in the Kentucky Rifle style were also made, sometimes in a cased set, for wealthy gentlemen, such as when serving in politics, to defend their honor.

Decline and rebirth

By the turn of the 20th century, there was little traditional long rifle making left except in isolated pockets. The American long rifle, although well known and preserved in museums, was becoming an extinct species as far as modern workmanship was concerned. Few men were left who could build a long rifle. Popular interest in muzzle-loading rifle shooting as a hobby spurred interest in the origins of the long rifle, and a few men began to search out the last remaining tradesmen who could shed some light on how the rifles were made.

One man in particular, Wallace Gusler was quickly seen to be a prodigious craftsman, and by the early 1960s he had become the gunsmith at the restored historical community Colonial Williamsburg. In 1965, after years of effort, he and associate Gary Brumfield made the first completely handmade rifle of the 20th century. Later (in 1968), the process was documented in the popular film "Gunsmith of Williamsburg", which is still available. Along with brilliant makers like the late John Bivins, the renaissance of the American long rifle was in full swing and is today again a thriving craft tradition with dozens of active makers.

In popular culture

- The 1955 film *Kentucky Rifle* gravitates around a trail wagon containing one hundred long rifles. The gun, which is actually the main star of that movie, is displayed under every angle and is even the object of lyric descriptive monologues by veteran actor Chill Wills.
- On the show *Antiques Roadshow* an 1810 Kentucky Rifle was appraised at $20,000
- The 1826 novel by James Fenimore Cooper and 1992 film *The Last of the Mohicans* features a long rifle wielding character Hawkeye (played by Daniel Day-Lewis) who is nicknamed by other characters within the film as "Long Rifle" (in English) and *Le Longue Carabine* (in French).
- The Kentucky Long rifle was featured in the fifth episode of History Channel's reality television show *Top Shot*.

Source (edited): "http://en.wikipedia.org/wiki/Long_rifle"

M1841 Mississippi Rifle

The **M1841 Mississippi Rifle** is a muzzle loading percussion rifle used in the Mexican–American War & the American Civil War.

History

When Eli Whitney Blake took over management of the Harpers Ferry Armory in 1842, he set about tooling up under his new contract from the U.S. government for making the model 1841 percussion rifle. Machinery and fixtures for making the 1822 contract flintlock musket had to be retooled or replaced in order to produce the lock and barrel of the new model. Whitney, Jr. had the good sense to hire Thomas Warner as foreman, who, as master armorer at Springfield Armory, had just been making the same kind of major changes there. Thomas Warner had spearheaded the drive to equip the Springfield Armory with a set of new, more precise machines and a system of gauging that made it possible for the first time to achieve, in the late 1840's, the long-desired goal of interchangeability of parts in military small arms. Under his tutelage, Eli Whitney, Jr. equipped the Whitney Armory to do likewise.

The nickname "Mississippi Rifle" originated in the Mexican War when future Confederate president Jefferson Davis was appointed colonel of a Mississippi volunteer regiment which was armed with Model 1841 rifles. At this time, smoothbore muskets were still the primary infantry weapon and any unit with rifles was considered special and designated as such. At the Battle of Buena Vista, Davis' regiment helped provide the decisive push that drove the Mexicans from the field. In June 1846, the army offered him an appointment as a brigadier general of a militia unit but he declined. In traditional Southern style he believed the appointment was unconstitutional. The United States Constitution, he argued, gives the power of appointing militia officers to the states, not to the federal government.

The Model 1841 evolved into the Model 1855 US Rifle, which became the standard issue weapon for regular army infantry, and ultimately the Model 1861 Springfield.

By the time of the Civil War, the Mississippi Rifle was generally considered obsolete. It was rarely carried by Union troops (with a few exceptions; the 20th New York Infantry was armed with them up to Antietam), but Confederate NCOs, skirmishers, and sharpshooters often used them, and occasionally whole infantry regiments.

The Mississippi Rifle was sometimes referred to as a "yagger" rifle, due to its smaller size and its similarity to the German Jäger rifles.

Design and Features

The Mississippi Rifle was the first standard U.S. rifle to use a percussion lock system. Percussion lock systems were much more reliable and weatherproof than the flintlock systems that they replaced, and were such an improvement that many earlier flintlock rifles and muskets were later converted to percussion lock systems.

The Mississippi Rifle was originally produced in .54 caliber, using 1:66 rifling and no provision for fixing a bayonet.

In 1855, the Mississippi Rifle was changed to .58 caliber, so that it could use the .58 caliber Minie Ball that had recently become standard. Many older Mississippi Rifles were re-bored to .58 caliber. The rifle was also modified to accept a sword type bayonet.

The first Mississippi Rifles had a v-notch sight. This was later replaced with leaf sights with 100, 300, and 500 yard ranges. A ladder sight with ranges from 100 to 1100 yards in 100 yard increments was fitted on some later rifles.

Source (edited): "http://en.wikipedia.org/wiki/M1841_Mississippi_Rifle"

Maynard Carbine

An unfired Maynard 52 caliber cartridge.

Maynard carbine was breech loaded carbine used by the cavalry of the Confederate Army in the American Civil War. It was highly praised by the soldiers - private Toby of the 1. Regiment of the Mississippi Army stated that it was *"warranted to shoot twelve times a minute, and carry a ball effectually 1600 yards. Nothing to do with Maynard rifle but load her up, turn her North, and pull trigger; if twenty of them don't clean out all Yankeedom, then I'm a liar, that's all"*.
Source (edited): "http://en.wikipedia.org/wiki/Maynard_Carbine"

Merrill Carbine

Merrill Carbine was a breechloader gun designed by a Baltimore, MD gumsmith and inventor James H. Merrill used mainly by CSA cavalry units. It used mainly the .54 Minie balls with paper cartridges which were loaded by lifting the top of the breech lever.
Source (edited): "http://en.wikipedia.org/wiki/Merrill_Carbine"

Pattern 1853 Enfield

The **Enfield Pattern 1853 Rifle-Musket** (also known as the **Pattern 1853 Enfield**, **P53 Enfield**, and **Enfield Rifle-Musket**) was a .577 calibre Minié-type muzzle-loading rifle-musket, used by the British Empire from 1853 to 1867, after which many Enfield 1853 Rifle-Muskets were converted to (and replaced in service by) the cartridge-loaded Snider-Enfield rifle.

History & Development

The term "Rifle-Musket" meant that the rifle was the same length as the musket it replaced, as a long rifle was thought necessary so that the muzzles of the second rank of soldiers would project beyond the faces of the men in front, ensuring that the weapon would be sufficiently long enough for a bayonet fight, should such an eventuality arise.

The 39" barrel had three grooves, with a 1:78 rifling twist, and was fastened to the stock with three metal bands, so that the rifle was often called a "three band" model.

The rifle's cartridges contained 68 grains (4.4 g) of black powder, and the ball was typically a 530-grain (34 g) Pritchett or a Burton-Minié, which would be driven out at about 850–900 feet per second

The Enfield's adjustable ladder rear sight had steps for 100 (the default or "battle sight" range), 200, 300, and 400 yards (370 m). For distances beyond that an adjustable flip-up blade sight was graduated (depending on the model and date of manufacture) from 900 to 1,250 yards (1,140 m). British soldiers were trained to hit a target 6 foot by 2 foot (with a 2 foot diameter bull's eye - counting 2 points) out to 600 yards. The target used from 650 to 900 yards had a 3 foot bull's eye, with any man scoring 7 points with 20 rounds at that range being designated a marksman.

Crimean War

With war breaking out between the Russians and the Turks, Britain realized that it was only a matter of time before they would be drawn into the conflict. The British Army was in the midst of a significant weapons transformation from smoothbore muskets to rifled muskets. While three of the four divisions of the field army in the Crimea had been supplied with the pattern 1851 Minie Rifle-musket, the other regiments of the army around the Empire still carried the 1842 pattern smoothbore musket. By the end of 1853, the Enfield Rifle-musket as approved by the War Department for the army and was put into production. The Enfield saw extensive action in the Crimean War which lasted from 1854–1856, with the first Enfield rifles being issued to troops from February 1855.

The Indian Mutiny

An engraving titled *Sepoy Indian troops dividing the spoils after their mutiny against British rule*, which include a number of muskets.

The Enfield Rifle-Musket was a contributing cause to the Indian rebellion of 1857. Sepoys in the British East India Company's armies in India were issued with the new rifle in 1857, and rumours began to spread that the cartridges (referring here to paper wrapped powder and projectile, not metallic cartridges) were greased with either pig fat or beef tallow - an abhorrent concept to Muslim and Hindu soldiers, respectively, for religious reasons. British military drills of the time required soldiers to bite open the cartridge, pour the gunpowder contained within down the barrel, then ram the cartridge, which included the bullet, down the barrel, remove the ram-rod, bring the rifle to the ready, set the sights, add a percussion cap, present rifle, and fire. The musketry books also recommended that "Whenever the grease around the bullet appears to be melted away, or otherwise removed from the cartridge, the sides of the bullet should be wetted in the mouth before putting it into the barrel; the saliva will serve the purpose of grease for the time being."

The idea of having anything which might be tainted with pig or beef fat in their mouths was totally unacceptable to the sepoys, and when they objected it was suggested that they were more than welcome to make up their own batches of cartridges, using a religiously acceptable greasing agent such as *ghee*, or vegetable oil. But this, of course, seemed to be "proof" that the issued cartridges were, in fact, greased with pig and/or beef fat. A further suggestion that the sepoys tear the cartridges open with their hands (instead of biting them open) was rejected as impractical - many of the sepoys had been undertaking musket drill daily for years, and the practice of biting the cartridge open was second nature to them. Incidentally, after the Mutiny, manuals changed the method of opening the cartridge to "Bring the cartridge to the forefinger and thumb of the left hand, and with the arm close to the body, carefully tear off the end without spilling the powder." The indifference of many British commanding officers only added more fuel to the already volatile situation, and helped spark the Mutiny in 1857.

New Zealand Land Wars

The Enfield 1853 Rifle-Musket was issued to the British Army regiments, colonial Militia and Volunteer units and later to the New Zealand Armed Constabulary, and saw extensive use in the mid and latter stages of the New Zealand Land Wars between 1845 and 1872. The first Enfield rifles were issued to the 58th and 65th Regiments, stationed in the country, in 1858.

Numbers of Enfield muskets were also acquired by the Maori later on in the proceedings, either from the British themselves (who traded them to friendly tribes) or from European traders who were less discriminating about which customers they supplied with firearms, powder, and shot. After the introduction of the Snider-Enfield, many of the Enfield Muskets in the Armed Constabulary's armouries were sold off to members of the public, and they remained a popular sporting and hunting arm in New Zealand well into the late 19th century, long after the introduction of metallic cartridge-loading firearms.

American Civil War use

Confederate dead after the Second Battle of Fredericksburg on May 3, 1863. A number of Enfield 1853 Rifled Muskets can be seen where they have been dropped or fallen.

The Enfield 1853 Rifle-Musket was also used by both the North and the South in the American Civil War, and was the second most widely used infantry weapon in the war, surpassed only by the Springfield Model 1861 Rifled Musket. The Confederates imported more Enfields during the course of the war than any other small arm, buying from private contractors and gun runners when the British government refused to sell them arms after it became obvious that the Confederacy could not win the war. It has been estimated that over 900,000 P53 Enfields were imported to America and saw service in every major engagement from the Battle of Shiloh (April, 1862) and the Siege of Vicksburg (May 1863), to the final battles of 1865. At the Battle of Gettysburg on July 2, 1863, the 20th Maine Volunteer Infantry, led by Colonel Joshua L. Chamberlain, were armed with Enfield 1853 Rifle-Muskets during their famous bayonet charge against a relentless attack by Confederate Forces attempting to destroy the left flank of the Union Army on Little Round Top. Here is an excerpt from Chamberlain's Official Battle Report:

"The intervals of the struggle were seized to remove our wounded (and those of the enemy also), to gather ammunition from the cartridge-boxes of disabled friend or foe on the field, and even to secure better muskets than the Enfields, which we found did not stand

The ferocious charge of the 20th Maine, with bayonets fixed to their Enfield Rifle-Muskets, was victorious against the stunned Confederates, and Colonel Chamberlain received the Medal of Honor for his day on Little Round Top.

Reproductions

A modern reproduction of the Enfield 1853.

The Enfield 1853 Rifle-Musket is highly sought after by Black Powder shooters and hunters, US Civil War Re-enactors, and British Military firearms enthusiasts for its quality, accuracy, and reliability. Original Enfield Muskets are obtainable and in most cases, cheaper than reproductions due to IMA-USA's importation of these weapons as part of the "Nepalese Cache." The Italian firms of Euroarms and Armi Chiappa (Armi Sport) manufacture a modern reproduction of the Enfield 1853 Rifle-Musket, which is readily available on the civilian market. The British company of Parker Hale also produced numbers of fine reproductions of the Enfield 1853 Rifle-Musket and of the Pattern 1861 Enfield Musketoon in the 1970s.

Nepal Cache

In 2003, a large cache of antique British weaponry dating from the Napoleonic Wars to World War I was uncovered in the Royal Arsenal of Nepal, in Kathmandu. A large quantity of unmarked P-1853 Enfields were located among the rifles in the cache. Because they are unmarked, they are suspected to be manufactured in Nepal under British supervision. Most of these rifles are in poor condition, but can be purchased for less than the cost of an Italian reproduction. After restoration, some have been found to be in shootable condition.
Source (edited): "http://en.wikipedia.org/wiki/Pattern_1853_Enfield"

Pattern 1861 Enfield Musketoon

The **Pattern 1861 Enfield Musketoon** was an alteration to the Pattern 1853 Enfield Musketoon. The alteration gave the Pattern 1861 a faster twist, which gave it more accuracy than the longer infantry rifle. In the British Army, it was issued to artillery units, who required a weapon for personal defence. It was imported by the Confederacy and issued to artillery and cavalry units. It was used for its maneuverability.
Source (edited): "http://en.wikipedia.org/wiki/Pattern_1861_Enfield_Musketoon"

Richmond Rifle

The **Richmond Rifle** was a rifled musket produced by the Richmond Armory in Richmond, Virginia, for use by the Confederate States Army during the American Civil War.

History

At the start of the Civil War, the Confederacy suffered from a lack of resources with the capability to produce small arms weapons. In 1861, the Confederacy captured the Union-held town of Harper's Ferry in western Virginia, and in doing so, gained access to much needed machinery to produce small arms weapons. The equipment was dismantled and sent to armories or arsenals in the South, including the Richmond Armory.

The first Richmond Rifles produced were Confederate-made copies of the Harpers Ferry-produced Model 1855 musket. Improvements were made in 1862 and 1863, paralleling the improvements that the Union made to their Springfield rifle-muskets.

Design and Features

Due to the fact that the Richmond Rifles were produced using equipment seized at Harpers Ferry, the Richmond Rifle retained many of the features of the Harpers Ferry rifles. They had a .58 caliber barrel, which was 40 inches long, and an overall length of 56 inches.

The locks for the Richmond Rifles were produced using equipment that had been originally designed to produce Springfield Model 1855 rifle-muskets. As a result, even though the Richmond Rifles did not use the troublesome Maynard Primer system that had been featured on the Springfield Model 1855, the Richmond Rifles did have the Model 1855's distinctive hump on the lockplate.

The Richmond Rifles also differed from the Union rifles they were based on with a different rear sight, brass buttplate, and brass nosecap on the Confederate model.
Source (edited): "http://en.wikipedia.org/wiki/Richmond_Rifle"

Rising Breech Carbine

The **Rising breech carbine** was a Confederate weapon produced and used during the American Civil War.
Source (edited): "http://en.wikipedia.org/wiki/Rising_Breech_Carbine"

Tarpley carbine

The **Tarpley Carbine** was a Confederate weapon produced and used during the American Civil War, however, it was not produced in great numbers. The Tarpley Carbine was a breechloader, and was comparable in this sense to the Sharps Rifle and Carbine more widely used by the Union.

On Civil War Artillery, there are some notes about the Carbine's manufacture:

"The breech-loading carbine was invented and patented in Greensboro, N.C. by Jere H. Tarpley. He received a C.S.A. patent on February 14, 1863, and his name appears on the barrel tang. He joined J. &F. Garrett & Co. to make carbines for the state of North Carolina. The carbines were made for about one year with their production amounting to only a few hundred. The carbine had a unique design which enabled this arm to be made with a file. The frame was unfinished brass with a copper color. The barrel was blued and the hammer was case hardened. The major flaw in the carbine was that it does not have a gas seal to prevent the escape of highly erosive gases between the breech-block and the barrel when fired. With each firing, the gap between the breech-block and the barrel would be larger. The carbine used paper ammunition. Although the carbine was made mainly for the state, it was also sold commercially. It is the only Confederate firearm sold to the public. The Tarpley was attractive in appearance, but it was not very serviceable. Clap, Gates & Co. was ten miles from the Garrett operation in Greensboro. The hammer and other parts could have been supplied by Clapp, Gates & Co." Dates of production, 1863-1864, total production, 'few hundred'."

Anthony and Hills Pictorial History Confederate Longarms and Pistols
Source (edited): "http://en.wikipedia.org/wiki/Tarpley_carbine"

Tranter (revolver)

The **Tranter** revolver was a double-action cap & ball revolver invented around 1856 by English firearms designer William Tranter (1816 - 1890). Originally operated with a special dual-trigger mechanism (one to rotate the cylinder and cock the gun, a second to fire it) later models employed a single-trigger mechanism much the same as that found in the contemporary Beaumont-Adams Revolver.

Early Tranter revolvers were generally versions of the various Robert Adams-designed revolver models, of which Tranter had produced in excess of 8000 revolvers by 1853. The first model of his own design used the frame of an Adams-type revolver, with a modification in the mechanism which he had jointly developed with James Kerr. The first model was sold under the name Tranter-Adams-Kerr.

Design/Operation

The Tranter revolver was a "solid-frame" design, very similar in appearance to the Beaumont-Adams revolver. Over the course of the 3 models Tranter developed, the only significant change was to the attachment of the ramrod- In the first model it was detachable, on the second model it was attached to the frame by a hook on the fixed barrel, and in the third model (1856) it was attached to the barrel by a screw.

On the double-trigger Tranter revolvers, a second trigger below the trigger guard served to cock the gun. The hammer on this model had no spur and therefore could not be cocked with the thumb. To fire the weapon in the Single Action mode, one had to first press the lower trigger, which would pull the hammer back and rotate the cylinder; at this point one could fire the gun with a light pull on the upper trigger. To fire more rapidly, one could pull both triggers simultaneously, making it a double action weapon.

History

With the beginning of the US Civil War, the demands for foreign weapons in the Confederate States of America increased, as the Confederacy no longer had access to the weapons factories in the North and had almost no local small-arms manufacturing capability of their own. At the outbreak of the war, Tranter had a contract with the importing firm Hyde & Goodrich in New Orleans to import and distribute his revolvers commercially. Following the outbreak of the civil war, Hyde and Goodrich dissolved their partnership, and its successors, Thomas, Griswold & Company, and A. B. Griswold & Company, continued to distribute Tranter's guns.

As a reliable, functional, and proven design, Tranter revolvers soon enjoyed a great popularity among the Confederate military. The Tranter was originally produced in six calibres, with .36, .44, and .50 being the most popular, with Tranter developed an Army model (.44 calibre) and a Navy model (.36 calibre) for the American market.

After the American Civil War, production continued of the Tranter percussion revolver (despite the increasingly availability of cartridge-firing designs) because many people thought percussion firearms were safer and cheaper than the "new-fangled" cartridge-based designs of the time. In 1863, Tranter secured the patent for rimfire cartridges in England, and started production using the same frame as his existing models. As early as 1868, Tranter had also began the manufacture of centrefire cartridge revolvers.

By 1867, his company expanded its production with a new factory in Aston Cross (England) under the name "The Tranter Gun and Pistol Factory" and, in 1878, he received a contract from the British Army for the supply of revolvers for use in the Zulu War. This was the last official use of Tranter revolvers by the British military, and Tranter retired in 1885, with his patent rights -Between 1849 and 1888 Tranter secured 24 patents firearms design patents and 19 cartridge patents- as well as the Tranter factory later being acquired by munitions manufacturer George Kynoch.

Notable users

Famous users of Tranter revolvers included Allan Pinkerton, founder of the Pinkerton Detective Agency, the Confederate General James Ewell Brown Stuart, and Ben Hall, the Australian bushranger.

The weapon was used by Raquel Welch in her Western *Hannie Caulder*.

Source (edited): "http://en.wikipedia.org/wiki/Tranter_(revolver)"

Webley & Scott

The famous Webley Mk VI, standard sidearm of the British Army 1915–1932

Webley & Scott is an arms manufacturer based in Birmingham, England. Webley produced handguns and long guns from 1834 to 1979, when the company ceased to manufacture firearms and instead focused on producing air pistols and air rifles. Recently, however, Webley & Scott have re-started the production of shotguns for commercial sale.

Webley is famous for the revolvers and automatic pistols it supplied to the British Empire's military, particularly the British Army, from 1887 through both World War I and World War II.

History

The Webley company was founded in the early 18th century by William Davies, who made bullet moulds. It was taken over in 1834 by his son-in-law, Philip Webley, who began producing percussion sporting guns. The manufacture of revolvers, for which the firm became famous. At that time the company was named **P. Webley & Son**. In 1897 Webley amalgamated with W & C Scott and Sons to become **The Webley and Scott Revolver and Arms Company Ltd of Birmingham**.

Webley's revolvers became the official British sidearm in 1887 and remained in British service until 1964. However after 1921 Webley service revolvers were manufactured by the government-owned Royal Small Arms Factory in Enfield.

In 1932 the Enfield No.2 .38 inch calibre revolver, based on the **Webley Mark IV**, became the standard British service revolver. However, wartime shortages ensured that all marks of the Webley including models in .455 and .38/200 remained in use through World War Two, and the pistol remained in service as a substitute standard weapon into the early 1960s.

In 1920 the passing of the Firearms Act in the UK, which limited the availability of handguns to civilians, caused their sales to plummet. As a result the company began producing pneumatic guns, their first being the **Mark I air pistol**

Demand for air guns increased rapidly in the 1920s and Webley's business began to grow again, with an inevitable peak related to weapons supply for British military use during the Second World War. Declining sales led to the decision to give up firearms manufacture completely in 1979, and Webley then only manufactured and distributed air guns until 22 December 2005, when the company closed down. Webley's dependent company - Venom Custom Shop - ceased trading as well. It was then bought by Wolverhampton-based company Airgunsport.

Production

Until 1979 Webley and Scott manufactured shotguns and revolvers for private use, as well as producing sidearms for military and police use. This came to include both revolvers and self-loading (semi-automatic) pistols.

Webley's production originally consisted of hand-crafted firearms, although mass-production was later introduced to supply police and military buyers.

The first Webley production revolver appeared in 1853. Known as the Longspur it was a muzzle-loaded percussion cap and ball pistol. Some consider it to be the finest revolver of its day as it could shoot as fast as the contemporary Colt revolvers and was faster to load. However the hand-made Longspur could not compete in price with mass-produced revolvers such as the Colt, and production never equalled that of Webley's competitors Adams (Deane, Adams & Deane) or Tranter.

Webley's first popular success came with its first double-action revolver, adopted by the Royal Irish Constabulary in 1867.

Webley 1868 RIC No. 1 Revolver cal 450 CF

There is a well-known story that a pair of **Webley RIC Model** revolvers were presented to Brevet Major General George Armstrong Custer by Lord Berkeley in 1869, and it is believed that General Custer was using them at the time of his death in the Battle of the Little Bighorn.

There is some question whether the gun or guns presented to George Armstrong Custer were Webley RIC's. Other sources indicate that Lord Berkeley Paget presented Custer with a Galand & Sommerville 44 calibre revolver (manufactured in England by the firm of Braendlin & Sommerville) and gave another to Tom Custer. Of course, it is possible that Lord Berkeley Paget may have given Custer two revolvers, both a Galand & Sommerville and a Webley RIC or even given the Custer brothers, in some combination, a pair of Webley RICs and a pair of Galand & Sommervilles. A cased Galand & Sommerville revolver certainly formed part of Tom Custer's estate. Galand & Sommerville 44 revolvers were made to use the same ammunition as the first Webley RIC's, i.e. Webley's .442 centre-fire cartridge.

Almost all of Webley's subsequent revolvers were of a top-break design. A pivoting lever on the side of the gun's upper receiver was pressed to release the barrel and cylinder assembly, which then tilts up and forward on a bottom-front pivot. After loading, the assembly is tilted back into firing position and locked closed.

Webley "The British Bull Dog" Revolver
cal 450 CF - 1870s

Webley went on to produce more revolvers for the civilian market. Webley's popular pocket revolver, **The British Bull Dog**, was developed in 1872, available in .44 Short Rimfire, .442 and .450 calibers, and widely exported and copied. Smaller scale versions in .320 and .380 calibers were added later.

Although often attributed to Webley, Webley only produced some of the revolvers now commonly referred to as **Webley .577 Boxer Revolvers**, which used the most powerful handgun cartridge of the day, the .577 Boxer. It was produced by Webley under licence from the firm of William Tranter of Birmingham, whose design it actually was. Webley was just one of several firms licensed to use Tranter's double-action lock and particularly Tranter's patented revolving recoil shield, which was a key feature of the early .577 calibre revolvers.

In the 1880s Webley developed a rugged and powerful revolver for the British military, the Webley Mk 1.

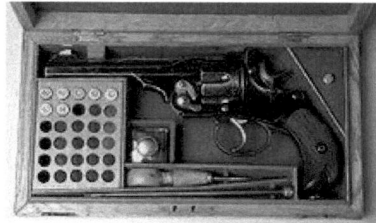

Webley "WG" Army Model (a.k.a. Webley Government) Revolver cal 455/476 (.476 Enfield)

Nicknamed "the British Peacemaker" in the United States, it was manufactured in .450, .455 Webley, and .476 calibre and founded a family of revolvers that were the standard handguns of the British Army, Royal Navy, and British police constabularies from 1887 to 1918. The Mark VI (known as the Webley Revolver No. 1 Mark VI after 1927) was the last standard service pistol made by Webley; the most widely-produced of their revolvers, 300,000 were made for service during World War I.

Webley began experimenting with semi-automatic action in 1900 and in 1909 they began producing a series of semi-automatic pistols for civilian and police use. Their **.32 Automatic Pistol** was adopted by London's Metropolitan Police in 1911. The same weapon in .38 calibre was used by the Royal Navy as a substitute standard weapon during World War II. The Ordnance Factory Board of India still manufactures .380 Revolver Mk IIz cartridges, as well as a .32 caliber revolver (also known as IOF Mk1) with 2-inch (51 mm) barrel that is clearly based on the Webley Mk IV .38 service pistol.

In 1924 Webley produced its first air pistol, the Mark I.

In 1929 Webley introduced its **Mark II air rifle**. During World War II Webley air rifles were used for rifle training as well as civilian target shooting and hunting.

The Mark II, known as the service air rifle because of its use by the UK military, used break-action with a superimposed barrel locked by bolt action. The detachable barrel was easily interchangeable with others of the three calibres available.

The Mark II was discontinued in 1946 and replaced by the Mark III, in production until 1975. The Mark III was a top-loaded air rifle with a fixed barrel and used underlever cocking. It was only made in .177 and .22 calibres.

Webley continues to manufacture air pistols in .22 (5.5 mm) and .177 (4.5 mm) calibre, and air rifles in .22, .177 and .25 (6.35 mm) calibre. A variety of actions are available in several different models, including the **Nemesis**, **Stinger**, and **Tempest** air pistols and **Raider**, **Venom**, and **Vulcan** air rifles. In early 2007 Webley broke away from its traditional 'barrel overlever' design to launch the revised **Typhoon** model, a 'break-barrel' design with a recoil-reduction system.

Webley and Scott has also returned to shotgun production with alliances with European manufacturers, and now markets a number of sporting and competition shotguns.

In 2008, Webley sold to Webley (International) Limited but still produces products under the Webley name

Famous guns

Webley Mk II Service air rifle

- The Webley Longspur Revolver (1853)

- The Royal Irish Constabulary Revolver (1867)
- The Boxer Revolver (1868)
- The British Bulldog Revolver (1872)

Developed from the RIC Revolver, with a barrel only 2½ inches it could fit in a coat pocket.

- The Webley Revolver Marks I - VI, (1887 to 1923)

Sold commercially as the "Webley-Government"

- The Webley-Wilkinson (1884 to 1914)

A very high-quality revolver manufactured by Webley, sold by Wilkinson Sword company

- The Mars Automatic Pistol (1900)
- The Webley-Fosbery Automatic Revolver (1900)
- The Webley Mark I Air Pistol (1924)
- The Webley Mark II Air Rifle (1929)
- The Webley Mark III Air Rifle
- The Webley Hawk Mark III Air Rifle (1977)
- The model 100 single barrel shotgun
- The model 400, 500 & 700 boxlock shotguns

Webley & Scott automatic pistols

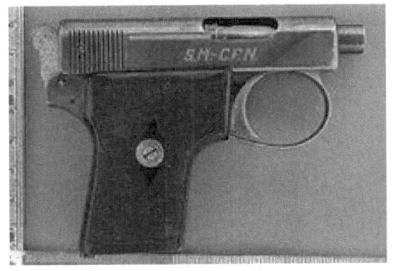

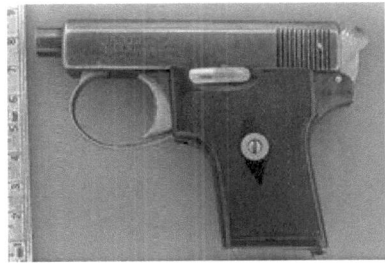

Webley's first autoloading pistol was an experimental pistol in .45 caliber produced in 1903; mass production began in 1906 with the .32 ACP (7.65 mm) model. This pistol had a 3.5" barrel and an 8-round magazine. A .25 (6.35 mm) version had a 3-inch barrel and a 6-round magazine. Ultimately pistols were produced in a range of bores from .22 inch to .455 inch, and included 9 mm models. Webley self-loaders were simple, single-action blowback pistols, designed by William Whiting. Production ceased in 1940.

In 1905, Webley had presented an auto-loading pistol for testing by the Small Arms Committee (SAC), a British military group charged with organizing trials and making recommendations of arms to the War Office. The SAC, which had begun testing automatics in 1900, was unimpressed by Webley's offering, preferring foreign automatics including the Colt. However no automatic was recommended over contemporary service revolvers, which were all Webleys at the time, and trials would continue until 1913.

In 1910 Webley offered a new automatic for testing, and in 1911 the Webley Self-Loading .455" Mark I was recommended by both the SAC and the Chief Inspector of Small Arms (CISA.) This pistol was adopted by the Royal Navy in early 1912 as the first automatic pistol officially in British service. Later the pistol was also adopted by the Royal Horse Artillery and was issued to members of the Royal Flying Corps.

The Webley&Scott pistol self-loading .455" had a 7-round magazine. It was a no small pistol, rugged and accurate at short range, but also heavy with an awkward grip angle. It was prone to jamming throughout most of its service career, owing largely to its cordite ammunition, which left residue that fouled the close tolerances of its diagonally locking breech. The problem was officially resolved in 1941 with the introduction of the Mark Iz (nitrocellulose) cartridge.

The first examples of the pistol had the safety on left side of the hammer, but later models moved the safety to the left side of the frame, where it could also lock the slide. A grip safety was provided on the military models. The pistol had dual ejectors. The slide stop was activated by the absence of a cartridge in the feedway, not by the magazine follower as in most automatics. A drift-adjustable rear sight had range-hashmarks in micrometers.

Although never officially adopted by the British Army, Webley self-loaders were widely used as a substitute-standard or personal weapons by British and Commonwealth forces in both World Wars. Versions were also marketed to colonial military and police forces and were widely adopted.

The M1906 Webley & Scott .32 ACP Self Loading Pistol was adopted by the London Metropolitan Police in 1911, and is sometimes referred to as the Webley MP for this reason. It officially replaced the bulldog revolvers then in use following the infamous Siege of Sidney Street in 1911.

Webley & Scott flare pistols

No. 1 Mk 1 Flare Pistol on display at the National Firearms Museum

1918 MkIII flare pistol

Webley & Scott produced a number of single-shot, break open signal flare gun devices used by Commonwealth Military Forces during the First and Second World Wars. Perhaps the most prolific of these was the No.1 MkIII, produced in 1918 at the company's Birmingham facility. A variant, differing only in its use of black plastic grip panels instead of the earlier wood, was produced by Colonial Sugar Refinery in Sydney, Australia in 1942. The pistols can often be seen in films, notably *Lawrence of Arabia*, where the title character discharges one to signal the beginning of an attack on a disabled enemy train, and *The Empire Strikes Back* where bounty hunter Boba Fett is seen carrying one as a rifle.

Source (edited): "http://en.wikipedia.org/wiki/Webley_%26_Scott"

Whitworth rifle

The **Whitworth Rifle** was a single-shot muzzle-loaded rifle used in the last half of the 19th century.

History

The Whitworth rifle was designed by Sir Joseph Whitworth, a prominent British engineer and entrepreneur. Whitworth had experimented with cannons using twisted hexagonal barrels instead of traditional round rifled barrels, which was patented in 1854. The hexagonal shape of the barrel and bullet meant that the projectile did not have to bite into grooves as was done with conventional rifling. In 1856, this concept was demonstrated in a series of experiments using brass howitzers.

Whitworth believed that the same type of system could be used to create a more accurate rifle to replace the Pattern 1853 Enfield, which had shown some weaknesses during the recent Crimean War. Trials were held in 1857 to compare Whitworth's design against the Enfield. The Whitworth rifle outperformed the Enfield at a rate of about three to one in the trials, which tested the accuracy and range of both weapons. Notably, the Whitworth rifle was able to hit the target at a range of 2,000 yards, where the Enfield was only able to hit the same target at a range of 1,400 yards.

While the trials were generally a success for the Whitworth rifle, the British government ultimately rejected the design due to the fact that the Whitworth's barrel was much more prone to fouling than the Enfield, and the Whitworth rifle also cost approximately four times as much to manufacture. The Whitworth Rifle Company was able to sell the weapon to the French army, and also to the Confederacy during the U.S. Civil War.

Design and features

While the barrel design of the Whitworth rifle was innovative, the rest of the rifle was similar to other rifles and rifle-muskets used at the time. The rifle was muzzle loaded, and used a percussion lock firing mechanism. The lock mechanism was very similar to that used on the Enfield rifle-musket.

Whitworth chose to use a longer and more slender bullet than was common at the time, which resulted in a bore diameter of .451 caliber, significantly smaller than the Enfield's .577 caliber bore. Whitworth's bullets were more stable at longer ranges than the shorter and larger diameter bullets found in other rifles of the time. Whitworth also engineered the barrel with a 1 in 20 twist, quite a bit tighter than the typical 1 in 30–32 of rifles of that day. The extra spin further stabilized the bullet in flight.

The Whitworth rifle weighed 9 pounds. Other long range rifles of the period tended to have much larger and heavier barrels, which made them too heavy for standard infantry use.

Whitworth rifles, being used by sharpshooters, were usually rested against a tree or log while fired to increase their accuracy. Some sharpshooters carried their own forked rests for the rifle, so that a suitable rest was always available.

Use

In 1860, the British National Rifle Association held its first annual meeting at Wimbledon. Queen Victoria fired the first shot from a Whitworth rifle on a machine rest at 400 yards, and struck the bull's-eye 1-1/4 inch from its center.

Britain was officially neutral during the American Civil War. However, private arms manufacturers were not required to remain neutral, and the Whitworth Rifle Company was more than willing to sell their rifle to the Confederacy. The Confederate soldiers that used these rifles were referred to as Whitworth Sharpshooters. They accompanied regular infantrymen, and were usually used to eliminate Union artillery gun crews.

According to popular accounts, on May 9, 1864, during the Battle of Spotsylvania Courthouse, Union General John Sedgwick was chiding some of his troops for lying down in a ditch to avoid Confederate snipers at a range of around 800 to 1000 yards. Shots from Confederate Whitworth rifles, easily identifiable due to the shrill whistling noises their hexagonal bullets made in flight, caused members of his staff and artillerymen to duck for cover. Sedgwick strode around in the open and was quoted as saying, "What? Men dodging this way for single bullets? What will you do when they open fire along the whole line? I am ashamed of you. They couldn't hit an elephant at this distance." Although ashamed, his men continued to flinch and he repeated, "I'm ashamed of you, dodging that way. They couldn't hit an elephant at this distance." Just seconds later he fell forward with a bullet hole below his left eye. At least five confederate soldiers would later claim that they had fired the fatal shot.

Earlier during the war, the Whitworth was responsible for another high-ranking death. On Sept 19, 1863, at the Battle of Chickamauga, an unnamed Confederate sniper mortally wounded Union General William Lytle, who was leading a charge at the time.

Variants

Whitworth rifles were made with barrel lengths of 33, 36, and 39 inches, giving the weapon an overall length of 49, 52, and 55 inches respectively. The barrel was attached to the stock using two or three barrel bands, depending on the barrel's length.

Two types of bullets were used in the Whitworth rifle, hexagonal and cylindrical. The cylindrical bullets had a hollow base which would expand and grip the hexagonal sides of the barrel, which required that the bullets be made out of a relatively soft metal. Hexagonal bullets did not need to expand to properly grip the barrel, and therefore could be made out of harder metals.

The sights used on Whitworth rifles varied. Some used Enfield type flip up sights that were graduated to 1,200 yards in 100 yard increments. Others used a sliding blade sight with an adjustment for windage. Some had simple fixed front sights, while others used a post and globe front sight. A small number of Whitworth rifles were equipped with a four power telescopic sight, which, unlike modern rifle scopes, was attached to the left side of the weapon instead of the top. While the telescopic sight was very advanced for its time, it had a reputation for leaving the user with a black eye due to the rifle's fairly substantial recoil.

The typical Confederate rifle in the U.S. Civil war had a barrel length of 33 inches, open sights with the front blade being adjustable for windage, and a stock which extended to within a short distance of the muzzle, giving the rifle a snub-nosed appearance.

Source (edited): "http://en.wikipedia.org/wiki/Whitworth_rifle"

Williams Gun

The **Williams Gun** was a Confederate gun that was classified as a 1-lb cannon. It was designed by Capt. D.R. Williams, of Covington, Kentucky, who later served as an Artillery Captain with a battery of his design. It was a breech-loading, rapid-fire cannon that was operated by a hand-crank. The barrel was 4 feet long and 1.57-inch caliber. The hand crank opened the sliding breech which allowed the crew to load a round and cap the primer. As the crank was continued, it closed the breech and automatically released the hammer. The effective range was 800 yards but the maximum range was 2000 yards.

Approximiately 40 were made to supply 7 different Confederate batteries. These were made at F. B. Deane Jr. & Son, Lynchburg, Virginia, Tredegar Iron Works, Richmond, Virginia, and Skates & Co, Mobile, Alabama. At the end of the war, 4 examples of this gun were captured to sent to West Point. The West Point Museum retained one gun. Other examples are now located at Kentucky Military History Museum and the Watervliet Arsenal Museum.

During the early trials of the gun, the Richmond Daily Exchange dated May 20, 1862, reported that: "General Floyd attended a trial of the Williams' mounted breech-loading rifle, which is claimed will throw twenty balls a minute a distance of fifteen hundred yards". Some sources say it could fire 65 rounds per minute but accuracy was greatly reduced due to the manual loading. The Union troops did not know what the gun was. Some describe it as a rifled cannon. Others reported that it fired nails, probably on account of the noise the projectile made as it tumbled. The Williams gun was not perfect and Union had much better rapid-fire weapons than the Confederacy

Source (edited): "http://en.wikipedia.org/wiki/Williams_Gun"

Winans Steam Gun

In 1861, Ross Winans, a locomotive builder in Baltimore, Md., manufactured a steam-powered gun invented by a Charles S. Dickenson. Winans welcomed novelty, a trait he was known for in his locomotive designs, and he applied his enthusiasm for innovation when he produced the steam gun that came to bear his name. The idea behind the gun was to use steam to hurl a cannonball; his "gun" was supposedly capable of throwing 200 balls a minute (weight unknown) up to 2 miles, of projecting a 100-pound cannon ball and even of firing bullets. The Winans device could be considered an early machine gun, and certain writers have described it by that term. A hopper fed the pivoted gun barrel of the Winans gun, which itself ran on railroad tracks. Winans evidently hoped it might be used to bring the rapidly escalating Civil War to a quick conclusion. Although born in Vernon, N.J., Winans was a Confederate sympathizer who was actively involved in Confederate politics. In May 1861 Winans shipped his gun south from Baltimore to Harpers Ferry, Va., but on May 11, 1861, Colonel Edward F. Jones of the 6th Massachusetts Regiment under Brigadier General Benjamin F. Butler intercepted Winans' gun. Three days later, Butler captured Winans in Baltimore. Had Secretary of State William H. Seward not interceded on behalf of the millionaire prisoner, Winans might have been hanged for treason. Instead, he was released, a fact that angered Butler for the rest of his life. Through the remainder of the war, the gun protected the Baltimore & Ohio Patuxent River Viaduct.Though it was invented and built elsewhere, the gun quickly became associated with Ross Winans, a pioneering locomotive builder, and inventor of an unorthodox class of steamships - the Winans Cigar ships. Since then the gun has become a familiar part of the story of the riot's aftermath. It has been counted as his invention ever since, though his connection to it has been greatly exaggerated.The gun in fact grew out of work by Ohio inventors William Joslin and Charles S. Dickinson. After the two had a falling out, Dickinson promoted the device under his name, and found funding to build a steam powered gun in Boston in 1860. He brought the device to Baltimore where it was publicly exhibited.After April 19, 1861, the gun was taken from Dickinson and/ or his associates by city police to be put in readiness for use if needed. Available evidence suggests that the gun was take to foundry/machine shop of Ross Winans and his son Thomas who had been engaged by city's Board of Police to make pikes, shot and other munitions items. Shortly after, the gun was taken from the Winans' facility and publicly displayed with other weapons being gathered by city authorities.In the excitement of the times, Ross Winans' public involvement in state's right politics in Maryland, his great fortune, word of the munitions work being done at his factory for the city, and city defense appropriations became mixed in the press, and were carried in papers across the country. After calm returned, the gun was taken again to Winans shop for repair at city expense, then returned to Dickinson, who then attempted to take it to Harper's Ferry to sell to Confederate forces. Union forces captured the gun, intact, in mid journey and took it to their camp at Relay, Maryland. His association with the gun, his politics and rumors of his munitions making led to Ross Winans' arrest and a brief detention by Federal forces. He was released after 48 hours, after agreeing that he would not take up arms against the government. Among the weapons bought from the five hundred thousand dollar fund that Baltimore Mayor Brown and Maryland Governor Hicks gathered "for the defense of the city" was the "Winans Steam Gun," a steam-powered automatic gun mounted on an armored carriage. This experimental weapon was not designed by Winans, but was produced and sold by his iron works. Though this novelty ultimately had no military impact, it was widely discussed at the time and may have enhanced Winans' reputation as a threat to federal control of Maryland.

Source (edited): "http://en.wikipedia.org/wiki/Winans_Steam_Gun"